AF540304

DAWN OF THE RAJ

THE COMPANY THAT RULED INDIA

RANJIT MISHRA

Srishti
PUBLISHERS & DISTRIBUTORS

Srishti Publishers & Distributors
A unit of AJR Publishing LLP
212A, Peacock Lane
Shahpur Jat, New Delhi – 110 049

editorial@srishtipublishers. com

First published by Bold,
an imprint of Srishti Publishers & Distributors in 2023

10 9 8 7 6 5 4 3 2 1

This is a work of non-fiction, based on the author's thorough research of Indian history. Some events have been fictionalised for dramatic effect. While due care has been taken to verify all information at press time, any inadvertent miss brought to notice shall be updated in the subsequent editions.

Printed and bound in India

Contents

Chronology

1498	Portuguese fleet led by Vasco da Gama arrived off the Malabar coast
1595	Dutch Compagnie Van Verre established to take the ocean route to the East
1600, 31 December	English East India Company (EIC) established
1602	Formation of the Dutch Verenigde Oostindische Compagnie (VOC)
1618	The English Company negotiated its first trade agreement with the Mughal Empire
1623	EIC merchants executed at Amboyna (Indonesia) by VOC forces
1639	Fort St George at Madras established by the English Company
1648	The EIC moved headquarters to East India House at Leadenhall Street
1657	The EIC became a permanent joint-stock corporation
1668	Bombay transferred to the EIC by King Charles II
1681	Josiah Child first elected as EIC governor (chairman)
1686-89	Child launched war with Mughal Empire
1690	Company established new base in Bengal at Calcutta
1695	First Parliamentary investigation into Company corruption
1698	Parliament awarded monopoly of Asia trade to the New Company
1709	Merger of New and Old Companies finalized

The Sequence of Events

1.	**1600** **31 December**	The Company of Merchants of London trading into the East Indies was founded by a Royal Charter signed by Elizabeth I. This charter gave them a monopoly on trade with any country east of the Cape of Good Hope and west of the Straits of Magellan. Sir Thomas Smythe was appointed Governor of the company commonly referred to as the East India Company. The Company's headquarters were at India House in Philpot Lane, London.
2.	**1601** **21 April**	Five ships commanded by James Lancaster, left Woolwich docks bound for the East Indies (Indonesia). They carried letters of introduction signed by the Queen to form trading partnerships. They managed to obtain spices and pepper which they brought back to England.
3.	**1603**	The East India Company founded a trading post in Bantam, Indonesia.
4.	**1604** **25 March**	Sir Henry Middleton commanded a Second Voyage that successfully traded in South Africa and reached Sumatra in Indonesia.
5.	**1607** **12 March**	A Third Voyage left England for the East. Commanded by William Keeling, this voyage reached Banda in Indonesia and discovered the Cocos Islands on the return trip to England.
6.	**1608** **14 March**	A Fourth Voyage of two ships commanded by Alexander Sharpeigh left Woolwich bound for the East.
7.	**1608** **24 August**	The first ships docked at Surat in the Gujarat region of India.

8.	**1609**	James I renewed the Company's charter with a stipulation that if it became unprofitable in three years, it would be null and void.
9.	**1611**	The East India Company founded a trading post at Machilipatnam in the Andhra Pradesh region of India. The Company began building factories in the Surat region of India.
10.	**1612**	King James I sent Thomas Roe to India. His instructions were to meet the Mughal Emperor Jahangir and arrange a commercial treaty.
	1612 29– 30 November	Battle of Swally.
11.	**1613 June**	The Clove, a ship belonging to the Company, commanded by John Saris, reached Japan. It carried a letter of introduction and gifts from King James I. The Company was given the right to establish a trading post on the island of Kyushu.
12.	**1615**	James I agreed to a commercial treaty with the Mughal Emperor Jahangir. The treaty gave the East India Company exclusive rights to build factories in Surat.
13.	**1616**	The East India Company had been unable to expand their trading activities in Japan, but they continued to trade out of Hirado and Nagasaki.
14.	**1619**	As agreed, under the treaty with Jahangir in 1615, the East India Company established a trading post in Surat.
15.	**1621**	Crosby Hall in Bishopsgate, London, became the new headquarters of the East India Company.

16.	**1623**	Unable to make headway in Japan, the Company closed its trading posts in that country.
	1623 9 March	Amboyna Massacre – rivalry between the Dutch and the English came to a head when the Dutch executed several English traders.
17.	**1634**	The Mughal Emperor invited the East India Company to trade in the Bengal region of India.
18.	**1638**	The Company moved its headquarters to Craven House in Leadenhall Street, London.
19.	**1640**	The Company established Fort St. George, a trading centre in Madras in South India.
20.	**1657**	Oliver Cromwell renewed the charter granting trading rights for the East India Company.
21.	**1667 April**	Cloth-makers and drapers in England, angry that imports of Indian cloth were threatening their livelihoods, rioted and attacked India House in London.
22.	**1668 27 March**	King Charles II leased Bombay, which he had acquired from the Portuguese as part of his wife's dowry, to the East India Company.
23.	**1670**	The power of the East India Company was increased when Charles II granted the Company the right to acquire territory, to mint money, to command fortresses, to make laws and use force to protect assets.
24.	**1673**	The East India Company made a loan of a substantial amount of saltpetre (an ingredient of gunpowder) to the king of England.
25.	**1682**	An attempt by the Company to obtain trading rights throughout the Mughal Empire was unsuccessful.

26.	**1683**	The Company's spice factory at Bantam was closed.
27.	**1684**	The East India Company began trading out of Guangzhou, China. Silk, tea and fine porcelain were brought back to England.
28.	**1690**	The Company established a trading post in the Calcutta region of India.
29.	**1694**	An act was passed that allowed any English company to trade with India.
30.	**1695 September**	An English pirate, Henry Every, led an attack on a fleet of Indian ships and pirated around £50,000 worth of treasure from one ship, the Fateh Muhammed, and around £400,000 from another, the Ganj-i-Sawai. The East India Company and the King's council put up a reward of £1,000 for the capture of the pirate Henry Every. The Mughal Emperor was furious and ordered the closure of four East India factories in India.
31.	**1696**	The Company built Fort William in Calcutta.
32.	**1698**	The East India Company was floated in a joint venture between the current stockholders and the State.
33.	**1700**	Chinese tea was extremely popular in England. The East India Company had paid for the tea with silver, but they became concerned that too much silver was leaving the country and so began using opium to pay for the tea.

The Who's Who

The Mughal Emperors

1.	**Akbar**	The third Mughal emperor, reigned from 1556 to 1605. In the year 1572-73, he conquered Gujarat. Akbar was conscious of the threat posed by the presence of the Portuguese and remained content with obtaining a cartaz (permit) from them for sailing in the Persian Gulf region. In 1573, he issued a firman directing Mughal administrative officials in Gujarat not to provoke the Portuguese in the territory they held in Daman. The Portuguese, in turn, issued passes for the members of Akbar's family to go on hajj to Mecca. In September 1579, Jesuits from Goa were invited to visit the court of Akbar. The emperor had his scribes translate the New Testament and granted the Jesuits freedom to preach the Gospel in his empire.
2.	**Jahangir**	The fourth Mughal emperor, ruled from 1605 until his death in 1627. Sir Thomas Roe, England's first ambassador to the Mughal court visited during his reign.
3.	**Shah Jahan**	The fifth Mughal emperor, reigned from 1628 to 1658. He was the Viceroy or Governor of Gujarat from 1618–1622.
4.	**Aurangzeb**	The sixth Mughal emperor, ruled over almost the entire Indian subcontinent for a period of 49 years from 1658-1707. During his reign, the Mughal empire reached its greatest extent, spanning nearly the entire Indian subcontinent. During his lifetime, victories in the south expanded the Mughal empire to 4

million square kilometres, and he ruled over a population estimated to be over 158 million subjects, with an annual revenue of $450 million (more than ten times that of his contemporary Louis XIV of France), or £38,624,680 (2,879,469,894 rupees) in 1690. At this time, India had surpassed Qing China to become the world's largest economy and biggest manufacturing power, worth nearly a quarter of the global GDP.

The Rulers of England

1.	Elizabeth I	Queen of England and Ireland from 17 November 1558 until her death on 24 March 1603.
2.	James I	He ruled from 24 March 1603 until his death in 1625. In October 1604, he assumed the title 'King of Great Britain', instead of 'King of England' and 'King of Scotland', though Sir Francis Bacon told him that he could not use the style in 'any legal proceeding, instrument or assurance'. The title was also not used on English statutes. The two Parliaments remained separate until the Acts of Union, 1707.
3.	Charles I	King of England, King of Scotland, and King of Ireland from 27 March 1625 until his execution in 1649. From 1642, Charles fought the armies of the English and Scottish Parliaments in the English Civil War. After his defeat in 1645, he surrendered to a Scottish force that eventually handed him over to the English Parliament. Charles I refused to accept his captors' demands for a constitutional monarchy, and temporarily escaped captivity in November 1647. Re-imprisoned on the Isle of Wight, Charles I forged an alliance with Scotland.

	However, by the end of 1648, Oliver Cromwell's New Model Army had consolidated its control over England. Charles was tried, convicted, and executed for high treason in January 1649. The monarchy was abolished and the Commonwealth of England was established as a republic. No monarch reigned between the execution of Charles I in 1649 and the Restoration of Charles II in 1660. Between 1649 and 1653, there was no single English head of state, as England was ruled directly by the Rump Parliament, with the English Council of State acting as executive power during a period known as the Commonwealth of England. After a coup d'etat in 1653, Oliver Cromwell forcibly took control of England from the Parliament. He dissolved the Rump Parliament at the head of a military force, and England entered a period known as The Protectorate, under Cromwell's direct control. He took on the title 'Lord Protector'.
4. Charles II	King of England, Scotland and Ireland from 1660, when the Restoration of the monarchy took place, until his death in 1685.
5. James II	Ruled from 6 February 1685, until he was deposed in the Glorious Revolution of 1688.

Presidents of the English East India Company Factory at Surat

The title of President came into use in 1618.

1.	**Thomas Aldworth**	1613-15
2.	**Thomas Kerridge**	1616-21
3.	**Thomas Rastell**	1621-25
4.	**Thomas Kerridge**	1625-28

5.	Richard Wylde	1628-30
6.	John Skibbow	Acting. April-September, 1630
7.	Thomas Rastell	1630-31
8.	Joseph Hopkinson	1631-33
9.	William Methwold	1633-39
10.	William Fremlin	1639-44
11.	Francis Breton	1644-49
12.	Thomas Merry	1649-52
13.	Jeremy Blackman	1652-55
14.	John Spiller	1656-57
15.	Henry Revington	1657-58
16.	Nathaniel Wyche	1658-59
17.	Matthew Andrews	1659-62
18.	Sir George Oxenden	1662

Travellers of the 17th century who have left accounts of the period

Name	Period of travel (in A.D.)	Under Reign	
1. Ralph Fitch	1585-1591	Akbar	first English traveller
2. John Linschoten	1583-1589	East India	Dutchman
3. Captain Hawkins	1608-1613	Jahangir	English traveller
4. William Fitch	1608-1612	Jahangir	English traveller
5. Thomas Coryat	1612-1617	Jahangir	English traveller
6. Sir Thomas Roe	1615-1619	Jahangir	English Ambassador
7. Edward Terry	1616-1619	Jahangir	English priest
8. Pietra Della Velle	1622-1660	Jahangir	from Italy

9. John Fryer	1627-1681	Shah Jahan	Englishman
10. Peter Mundy	1630-1634	Shah Jahan	from Italy
11. Jean-Baptiste Tavernier	1641-1687	Shah Jahan & Aurangzeb	French jeweller
12. Niccolao Manucci	1656-1687	Aurangzeb	from Italy
13. François Bernier	1658-1668	Aurangzeb	French doctor
14. Jean Thevenot	1666-1668	Aurangzeb	from France
15. John Ovington	1689-1692		English Chaplin hired by the East India Company. Travelled to Bombay and settled in Surat.
16. Johan Albrecht de Mandelslo	1616–1644		17th century German adventurer. Travelled to Isfahan (Persia) with a diplomatic mission, separated from the party and made his way to India, where he made interesting observations on the Mughal Empire, then ruled by Shah Jahan. Arriving at the port of Surat in April 1638, he moved on to Ahmedabad and Agra. He left India in 1644.

Introduction

Today, more than 160 years after the English East India Company wound up its business in India, its name still evokes a train of emotions in every Indian. From parliamentary debates to discussions at roadside tea-stalls, the East India Company is a synonym for any and all corporate excesses. The human rights abuses and corruption associated with the Enron power project at Dabhol brought these fears to a head in the late 1990s. "It's the second coming of the East India Company," argued Justice Daud, a retired judge of the Mumbai High Court, who led a fact-finding team following a series of violent incidents at Dabhol in March 1997. Again and again, 'the return of the East India Company' is used as a catch-phrase to describe the influx of multinationals into India post-liberalisation, whether global mining corporations or business in general.

The East India Company was the ultimate model and prototype for many of today's joint-stock multinational corporations. It remains history's most ominous warning about the potential for the abuse of corporate power, and the insidious means by which the interests of shareholders can seemingly become those of the State.

We are living at a time when the majority (about two-thirds) of the largest economies in the world are multinational corporations. The Itochu Corporation's sales, for instance, exceed the gross domestic product of Austria, while those of Royal Dutch/Shell equal Iran's GDP. Together, the sales of Mitsui & Co and General Motors are greater than the GDPs of Denmark, Portugal and Turkey combined, and US$50 billion more than all the GDPs of the countries in sub-Saharan Africa. Partly as a result of their size, these multinational corporations tend to dominate in industries where the output and markets are oligopolistic, or concentrated in the hands of a relatively small number of firms. The top five car and truck manufacturers are responsible for nearly 60 per cent of the worldwide sales of motor vehicles. The five leading oil majors account for over 40 per cent of that industry's global market share. For the chemicals sector, the comparable percentage is 35 per cent, and for both electronics and steel, it is over 50 per cent.[i] Not only are these multinational corporations seizing the power of governments, but they are also pulling the strings behind the scenes: bribery, blackmail, cronyism, etc. Acting beyond the level of nation-states, they are creating something entirely new – a global network of corporate governance that lacks any and all democratic procedure, transparency and accountability.

There are countless histories of the East India Company, yet none address its social record as a corporation. Leading lights of its own times examined its practices and found them wanting. Adam Smith, Edmund Burke and Karl Marx were all united in their critique – for quite different reasons – of this domineering, overbearing corporation. From the right to the left of the political spectrum, those who lived with the Company saw the corporation as a fundamentally problematic institution. For Adam Smith, the corporation was one of the great enemies of the open market, while for Edmund Burke, it posed a revolutionary threat to the established order in Britain and India. It also exhibited ethical failings of a structural nature. "Every rupee of profit made by an Englishman," Burke told the Parliament, "is lost forever to India." And for Marx, writing 70 years later as the Company was on its last legs, it was the standard-bearer of Britain's 'moneyocracy', a more terrible creation than "any of the divine monsters startling us in the Temple of Salsette near Mumbai". What makes the Company's story so unique

i 'Everybody's Favourite Monsters', *The Economist*, Survey of Multinationals, 27 March 1993.

is the way that its bid for unbounded economic power was repeatedly met by individuals such as these, struggling to make it accountable. As a result, the Company provides timeless lessons on how (and how not) to confront corporate excess through reform, protest, litigation, regulation, and ultimately, through corporate redesign.

Corporate imperialism is now a global phenomenon. The East India Company remains the prototype for almost all of these multinational corporations, providing a readymade template for them to follow. So, when the United Fruit Company – an American multinational corporation that traded in tropical fruit (primarily bananas) grown on Latin American plantations – was threatened by the agrarian reform legislation of the democratically-elected Guatemalan government of Colonel Jacobo Arbenz Guzmán, which would result in 40per cent of its land getting nationalised, it lobbied with the CIA (allegedly paying over a million US dollars), which arranged an invasion by US-backed forces led by Colonel Carlos Castillo Armas from the Honduras. The East India Company had basically invented corporate lobbying in 1692. Its records of that year show earmarking £1,200 for payments to various Members of Parliament who would vote for the Company to extend its monopoly. That was the first time a proper corruption scandal was associated with a corporation. Within 50 years, 40 per cent of British Parliamentarians actually had shares in the Company, and in turn, they worked as a block in Parliament to push through military support for the Company, an extension of its monopoly, and so on.

Added to this was the military might of the East India Company, which none of the modern multinational corporations possess. The East India Company had been authorized by its founding charter to "wage war" and had been using military and naval power to gain its ends since it boarded and captured a Portuguese vessel on its maiden voyage in 1602. But it was not until 1765 that the Company ceased to resemble a conventional trading corporation dealing in silks and spices, and became something altogether more unusual. In that year, in the Mughal fort of Allahabad, the young Mughal emperor Shah Alam, exiled from Delhi and defeated by the Company's troops, was forced into what we would now call an act of involuntary privatisation. He was forced to issue an order to dismiss his own Mughal revenue officials in Bengal, Bihar and Orissa, and replace them with a set of English traders appointed by Robert Clive, the new governor of Bengal and the directors of the Company, whom the document describes as "the high and mighty, the chief of illustrious warriors, the English Company". The collecting of Mughal taxes was henceforth subcontracted to a powerful multinational corporation whose revenue-collecting operations were protected by its own private army. Within a few months, 250 Company clerks backed by the military force of 20,000 locally-recruited Indian soldiers had become the effective rulers of the richest Mughal provinces. An international corporation was, for the first time, transforming itself into an aggressive colonial power. By around 1799, the East India Company had an army of 200,000 men, mostly sepoys in India, more than double the size of the British army at that time.

Perhaps the most crucial factor of all was the support that the East India Company enjoyed from the British Parliament. The relationship grew more symbiotic through the 18th century, until eventually it turned into what we might today call a public-private partnership. Returned nabobs such as Clive used their wealth to buy both Members of Parliament and Parliamentary seats. In turn, Parliament backed the Company with State power: the ships and soldiers that were needed when the rival French and British East India Companies trained their guns on each other. But the Company always had two targets in its sights; one was the lands where its business was conducted; and the other was the country that gave it birth, as its lawyers and lobbyists and MP shareholders slowly and subtly worked to influence and subvert the legislation of Parliament in its favour. The Parliamentary investigation into this, the world's first corporate lobbying scandal, found the East India Company guilty of bribery and insider trading, and led to the impeachment of the Lord President of the council, and the imprisonment of the Company's governor. Though other companies such as Cecil Rhodes and the British South African Company, acted as Pied Piper in the march towards exploitation and empire, the East India Company's conquest of India almost certainly remains the supreme act of corporate violence in history. For all the power wielded today by the largest corporations, whether Walmart or Google, they are tame beasts compared to the ravaging territorial appetite of the militarized East India Company.

The East India Company no longer exists, and it has thankfully, no exact modern equivalent in military terms. Walmart, which is the world's largest corporation in revenue terms, does not number among its assets a fleet of nuclear submarines; neither Facebook nor Shell possesses regiments of infantry. The most powerful among them do not need their own armies; they can rely on governments to protect their interests and bail them out. Many corporations nowadays, from Exxon to Coca-Cola, lobby for coups or hire mercenaries to protect their profits, acting as mini-empires in their own right. Now, several billionaires claim they intend to use their immense wealth to colonise space.

Four hundred and twenty years after its founding, the story of the East India Company has never been more current. The 400-year-old question of how to cope with the power and perils of large multinational corporations remains unanswered even today. It is not clear how a nation state, especially a fragile or impoverished one, can adequately protect itself and its citizens from corporate aggression.

On 28 February 1785, Edmund Burke delivered a now-famous speech, 'The Nabob of Arcot's Debts', wherein he condemned the damage to India by the East India Company. He correctly identified what remains today one of the great anxieties of modern liberal democracies: the ability of a ruthless corporation to corruptly buy a legislature. And just as corporations now recruit retired politicians in order to exploit their establishment contacts and use their influence, so did the East India Company. So it was, for example, that Lord Cornwallis, the man who oversaw the loss of the American colonies to Washington, was recruited by the EIC to oversee its Indian territories. Burke claimed, "Of all human conditions, perhaps the most brilliant and at the same time the most anomalous, is that of the Governor General of British India. A private English gentleman, and the servant of a joint-stock company, during the brief period of his government, he is the deputed sovereign of the greatest empire in the world; the ruler of a hundred million men; while dependant kings and princes bow down to him with a deferential awe and submission. There is nothing in history analogous to this position."

However, the corporation – a revolutionary European invention contemporaneous with the beginnings of European colonialism, and which helped give Europe its competitive edge – has continued to thrive long after the collapse of European imperialism. When historians discuss the legacy of British colonialism in India, they usually mention democracy, the rule of law, railways, tea and cricket. Yet the idea of the joint-stock company is arguably one of Britain's most important exports to India, and the one that has for better or for worse, changed South Asia as much any other European idea. Its influence certainly outweighs that of communism and Protestant Christianity, and possibly even that of democracy.

The Beginnings

Colonial rule was certainly the final outcome of the Company's adventurism in Asia. But it was the hunt for personal and corporate profit that had drawn the Company inexorably on. The results of this enduring dynamic were world-shattering. By the time of its demise, the Company had changed the course of economic history, reversing the centuries' old flow of wealth from west to east. From Roman times, Europe had always been Asia's commercial supplicant, shipping out gold and silver in return for spices, textiles and other luxury goods. European traders were attracted to the East for its wealth and sophistication at a time when the Western economy was a fraction the size of Asia's. And for its first 150 years, the Company had to repeat this practice, as there was almost nothing that England could export that the East wanted to buy. Then, first in Bengal in the decades that followed Plassey, and then in China through the opium trade, the Company broke this long-standing pattern of trade and wealth. By the time of its demise, Europe's economy was double the size of those of China and India, a complete reversal of the situation in 1600. There are many elements in this turnaround, but the East India Company was certainly one of the chief agents that engineered the great switch in global development that marked the birth of the modern age.

From 1600 to 1858, the life span of the Company, there occurred its dramatic metamorphosis from a small commercial group sponsored by Queen Elizabeth into a cumbersome organization that controlled enormous revenues, vast properties, armed forces, innumerable ships and countless trading posts. What the East India Company accomplished, however, was not achieved without vicissitudes and constant obstacles. It was harassed by wars, both foreign and internal. The Dutch, the Portuguese and the French traders sought at all times to force their English competitors out of the Far East. Pirates marauded East Indiamen, looting cargoes, and torturing and killing the crews. The home office was faced by apathy, then opposition, and finally violent protests against "the wrongs of a monopoly". And yet, despite the hazards that blocked its progress, the Company prospered. By 1700, its trading posts were established up and down both sides of the Indian coast, at isolated places on the Malay Peninsula, and on many of the remote islands lying south and east. It was in these decades that the foundations of the Company were firmly established.

The 18th century saw fruition: trading posts became the nuclei of permanent settlements – colonies that became ultimately Calcutta, Bombay and Madras. This was the time of the Company's major triumphs, its military victories, its invaluable treaties with local potentates, its first acquisition of rich revenue-producing properties. It was also the time of menacing opposition on the part of the British public. As the renowned historian and able compiler of valuable state papers preserved in the Bombay Secretariat, G.W. Forrest has pointed out, the English enterprise, after roaming over the Indian seas, first furled its wandering sail at the port of Surat and there founded a small factory, which afterwards grew into that stately fabric of an empire in the East.

To begin with, the English Company was more interested in spice trade with Moluccas. Its first two voyages did not even touch the Indian mainland. And on the Third Voyage, only one of three vessels under Hawkins was to land at Surat to explore trade possibilities, and it did land there on 4 August 1608. Surat was the most important port of the Mughal Empire, the richest and the most powerful monarchy in the world. India, at that time, had more than a quarter of the world's GDP, more than China. The Mughal Emperor, with a standing army of 4 million, was the most powerful monarch on the face of the earth. But they were weak at sea, which was controlled completely by the Portuguese who had been trading in these parts for more than a century when the first English ships arrived.

Almost at the same time as the English East India Company was born, the Dutch East India Company, or the VOC, was also formed in 1602, which proved to be a tough rival. They started with a capital base of almost ten times that of the English East India Company, and considerably more military power and State support. By 1623, they had completely ousted the English East India Company from the Spice Islands by force, massacring Englishmen and others at Amboyna. Both militarily and financially, they could not match VOC. Added to that, there was trouble at home from the English rulers. After Queen Elizabeth's death, James I became the king of England in 1603. Both James I, and his successor Charles I, created problems for the Company till 1649 when Charles I was executed, by financially squeezing the Company as often as possible, and constantly propping up rival companies to seriously undermine their monopoly rights. As per the Company records, there were at least four instances during this period when the directors of the Company were on the brink of winding up operations, unable to cope with the pressure from the king, or otherwise.

Another problem for the East India Company was that it had established its base at Surat, inside Mughal dominion. The Portuguese and the Dutch began by establishing factories and forts outside Mughal Empire, particularly the Malabar region in southern India, where they could overpower local rulers. This was a distinct disadvantage for the English to begin with. Though the English had a factory at Masulipatnam, and by 1639, Francis Day would lay the foundations of Madras, Surat remained their Eastern headquarters during the entire 17th century.

During the second half of the 17th century, two new threats emerged. The Marathas, as part of their war of independence against the Mughals, raided Surat twice, in 1664 and in 1670, and completely ruined the English trade. And at sea, there emerged the menace of pirates. But the East India Company managed to endure all these, and survive.

One crucial aspect in the study of history in India as well as in England has been its complete focus on polity. When dealing with a particular period, politics remains the central theme, followed by social condition, art and culture, etc. But the East India Company, essentially being an economic entity, a closer look at trade in India and Surat is crucial for the understanding of the struggle and survival of the Company during the 17th century. In fact, the reason why most contemporary literature on the narrative of Modern India begin with the British era after the arrival of Robert Clive and the battle of Plassey, is precisely because of this. The Company was not a political entity before Clive. However, understanding the trade ecosystem of the period is key to understanding the reason for the success of the Company, when so many odds were stacked against it.

The story of the first English factory at Surat is, therefore, the story of survival of a relatively weaker company against two formidable European rivals, entangled in the interplay between the most powerful monarch in the world and some of the richest merchants in the world. Added to that are two hostile successive rulers at home, some of the most dreaded and the most celebrated, pirates of all times, and the Marathas in ascendancy. The story of the English factory at Surat, the original headquarters of the Company in India, is not a long one. The importance of the factory, the centre from which the whole of the Company's operations in the East were controlled, faded gradually before the rising star of Bombay. Surat had many disadvantages: by sea it was crippled by the lack of a good harbour, and by land it was open to incursions by the Mughals and the Marathas. But it existed and survived for nearly a century. This is the story of that first English establishment on Indian soil.

Chapter 1
The Quest for the Indies

On 29 May 1453, the forces of the 21-year-old Ottoman Sultan Mehmed II captured Constantinople, the capital city of the Byzantine Empire, ending a 53-day siege that had begun on 6 April 1453. Hailed in the Islamic history as a victory next only to the recapture of Jerusalem by Saladin in 1187 during the third Crusades, the capture of Constantinople changed the course of world history. For Christian Europe, Mehmed's victory at Constantinople represented a serious shift in its dealings with the East. Many modern scholars agree that the exodus of Greeks to Italy as a result of this event marked the end of the Middle Ages and the beginning of the Renaissance in Europe.

The fall of Constantinople severely hurt the trading and mercantile activities in the European region. The Ottoman conquest affected the highly lucrative Italian trade, and gradually ruined the trade bases in the region. This commerce, dating back to the Roman era, started from the marts of Eastern Asia and reached the Mediterranean by three main routes. The northern tracks by way of the Oxus and Caspian, converged on to the Black Sea. The middle route lay through Syria to the Levant. And the southern one brought the products of India by sea to Egypt, and from there, they passed to Europe through the mouths of the Nile. The struggle for these trade routes had, for centuries, formed a key to the policies and wars of many nations throughout history. After 1453, a great necessity arose in Europe to search out new lines of approach to India. From that quest begins the history of modern commerce.

The Ottoman seizure and subsequent obstruction of the Indian trade routes had brought disaster to the

Mediterranean republics. The blow fell first on Genoa and Venice, and it sent a shock throughout the entire system of European commerce. In 1453, very few Christian rulers in Western Europe cared for the fate of Constantinople to send any real military help against the Ottoman Turks. However, these European countries depended upon Constantinople for much of their economic livelihood. A huge part of the medieval world economy was powered by spices, silk and gold coins that travelled on this road. After 1453, travel by Europeans on the Silk Road virtually ended. Europe fell into what we might today call a recession. Asian goods were not reaching the markets in Europe. Something had to be done.

In 1453, while Constantinople fell, Christopher Columbus was just a boy in Genoa. But the fall of Constantinople had already shaped his fate, jump-starting as it did the Age of Exploration. The Portuguese pioneered the idea of reaching the Orient over water as opposed to a land route. Making use of what the Europeans knew about the world in the late 15th century, the Portuguese decided to sail east around the horn of Africa to reach India, South East Asia and China. The Indian Ocean had been a hub of trade for much of the Middle Ages and they decided to exploit it.

The existence of this trade route around Africa had long been suspected in Europe. Herodotus (c. 484 BC-c. 425 BC), the 'Father of History', in his book[1] speaks of two attempts to circumnavigate Africa. The first was by Pharaoh Necho (610 BC-595 BC) who sent an expedition consisting of Phoenician[i] mariners, who sailed down the Red Sea, and after three years, returned through the Strait of Gibraltar. The second attempt was by Xerxes (519 BC-465 BC), the Persian Emperor who had permitted a Persian noble named Sataspes, who was lying under a sentence of death, to expiate his crime by a similar feat. He set out in the opposite

i Phoenicia was a region around Levant that is present-day Lebanon and Syria.

direction through the Strait of Gibraltar, but returned after reaching a point called Soloeis, the modern Cape Spartel in present-day Morocco.

There were several such attempts throughout the history of Europe, but they all failed. The real value of the early explorers lay not so much in their actual achievements, as in the information which they had collected for the Portuguese, to be used in the latter half of the 15th century.

Apart from economic necessity, the race for exploration of sea routes to Asia had the fervour of religious zeal too. The Portuguese were more inclined on instituting a new crusade against the Mohammedans by carrying the war into their own backyard. They crept farther and farther down the African coast, erecting crosses, converting natives, kidnapping them for slaves, or searching for the kingdom of the legendary Prester John until in 1487, Bartholomew Diaz discovered the famous Cape, which, for his manifold troubles, he termed Cabo Tormentoso, or the tempestuous Cape. But King John II of Portugal (1481-95), hoping to discover the Indies, named it the 'Cape of Good Hope'.

The Search for Prester John

Prester John, also called Presbyter John or John the Elder, was a legendary Christian ruler of the East, popularized in medieval chronicles and traditions as a hoped-for ally against the Muslims in the crusades. Prester John was at the centre of a number of legends that hark back to the writings of 'John the Elder' in the New Testament. There was a long-standing Christian tradition about Apostle Thomas preaching in India in the first century A.D., in the present-day Indian states of Kerala and Tamil Nadu. Itself based largely on oral tradition, this had given rise to many legends of a faraway and mysterious 'Christian' India. This India was believed to be a Christian kingdom, ruled by a certain 'Prester (priest) John'. This legend, widespread especially in the late Middle

Ages, even reached Russia, where this legendary priest-king was known as 'The Tsar and Priest Ivan'. The first historical mention of Prester John is found in the Chronicle of Otto by Bishop of Freising, also known as Otto van Freisingen (1145), which reports that the emperor (Prester John) had set out with an army to help the Crusaders in Jerusalem, but was unable to cross the Tigris. In 1177, Pope Alexander III sent a letter to this (legendary) emperor, but no response was received. The Bishop of Gabala spoke of a Christian ruler in the distant lands of the East. At roughly the same time, someone calling himself 'Prester John', descendant of one of the Three Magi and King of India, wrote a letter to the Byzantine Emperor Manuel I Komnenos (28 November 1118 – 24 September 1180).[2]

The mythical emperor was, most importantly, a Christian: Prester signified 'priest'. It was thought that he had descended from one of the Three Magi,[ii] and from the queen of Sheba, and that his empire was vast, with 72 dependent kingdoms. Thus, it was believed, he had massive military power and untold wealth. The sultan of Cairo was said to pay tribute to him owing to his power to change the course of the Nile, which had its source in his kingdom.

This 'India' ruled by Prester John was a half-legendary country. Even its exact location wasn't clear, and different maps showed it in different places. In Medieval Europe, there were as many as three Indias. The Prester John who wrote the letter to the Byzantine Emperor Manuel I Komnenos, claimed himself to be the ruler of all three, including the one where the body of Apostle Thomas was buried. Fascinated by this mysterious Christian ruler, travellers and missionaries from Europe repeatedly tried to find his

---

ii As per Christian tradition, these were three wise men or three kings who visited Jesus after his birth, bearing gifts of gold, frankincense and myrrh.

descendants. The lands of this Prester John were said to be filled with all manner of strange creatures and peoples.

Not having found the legendary kingdom in Asia, at the end of the 13th century, Europeans began to seek it in Africa. The 'third India' was supposed to be located there. In 1321-1324, a Dominican missionary named Jordanus de Severac wrote a book called the *Mirabilia*. In it, he described the 'far India', which he equated with the Ethiopia of Prester John. Interestingly, the search for the treasures of the Indies was at least partially a search for the kingdom of Prester John.

In works such as 'The Travels of Sir John Mandeville'[3] and 'Historia Trium Regum' by John of Hildesheim[4], Prester John's domain is refreshed in its fantastic aspects, and finds itself located not on the steppes of Central Asia, but back in India proper, or some other exotic locale.

> *"This emperor, Prester John, holds full great land, and hath many full noble cities and good towns in his realm and many great diverse isles and large. For all the country of Ind is devised in isles for the great floods that come from Paradise, that depart all the land in many parts. .... In the land of Prester John be many diverse things and many precious stones, so great and so large, that men make of them vessels, as platters, dishes, and cups. ... In that desert be many wild men, that be hideous to look on; for they be horned, and they speak nought, but they grunt, as pigs. And there is also great plenty of wild hounds."*[5]

Prester John and his son David were described as kings of India to whom the Mongols used to pay tribute. Genghis Khan, it was rumoured, had put an end to this practice by invading the land of Prester John and defeating King David.

The Portuguese voyages to Africa from the late 15th century led to the modification and ultimately the dispelling of the myth, which had partly inspired them. In 1484, the king of Benin told the Portuguese of a ruler named Ogàmé, a

'Lord of lords', who lived 250 leagues east of Benin, and gave his dependents a little cross to cement their friendship. This gave the Portuguese hope that they were close to finding the legendary ruler. In 1521, King Manuel of Portugal wrote to Pope Leo X to tell him that Portuguese captains had found Prester John in Ethiopia. Francisco Alvarez, who spent six years at the Ethiopian court of Lebna Dengel (David II) and Queen Helena, wrote an account which exploded many of the myths. 1530 was the last year that a 'letter from Prester John' made its way across Europe. People were basically fed up with the legend. All the same, in European cartography, the kingdom of Prester John continued to be drawn until the 17th century. Europeans began to realize that the Prester's territory was not so vast, that his people were not so Christian, nor was his treasury as bottomless as they had dreamed. It gradually became clear that even the name 'Prester John' was a European invention rather than an Ethiopian reality, but the myth lived on, inspiring writers from Shakespeare and Samuel Johnson to John Buchan and Umberto Eco. Even today, the legend continues to fascinate. Umberto Eco wrote a novel *Baudolino,* inspired by it.

Sea Navigation in Medieval Europe

In the ancient days, sea navigation used the position of the stars and the coasts as guides. Later on, the invention of the compass with the magnetic needle directed travellers on their journeys through land and through the vast seas. The Italians were the inventors of the art of printing, making guns, and perhaps also of the compasses. When the Portuguese entered the waters of the Indian Ocean, they found that the compass was being used by "the Moores, together with Cards and Quadrants to observe both the Heavens and the Earth".[6] The Arab navigators who were basically merchants, guided the Portuguese in their search for exotic spices, and were the dominant group in the Indian

Ocean trading world. Afonso D'Albuquerque, for example, found it absolutely necessary to obtain the services of an Arab pilot by force or fraud, when he made his way into the Red Sea in 1513.

One of the earliest human-made navigational tools used to aid mariners was the mariner's compass, which was an early form of the magnetic compass. Early mariners thought the mariner's compass was often inaccurate and inconsistent because they did not understand the concept of magnetic variation, which is the angle between true north (geographic) and the magnetic north. During the mid-13th century, mariners began realizing that maps could be helpful and began keeping detailed records of their voyages. Thus, the first nautical charts were created. These first charts were not very accurate, but were considered valuable and often kept secret from other mariners. There was no latitude or longitude labelled on the charts, but between major ports, there was a compass rose indicating the direction to travel.[iii] In the South China Sea and the Indian Ocean, a navigator could take advantage of the fairly-constant monsoon winds to judge direction. This made long one-way voyages possible twice a year.

Islamic geography and navigational sciences made use of a magnetic compass and a rudimentary instrument known as a 'kamal', used for celestial navigation and for measuring the altitudes and latitudes of the stars. Another instrument available, again developed by the Arabs, was the quadrant. Also a celestial navigation device, it was originally developed for astronomy and later transitioned to navigation. When combined with detailed maps of the period, sailors were able to sail across oceans rather than skirt along coasts. Muslim sailors were also responsible for the use and development of the lateen sails and large three-

---

iii The term 'compass rose' comes from the figure's compass points, which resemble rose petals.

masted merchant vessels to the Mediterranean. The origins of the caravel ship, developed and used for long-distance travel by the Portuguese since the 15th century, and later by the Spanish, also date back to the qarib used by Andalusian explorers during the 13th century. Vikings used polarization and the sunstone to help the navigation of their ships, by locating the sun even in a completely overcast sky.[7]

Spain Joins the Race

In the 15th and 16th centuries, the Crown of Castile and then the 'unified' Crown of Spain, was also at the vanguard of European global exploration and colonial expansion. The Spanish Crown opened trade routes across the oceans, especially the transatlantic expeditions of Christopher Columbus on behalf of Castile, from 1492 onwards. The Crown of Castile, under Charles I of Spain, also sponsored the first expedition of world circumnavigation in 1521. The enterprise was led by the Portuguese navigator Ferdinand Magellan, and completed by the Spanish Basque Juan Sebastián Elcano. The trips of exploration led to trade flourishing across the Atlantic Ocean between Spain and America, and across the Pacific Ocean between the Asia-Pacific and Mexico via the Philippines.

The Papal Bull

At around the same time as Bartholomew Diaz discovered the Cape of Good Hope, one Peter Covilian, travelling via Constantinople and Aden, had actually managed to reach Goa and Calicut. Peter Covilian was sent by King John II in May 1487 to the land of the legendry Prester John, through the land route of Alexandria-Cairo-Aden. Having reached Aden, Covilian took the sea route near the Straits of the Red Sea, to Cannanore, and from there to Calicut and Goa. On his return, he was detained at the Abyssinian court, but he managed to send back to his master a map of the coast of East Africa and the way to India.

Armed with Covilian's map, Vasco da Gama, after many anxious months of training and utmost care in the selection of tackle, stores, medicines and charts, sailed with splendid pomp from Lisbon with three ships and 160 men on 9 July 1497. On 20 May 1498, he cast anchor at Calicut, and the Cape route to India was opened.

Meanwhile, something interesting had happened in Europe. Christopher Columbus, a Genoese, had offered his services to Portugal for the discovery of a western route to India. But finding himself ignored, he made the same offer to Spain and discovered land. Spain became the claimant of the Americas. The discovery of the Americas caused much anxiety in Portugal, as it was believed that the West Indies were actually the outworks of the Asiatic continent, and that Columbus had actually found a short cut to India. Columbus' arrival in supposedly Asiatic lands in the western Atlantic Ocean in 1492, threatened the unstable relations between Portugal and Spain. With word that King John of Portugal was preparing a fleet to sail to the west, Queen Isabella and King Ferdinand of Spain initiated diplomatic discussions over the rights to possess and govern the newly-found lands. The matter was referred to the Vatican. The Pope at that time was Alexander VI or Rodrigo de Borgia, one of the most controversial Popes of all time, so much so that the word Borgia has become a byword for libertinism and nepotism.

Pope Alexander VI was a Spaniard, a native of Valencia, and as ruler of the Papal States, was embroiled in a territorial dispute with Ferdinand's first cousin, Ferdinand I, King of Naples. Therefore, he was amicable to any requests of Isabella and Ferdinand. Spain was able to secure a Papal Bull also called *Inter caetera*, which stated:

"...[W]e... assign to you and your heirs and successors, kings of Castile and Leon,... all islands and mainlands found and to be found, discovered and to be discovered towards the west and south, by drawing and establishing a line from... the north,... to... the south,... the said line to be distant one hundred leagues towards the west and south from any of the islands commonly known as the Azores and Cape Verde."[8]

This settlement was not very definite and complications arose from time-to-time. However, these were finally settled when the Spanish and Portuguese crowns were united in 1580.

The First Europeans in India

When Vasco da Gama arrived at Calicut, he saw that the open harbour was filled with vessels of all sizes, and the beach was lined with shops and warehouses. When the Europeans arrived, many boats rowed up to sell them coconuts, chicken and other fresh produce. Families of curious sightseers along with their children, were out to see the ships that looked quite different from those usually plying the Indian Ocean. A crowded street called the Avenue of Trees led to the palace of the Samudrin[iv] of Calicut. The ground was strewn with white blossoms from the trees. The rich and powerful were carried about in palanquins, and were preceded by men blowing trumpets to clear the way.[v] On his way to the palace, Vasco da Gama even stopped to pray at a Hindu temple under the mistaken belief that the Hindus were heretical Christians!

The opulent palace of the Samudrin was spread over a square mile and surrounded by lacquered walls. The Samudrin received Vasco da Gama in his royal chamber

---

iv Zamorin

v This may be the reason why people in India love to blow their car horns today; it is an assertion of self-importance!

while seated on a green couch below a silk canopy. He was bare-bodied above the waist, except for a string of pearls and a heart-shaped emerald surrounded by rubies, the insignia of royalty. Vasco da Gama knelt and presented a letter from King Manuel[vi]. He also laid out the gifts he had brought with him. The Samudrin was evidently not impressed with the gifts, but agreed to trade in pepper and other spices in exchange for gold and silver.

The Arab merchants of Calicut were understandably unhappy to see their monopoly being broken. They even arranged to kidnap da Gama before he could return to his ship, but the Samudrin intervened and had him freed. The prosperity of Calicut depended on free trade, and the Samudrin had to ensure that the principle was upheld even though he felt uneasy about these newcomers. The Portuguese fleet, however, did not wait for long. After purchasing pepper, they lifted their anchors and headed home. Vasco da Gama wanted to get home as soon as possible to tell his king about his discoveries. He received a rapturous welcome back home and was showered with honours, as well as 20,000 gold cruzados.[vii] However, the human cost of the expedition had been great – two-thirds of the crew had perished during the voyage, including Vasco da Gama's brother. This did not deter King Manuel from declaring himself 'Lord of Guinea, and of the Conquest, the Navigation and Commerce of Ethiopia, Arabia, Persia and India'.

Preparations now began for sending a much larger fleet to India. Thirteen ships armed with cannons and 1,200 men, under the overall command of Pedro Alvares Cabral were mobilized. Despite the loss of some ships along the way, the fleet arrived in Calicut in September 1500, and demanded that the Samudrin expel all the Arabs and trade exclusively

---

vi John II's successor

vii Coins in Portugal in those days.

with Portugal. The Samudrin, understandably, was not keen on such an arrangement. While prolonged negotiations were continuing, a large Arab ship loaded with cargo and pilgrims for hajj decided to set sail for Aden. Cabral seized the ship and the Arabs retaliated by attacking a Portuguese contingent that was in the city. The Portuguese now seized ten more Arab ships in the harbour and burned their crew alive in full view of the people ashore. Next, they bombarded the city for two days, and even forced the Samudrin to flee from his palace – a humiliation that the rulers of Calicut would never forget. Cabral loaded his ship with pepper and other spices, made payments in gold coins and headed home. In order to gauge the potential profits, pepper that made its way to Venice by the traditional Rea Sea route used to cost sixty to hundred times its price on the Kerala coast. With the discovery of this new route, it was clear that Venice was ruined.

Using the profits from these successful voyages, the Portuguese now rapidly scaled up the number of fleets operating in the Indian Ocean. Within a couple of decades, they sacked or occupied most of the important ports in the western Indian Ocean region – Muscat, Mombasa, Socotra, Hormuz, Malacca and so on. And in the process, even by the standards of that time, they established a well-deserved reputation for extreme cruelty. For example, when Vasco da Gama returned on a second voyage to Calicut, he refused to negotiate and simply bombarded the city. He seized all the ships he found in the harbour and their crews – 800 men in all. They were paraded on ships' decks and then killed by having their arms, noses and ears amputated. The body parts were piled into a boat and sent ashore. When the Samudrin sent a Brahmin to negotiate for peace, he was gruesomely killed. The Brahmin's two sons and a nephew who had accompanied him were hanged from the mast. In other words, the maritime world of the Indian Ocean rim, now experienced a shock similar to what had been experienced by the inland cities of Asia during the Mongol invasions.

The Islamic world clearly needed to respond. It fell on the Turks to provide a comeback. The Ottoman Turks were the most powerful Muslim empire of that time and had taken Constantinople[viii] in 1453, thereby ending the last vestige of the Byzantines. Although their military tactics were derived from the Central Asian steppes, they had recently developed naval capability in the Mediterranean. However, they were aware that their galleys were not capable of dealing with the much more demanding conditions in the Indian Ocean. The traditional vessels of the Arabs were also deemed unsuitable, as the stitched ships could not take the shock wave from the recoil of firing cannons. Twelve large warships were custom-built on the Red Sea and fitted out with cannons. Interestingly, Venice provided the Turks with inputs from their spies in Portugal, and even put a team of gunners at the Turkish Sultan's disposal. Clearly, economic interests trumped all religious differences.

The Turkish fleet sailed down the Red Sea in early 1507 under the command of Amir Husayn and headed for the Indian coast. Together with reinforcements sent by the Samudrin of Calicut, the Turks won the battle against a small and unprepared Portuguese fleet anchored at Chaul.[ix] The Portuguese were enraged, and a larger fleet was assembled. The two sides met near the island of Diu just off the coast of Gujarat, in February 1509. In the battle that followed, the superiority of European ship and cannon designs was fully displayed. Within hours, Husayn's defensive line had been shattered and the Turks were forced to flee. An additional factor that helped the Portuguese was the fact that the forces sent by the Sultan of Gujarat remained neutral, rather than helping their fellow Muslims. The Turkish admiral would

viii Istanbul

ix Near modern-day Mumbai

complain bitterly about this treachery when he faced the Ottoman Sultan in Istanbul. But this victory ensured that for the next hundred years, the Portuguese would remain unchallenged on both sides of the Arabian Sea, the Persian Gulf and the Red Sea.

The Portuguese made a great success of their trade in India. Under Albuquerque (1509-15) their power reached its zenith. Albuquerque captured Goa in 1510. He conquered Ormuz, in the Persian Gulf in 1515 and put the control of the Persian Gulf route in the hands of Portugal. He almost succeeded in seizing Aden, the key to the Red Sea, and also occupied Socotra[x]. Along the west coast of India, a string of Portuguese forts stretched from Diu to Cochin, while on the east coast they held St. Thome and Negapatam. In Ceylon, it was Manaar, Colombo and Galle, while in the Far East, they took over Amboyna, Tidore, Macao, and Manilla; and on the coast of Africa, Sofala and Mozambique.

The Portuguese had come to India not as mere merchants or colonists, but as crusaders. This led them to commit acts of cruelty, which ensured that they were detested by the locals. The massacre, mutilation and torture of captives was the rule rather than the exception. They thought nothing of stuffing an Arab merchant's mouth with dirt and fastening it up with a slice of pork; or cutting off the ears of a Brahmin spy and sewing dog's ears to his head. Almeida did this at Diu in 1509. While at Cannanore, he stuffed his prisoners into his ships' guns and blew them out. The horrors of the Inquisition were afterwards added to the brutalities of forcible conversion, and were applied even to the unoffending Nestorian Christians who had been living in the region around the Malabar Coast since 52 A.D., when St. Thomas was said to have landed there. Temples were plundered as a religious duty. The sacred Tooth of the Buddha, revered by millions in Ceylon, Burma and Siam, was pounded in a mortar and hurled into

x Part of Yemen

the sea. It was only adverse winds which saved Albuquerque from attempting a raid upon Medina, where he had planned on holding up the body of the Prophet to ransom in exchange for the surrender of Jerusalem and the Holy Sepulchre.[xi] Albuquerque even had plans to divert the Nile into the Red Sea, leaving Cairo high and dry![9]

Although there was always an air of uncertainty, things were tolerable till the arrival of Francis Xavier, a Jesuit missionary, in 1542. Xavier, later to be canonized as a saint, is known today in India for the numerous Jesuit schools and colleges named after him. However, it was he who invited the Inquisition to Goa before leaving for Malacca. At the time the Inquisition arrived in Goa, the vast majority of the local population practised Hinduism, and there were numerous temples dedicated to the goddess Shanta-Durga. Egged on by the Jesuits, the Portuguese would destroy hundreds of temples. Thousands of Hindus would be killed or forcibly converted to Christianity. Many small children were forcibly taken away and baptized. The remains of destroyed temples can still be seen in Goa, some with churches built over them. One example is the Mahalasa Narayani temple in the village of Verna, which was destroyed in 1567, and was rebuilt in 2000-05.[xii]

The Inquisition soon turned on the communities of the Syrian Christians who had lived peacefully on India's west coast for over a thousand years before the arrival of the Portuguese. Their ancient rituals were condemned as heretical and they were forced to convert as well.

But Portuguese supremacy began to decline in the second half of the 16th century. The fall of the Vijayanagar Empire in 1565 had a disastrous effect on their prosperity. Goa was

xi According to the Bible, the Holy Sepulchre refers to the temporary tomb in which Jesus was reportedly buried following his crucifixion.

xii Incidentally, the site also has a large stone carving of a female figure that may date back to the Neolithic age.

besides a rather unhealthy spot, and was devastated by periodical epidemics – cholera in 1543 and epidemic fever in 1570 and 1635.[10] It is true that after 1570, the Portuguese secured the patronage of the Mughal court, but this was due to the unwearied diplomacy of the Jesuit Mission which had settled in Agra in the time of Akbar, and had maintained for the next fifty years, an unceasing struggle against English attempts to procure a firman to trade from the Mughal Emperor. The Mughals were too powerful and too distant to feel the effects of Portuguese fanaticism.

At Goa and throughout Portuguese India, corruption and venality were widespread. The Portuguese, too proud to earn money honestly by trade, were driven to make it by less honourable means. The civic virtues of Albuquerque and Dom João de Castro were supplanted by corruption and venality. Justice was bought, public offices were put up for sale, and the martial spirit degenerated into effeminacy, sloth and indolence.

This same story is told by John Linschoten, a Dutch merchant, trader and historian, who speaks of Portuguese women as being secluded in privacy, and indulging in intrigues before the very eyes of their husbands, whom they drugged with datura.[11] An English doctor, John Fryer, writing in 1681, confirms this. "The Portugals," he writes, "generally forgetting their pristine virtue, lust, riot and rapine, the ensuing consequences of a long undisturbed peace where wealth abounds, are the only remarkable reliques of their ancient worth; their courages being so much effeminated that it is a wonder to most how they keep anything, if it were not that they have lived among mean-spirited neighbours."[12]

The English came to India in a very different spirit from the Portuguese. At first, they sought neither colonies nor converts. They came neither as crusaders nor as conquerors, but as simple merchants. "A war and traffic are incompatible," wrote Sir Thomas Roe to his employers, the directors of the East India Company. "It is the beggaring of the Portuguese, notwithstanding their many rich residences and territories, that they keep soldiers that spend it. They never profited by the Indies since they defended it."[13]

The first Englishmen were plain merchants, very different from the haughty hidalgos of Goa. They had little liking for the upper classes. The English East India Company had even requested the Crown "to be allowed to sort their business with men of their own quality, lest the suspicion of the employment of gentlemen, being taken hold of by the generality, do drive a great number of the adventurers to withdraw their contributions!"[14] They were not out to fight, but would defend themselves if molested when in pursuit of their calling.

England Under Elizabeth Joins the Race

At first, England, bound by the Papal Bull, had to confine her efforts to attempts to discover a North West or North East passage to India through the Arctic Ocean. However, things began to change when in 1558, Elizabeth I succeeded her half-sister, Mary, as queen of England. Elizabeth I depended heavily of a group of trusted advisers led by William Cecil, the first Baron Burghley. One of her first acts as Queen of England was the establishment of the English Protestant Church, of which she herself became the Supreme Governor. She passed an act in the English Parliament, the Act of Supremacy 1559 which did three things – firstly, Elizabeth became the head of the Church of England; secondly, asserting the authority of any foreign prince, or prelate[xiii] was declared a crime, thereby abolishing the authority of the Vatican Pope in England; and thirdly, high treason[xiv] was made punishable by death.

---

xiii Any high-ranking church, including the Bishop of the Church.

xiv Roughly, treason against the monarch.

The Pope at the Vatican waited nearly eleven years to react, the delay being caused in part by a number of royal Catholic suitors who hoped to marry Elizabeth, and also because she had tolerated the Catholic way of worship in private. But the revolt by the Northern Earls, and the Desmond Rebellions in Ireland that was aimed at replacing Elizabeth with Mary, Queen of Scots, hardened Queen Elizabeth, and the persecution of the Catholics began. In their support, Pope Pius V issued a papal bull called *Regnans in Excelsis* on 25 February 1570, declaring "Elizabeth, the pretended Queen of England and the servant of crime", to be a heretic and releasing all her subjects from any allegiance to her, even when they had "sworn oaths to her", and excommunicating anyone who obeyed her orders.

The Excommunication Year has been taken as marking a distinct departure in the policy of England towards sea trade. The queen's title to the crown she was now wearing had been called into question by the titular head of Christendom, one of whose predecessors Pope Alexander VI, had divided the whole world outside Europe between the Kings of Portugal and Spain through the papal bull. A series of political events that followed this – including attempts on her own life, the massacre of Bartholomew's Day (1572) and the Spanish Fury at Antwerp (1576) – hardened Elizabeth to declare herself independent of the directions of the Vatican.

Another consequence of this was the royal support that sea piracy received, particularly in the English Channel. These pirates were, however, referred to by a polite Elizabethan euphemism – Privateers. This was the period of renaissance for the Royal English Navy, in which the queen exhibited the liveliest interest. By 1578, she had succeeded in forming a fleet of 24 vessels with a total of 7,000 men, the largest being the Triumph, which was 1,000 tonnes, while there were two of 900 tonnes, two of 800 tonnes, five of 600 tonnes and so on down to 60 tonnes. Sir John Hawkins was at its helm as Treasurer of the Navy, despite there being some suspicion of his financial practices. As far back as 1532, William Hawkins of Plymouth, father of Sir John Hawkins, had sailed to the Guinea Coast and became a pioneer in a style of trade in which Martin Frobisher and Francis Drake subsequently served apprenticeship. Hawkins' plan was to make a round voyage from England to Guinea, and thence to Brazil – where, after Sebastian Cabot, now in the Spanish service, he was the first English representative – and then home. By 1562, William Hawkins, along with his son John, had become the biggest exponents of the slave trade, trading between Africa and the Spanish colonies in Brazil. In 1578, Drake voyaged into the Southern Ocean, and reached Tidore in the heart of the Spice Islands in modern-day eastern Indonesia, on his homeward voyage. Cavendish repeated the feat in 1586. The defeat of the Spanish Armada two years later finally asserted England's supremacy at sea and laid the foundations of her overseas empire.

Decline of the Portuguese in Indian Ocean region – The Merchant's Daughter

One of the important power shifts of the 17th century was the decline of the Portuguese in the Indian Ocean region. This was partly due to the entry of other Europeans in the Indian Ocean, and partly due to the fact that local rulers adopted cannons and learned to deal with European military tactics. The Portuguese lost Hormuz to the Persians in 1622, and shifted their base to Muscat in Oman that was defended by two mud forts – Mirani and Jalali – both built on craggy rock outcrops overlooking the harbour. The forts still exist and can be seen standing on either side of the Sultan's Palace.

Despite the shift to Muscat, the Portuguese found that their position was not secure. Led by Imam Nasir ibn Murshid, the Omanis had regrouped in the interiors and were steadily reclaiming the coastline. The Portuguese were left only with Muscat when Murshid died in 1649. He was succeeded by his cousin, the equally aggressive Sultan ibn Saif, who wanted to recapture this last outpost. Unfortunately, this proved difficult as long as the Portuguese controlled the harbour, and could resupply themselves from Goa. This problem was solved by a very unusual turn of events.

The Portuguese depended on an Oman-based Indian merchant called Naruttam to supply their provisions. He had a beautiful daughter that the Portuguese commander Pereira coveted. Naruttam and his daughter were not keen on the match, but Pereira kept up the pressure. At last, under threat, the merchant agreed and requested some time to prepare for a grand wedding. Meanwhile, he convinced the authorities that the Mirani fort in the harbour of Muscat needed to be cleared out so that he could do some repairs. Using this as the pretext, Naruttam removed all the provisions from this Portuguese fort, and then informed Sultan ibn Saif that the garrison was unprepared for a siege. The Omanis attacked immediately. They took the fort and Muscat town in 1650. Thus, an Indian father's determination to protect his beloved daughter led to the demise of Portuguese colonialism in Oman, and ended their supremacy in the Arabian sea.

In India, the Portuguese were similarly squeezed out, first by the Mughals and later by the Marathas. Pushed out of their base in Hugli, they were reduced to piracy in Bengal. They withdrew to Chittagong where they formed an alliance with the Arakanese king Thiri, who believed that he was an incarnation of the Buddha and was destined to unite the world under him. Together, they carried out murderous raids into the riverine delta of Bengal.

As they lost control over the spice trade, the Portuguese were reduced to trading in African slaves, although they were not above kidnapping Indian children and selling them in faraway markets.

The First Englishmen in India

The first Englishman to visit India was Sighelm or Sigelinus, Bishop of Sherborne, in A.D. 883. He was sent by King Alfred on a pilgrimage to India, believed to be the land of St. Thomas. Sighelm returned to England after a few years with strange tales, precious pearls and costly spices. His adventures included a visit to the Well of Youth at Polombe, identified as Quilon on the Malabar Coast.

After the discovery of the sea route to India by the Portuguese, the first Englishman to set foot in India was Father Thomas Stevens.[15] He was born at Bulstan in Wiltshire in South West England in 1549, and educated at Winchester.[16] He was brought up as a Catholic, and when the persecution of the Catholics by Queen Elizabeth became bitter, he and his friend Thomas Pound resolved to flee to Rome. Pound was arrested but Stevens escaped. He enrolled as a novice at the Seminary of Santa Andrea in October 1575. A perusal of the works of St. Francis Xavier had filled him with dreams of the East, and he applied for permission to go as a missionary to Goa. He went to Lisbon and sailed with a fleet of five ships to India on 4 April 1579. Upon his arrival, he wrote a letter[17] to his father, dated 10 November 1579, which contained a long description of his adventures. Stevens' father was a prominent London merchant and this letter, arriving at a time when every London merchant's mind was intent upon India, aroused great interest. Stevens wrote another letter in Latin, in 1583, to his brother in Paris, throwing light upon the missionary methods in those early days in Goa. Stevens wrote of a certain Peter Bruno, who burnt the temple at Cuncolim after slaying a cow upon the altar of the idol, and was torn to pieces by an enraged mob.[18]

The first letter of Father Stevens, which he had written to his father in 1579, inspired two men – Richard Staper and Sir Edward Osborne, then Lord Mayor of London – to send an expedition to India. Staper had been on an embassy to Constantinople in 1579, and had established the Levant Company of 1582 along with Osborne. The Levant Company established an English consul at Tripolis[xv] in 1583, and later at Aleppo. Apparently, the original idea in Staper's mind was to revive the old overland trade with India by way of Aleppo, which had made the fortunes of Venice in the Middle Ages. But this idea was not practical. The Portuguese at Ormuz, and the Spanish at Gibraltar, controlled the two strategic points on the route. So, they decided upon a sea voyage. A team of four English merchant-adventurers was put together for the purpose – John Newbery, Ralph Fitch, William Leedes and James Story.

John Newbery knew Arabic and had been to Tripolis twice before. In 1579, he had visited Syria, and in 1582, through Turkey in Asia, as far as Ormuz, where he made a few enemies. Immediately on his return he was requisitioned by Staper for his new venture. His companions were Ralph Fitch, also a merchant, William Leedes, a jeweller, and James Story, a painter. Newbery carried with him a letter of introduction to the Emperor Akbar from Queen Elizabeth which read as follows:[19] [xvi]

"Elizabeth by the grace of God etc.
To the most invincible and most mightie prince, lord Zelabdim Echebar king of Cambaya. Invincible Emperor etc. The great affection which our subjects have to visit the most distant places of the world, not without good will and intention to introduce the trade of marchandize of al nations whatsoever they can, by which meanes the

xv Old name of Tripoli in Libya.

xvi Ironically, Queen Elizabeth referred to Akbar as king of Cambay.

mutual and friendly trafique of marchandize on both sides may come, is the cause that the bearer of this letter John Newbery, jointly with those that be in his company, with a curteous and honest boldnesse, doe repaire to the borders and countreys of your Empire, we doubt not but that Your imperial Majestie through your royal grace will favorably and friendly accept him...."

The party sailed for Tripolis on the ship named Tyger in early 1583. On the Tyger, they met two other English merchants – William Shales and John Eldred. The Tyger reached Tripolis on 1 May. They then proceeded by caravan to Aleppo and travelling on a camel back to the Euphrates river, they drifted downstream to Feluja on the Euphrates, 70 kms North West of Baghdad. On the way they were attacked a couple of times by highway robbers, but they managed to escape. The party eventually reached Baghdad.

At Basra, four weeks' journey from Bagdad, Eldred and Shales stopped. Newbery and his party boarded a ship to the port of Ormuz, which they reached on 5 September. Ormuz in those days, was the key port on the Persian Gulf, and had been captured and fortified by Albuquerque in 1515. Here, the party invested considerable sums in jewels, particularly the famous Bahrain pearls, which they procured locally at cheap rates under the expert guidance of William Leedes, the jeweller. Newbery's share in the adventure was £400.[20] It was here at Basra that their good fortune ended. The markets were covered by mercenary spies, whose easiest way of making money was spotting traders of hostile nations and reporting them to the Portuguese officials, as well as to whosoever could pay for such information. Established traders looked upon these newcomers with jealousy and suspicion. Among them was a Venetian named Michael Stropene, whose enmity Newbery had somehow incurred on his former visit to Ormuz. Stropene had already been warned by his men at Aleppo of the Englishmen's coming. He denounced them to the Captain of the Castle, Don Mathias de Albuquerque, as spies.[xvii] [21]

The Portuguese had an additional cause to hate the presence of the English in the east, as reports had just arrived that Drake had fired on a Portuguese vessel in the Spice Islands and had captured a cargo of cloves. Don Mathias, however, refused to punish them. But as the charges demanded investigation, he decided to refer the matter to the Viceroy at Goa. The party was put under arrest to be despatched by the next boat to Goa, which was due in another four days. Meanwhile, they were allowed to trade, but under surveillance.

Monsoon ensured that the party could start sail only on 11 October, touching Diu, Daman, Bassein, Thana, and Chaul *en route*, and finally reaching Goa on 29 November.[22] Fitch noted with surprise the usual marvels of Indian life, which fill the pages of contemporary travellers' notes – sati, the sacred cow, the palm and the Brahmins. At Goa, however, they did not meet with the savage treatment they had feared. They, like many other Englishmen of Elizabeth's time, had been brought up in the Old Faith. Thus, they wisely "*behaved themselves very Catholikely and devoute, everie day hearing Mass with Beades in their hands*". And one fine day, an offer was made to them to either join an Order or be shipped off to Lisbon for trial. Only one of them yielded – James Story, the painter – who was admitted as a novice to the monastery of St. Paul, and was employed in decorating the magnificent churches with which Goa abounded.

At Goa, though still under surveillance, they befriended the archbishop and two other Padres or Jesuits of St. Paul's College. The archbishop had two young Europeans as servants, one being John Huyghen van Linschoten, the Dutch

---

xvii Don Mathias de Albuquerque later became the Viceroy of Goa 1591-1597.

traveller, who had come to Goa with the archbishop and stayed there from 1583 to 1589. He later published *Itinerario,* one of the best books on India written till that time, in 1595-96. And of course, the other was Thomas Stevens. On the recommendation of Linschoten and Stevens, they were set free on 22 December, putting in sureties for two thousand ducats[xviii] each. They were not to leave Goa. The surety's name was Andreas Taborer and he had been arranged by Father Thomas Stevens.

Six months later, they obtained permission from the viceroy to set up a small jewellery shop in the Goa market, again with the help of Father Stevens. One year later, on 5 April 1585, Newbery, Fitch and Leedes arranged a picnic in the countryside, leaving a Dutch boy in charge of their shop.[23] From there, with the help of a patimar, one of the Indian post carriers,[24] they escaped to Belgaum, away from Portuguese control. Story did not join the escape. He married a Mestico's or a half-caste's daughter and settled down at Goa. Fitch, Newbery and Leedes travelled through Bijapur, Golconda, where they did some business in stones, and went on to Ujjain. Finally, they reached Agra, which they described as *"a very great city and populous, built with stone, having fair and large streets, with a fair river running by it, which falleth into the gulf of Bengala. It hath a fair castle and a strong, with a very fair ditch"*.

From Agra, they went to Fatehpur Sikri, and were struck by its prosperity, and by the splendour of the Mughal court.

> *"All the way from Agra to Fatehpur was a market of victuals and other things, as full as though a man were still in a town, and so many people as if a man were in a market. Both cities were much greater than London and very populous. In the royal stables are 1,000 elephants, 30,000 horses, 1,400 tame deer, and such store of ounces,*

xviii The Venetseander or the Venetian ducat, was equivalent to 6s. 8d. sterling at that time.

tigers, buffles, cocks and hawks that is very strange to see. In the royal harem, eight hundred concubines. In the markets was a great resort of merchants from Persia and out of India, and very much merchandize of silk and cloth and of precious stones, both rubies, diamonds, and pearls."

Apparently, they were able to reach the court of Akbar, for Fitch describes him as simply attired in *"a white cabie (or tunic), made like a shirt tied with strings on one side, and a little cloth on his head, coloured often times with red or yellow"*. But regarding the delivery of Elizabeth's letter, Fitch tells us nothing. At Fatehpur Sikri, they stayed till 28 September 1585. William Leedes managed to enter Akbar's services *"who did entertain him very well and gave him a house and five slaves, a horse, and every day six shillings in money"*.

John Newbery travelled towards Lahore, and from there to Persia, and then for Aleppo and Constantinople. He was not heard of after that. Perhaps, he perished in his journey from Aleppo to Constantinople. *"He dyed in his travels,"* notes Samuel Purchas (c. 1577–1626), an English Anglican cleric who published several volumes of reports by travellers to foreign countries, *"unknown how and where, the first of the many Englishmen who have perished in the quest of new scenes of adventure and conquest in the East"*.

Fitch decided to travel eastwards, having heard about the riches of Bengal. From Agra, he travelled along the Yamuna and Ganges rivers. He visited Benares and Patna, and then travelled on to Cooch Behar at the foothills of the Himalayas, where he hoped to learn about Tibetan trade across the mountains. After travelling through East Bengal, he sailed for Myanmar[xix] in November 1586. He visited the Yangon[xx] region; sailed up the Irrawaddy River; stopped at Pegu, fabled for its splendour; and ventured into the Siamese

---

xix Burma

xx Rangoon

Shan states[xxi] in 1586-87. In 1588, Fitch visited the Malay Peninsula and Malacca[xxii] where he learned much about trade with China and the Spice Islands, making inquiries about trade and about the route to China and Japan. Returning to Bengal and hearing nothing of Newbery, he decided to return home to England. He started the journey back in 1589 and travelled via Ceylon, Goa (where he was, curiously enough, not arrested), Ormuz and Aleppo, finally reaching England on 29 April 1591. He resumed his employment with the Leather-sellers' Company, becoming a Liveryman in 1599, serving as Warden in 1607, and joined the East India Company's Court of Assistants in 1608. His travel experiences were greatly valued by the founders of the East India Company, including another of Elizabeth's adventurers, Sir James Lancaster, who always consulted him on Indian affairs. Thus ended the first organized English expedition to India. The knowledge obtained was of great value, inspiring further journeys. Fitch, on his return, became such a celebrity in London that his ship Tyger was mentioned by Shakespeare in Macbeth as "her husband is to Aleppo gone, master o' the tyger".[xxiii]

References

[1] Herodotus, Book IV, ch. 42-3.

[2] Michael Uebel, *Ecstatic Transformation: On the Uses of Alterity in the Middle Ages, Palgrave/Macmillan* (2005), contains a full English translation and a discussion of the Letter.

[3] Halsall, Paul (March 1996). "Mandeville on Prester John". Internet Medieval Sourcebook.

[4] John of Hildesheim (1997*). The Story of the Three Kings*. Neumann Press. ISBN 0-911845-68-2.

[5] Extracts from Chapter XXX of Mandeville's text, titled "Of the

xxi In present-day Myanmar

xxii Now in Malaysia

xxiii Act I, scene 3 of William Shakespeare's Macbeth.

Royal Estate of Prester John. And of a rich man that made a marvellous castle and called it Paradise and of his subtlety".

[6] Purchas, Samuel, *Purchas His Pilgrimes,* Volume II, The Hakluyt Society publication, Glasgow, MCMV,p. 5.

[7] John M. Hobson (2004), *The Eastern Origins of Western Civilisation,* p. 141, Cambridge University Press, ISBN 0521547245.

[8] https://www. papalencyclicals. net/Alex06/alex06inter. htm

[9] Robin Leonard Bidwell, *The Two Yemens,* Chapter 2, p. 17.

[10] Fonseca, *Historical Sketch of Goa,* p. 146, p. 149, p. 169.

[11] Ibid. Fonseca, p. 162.

[12] New Account, ed. Crooke, Hakluyt Society, vol. I. p. 165.

[13] Roe, ed. Foster, p. 344.

[14] Quoted in Mill, *History of India* (1826 ed.), i. 123.

[15] The following details are mainly borrowed from the Introduction to the *Christian Purana* by J. L. Saldanha (Mangalore, 1907), and the notice in the *Dictionary of National Biography,* Supplement, vol. III, p. 355. The name is also spelt Stephens.

[16] Kirby, Winchester Scholars, p. 139.

[17] Given in Hakluyt, *Principal Navigations,* ed. MacLehose, vol. vi, p. 377 ff. ; also in Purchas.

[18] In the same massacre perished the famous Father Rodolfo Aquaviva, the friend of Akbar (V. A. Smith, Akbar, p. 206) with three other priests, July 15, 1583. The "Martyrs of Cuncolim" were beatified in 1893 (Fonseca, Historical Sketch of Goa, p. 47).

[19] *Hakluyt,* ed. MacLehose, v. 450, quoted by Ryley, p. 44.

[20] Eldred in Ryley, p. 218.

[21] Fonseca, p. 90.

[22] Ryley, p. 65.

[23] Fitch apud Ryley, p. 73.

[24] Ibid.

Chapter 2
A Company is Born

An organisation named the 'Merchant Adventurers' had been involved in the overseas trade of England since as early as the 13th century. There were several distinct bodies or groups within this organisation, mostly based on the region they traded with or the item they traded in. The group of Merchant Adventurers that traded with the 'Low countries', that is Netherlands, Flanders or Belgica[i] had their offices at Bruges and Antwerp. By the 16th century, Antwerp had developed as the most important depot for the sale of Asian commodities, mostly spices and silk, brought by the Portuguese merchants, who in exchange, purchased from these Merchant Adventurers considerable quantities of English cloth for export back to the East. The profit margin in trade in Asian commodities encouraged the English Merchant Adventurers to seek ways for direct contact with the East. These Merchant Adventurers were the pioneers in the development of English overseas trade with Asia.

A group of these English Merchant Adventurers formed an association called the Venice Company in the mid-16th century. It had commercial contacts with Venice and supplied Asian commodities to the English markets. In 1553, a few prominent London merchants, in consultation with Sebastian Cabot, the famous navigator, explorer and cartographer, decided to jointly send shipping expeditions to Russia for trade and whale-fishing. For this purpose, they set up the Muscovia or Muscovy Company, commonly referred to as the Russia Company. This was the foundation of the first of the great English joint-stock companies for overseas trade. Previously, the regulated companies were

---

i The region lying in coastal North West Europe in the lower basin of the Rhine-Meuse-Scheldt delta.

being organized so as to enable certain individual traders to carry on their businesses either personally or through their factors, within certain specified geographical limits. Since this particular expedition was being fitted out to penetrate into other countries that were considered either "altogether savage or of a low degree of civilization", it was felt that the type of company which was adapted to trade with a neighbouring and developed region (of Europe) would be unsuitable in this case. Therefore, while the form of management in its essentials remained same as the regulated company, it was decided that instead of each person participating by trading on his own capital, a joint stock should be established.

With a modest capital of £6,000, the enterprise was started in May 1553. Three ships were sent to explore trading opportunities with Russia. Two of the three ships were frozen in the ice and all lives on it were lost; but the third, under the command of Richard Chancellor succeeded in landing near Archangel[ii]. Chancellor sought an interview with the ruler of this new country, which he believed he had discovered, which only later on, he realised, was a coastal province of Russia. Ivan the Terrible, the first Czar of Russia[iii], was favourable to these strange merchants, because Russia at that time, had no outlet to the Baltic Sea. Its goods found their way to Europe with great difficulty through Livonia. The Czar formally authorized the free passage of English ships to Russia "with good assurance on our part to see them harmlesse".[1]

Upon Chancellor's return, the Muscovy Company believed that there were very good prospects of a profitable trade with Russia. Steps were taken to secure the sole right of the concession for the persons who had undertaken the risk. A charter was sought and duly received, signed by

ii Present-day Arkhangelsk

iii From 1547 to 1584

Queen Elizabeth, on 6 February 1555. This document is of considerable interest as an early example of the creation of a trading corporation. The charter concluded with the recapitulation of the privileges already granted by the Czar, and conferred the sole rights of entry into Russia upon the Muscovy Company. It also granted the Company the sole rights of entry into any other countries that would be discovered by it in the future, and which were not 'commonly frequented' by Englishmen. The Muscovy Company became the first company to employ joint stock and to own ships corporately. In the same year, it was successful in negotiating an agreement with the Russian Czar, "whereby it was to enjoy the sole right of trading with Muscovy by the White Sea route, and to establish depots at Kholmogory and Vologda". In 1557, an employee of the Company went to Persia and Bokhara, and by 1567, the Company "obtained the right to trade across Russia with Persia through Kazan and Astrakhan".[2] The Muscovy Company retained the monopoly in Russo-English trade until 1698.

In the same year in which the Muscovy Company obtained its charter, the Royal Africa Company was formed. It prospered on the lucrative enterprise they took up, 'to kidnap or purchase and work to death without compunction, the natives of Africa'.

The first practical step to obtain a share of the Eastern trade was taken in the year 1579, when Queen Elizabeth sent William Harburn, an English merchant, to Turkey. He obtained permission from the Turkish Sultan, Amurath III, for the English merchants to trade freely there, just like the French, the Venetians and the Germans. The success of this venture brought Queen Elizabeth to declare openly in 1580 to the Spanish Ambassador, that "the Ocean was free to all, for as much as neither nature nor regard of public use do permit the exclusive possession thereof". And, then in 1581, letters of patent were granted by the English Crown to four gentlemen to trade with Turkey, which was the origin of the Turkey Company, which later became the Levant Company in 1592, after merger of the Turkey Company with the Venice Company. It included Queen Elizabeth as one of its leading shareholders. This venture brought the commodities of the East directly to England. This company had another agenda. From the time the Portuguese merchants had forayed into India, they had their eye on the subcontinent, and were devising ways and means to get there too. The English sent two expeditions to China via the Cape of Good Hope. The first one was in 1582, and the second in 1596; the latter carrying Queen Elizabeth's letters to the Emperor of China. But both these expeditions were a fiasco. These adventures took place under the banner, the Company of Cathay.

Meanwhile, in 1580, Captain Drake[iv], completed his 'round the world voyage', by sailing via the New Hemisphere and returning via the Cape of Good Hope, "with half a million pounds worth of loot, as much as the whole revenue of the Crown for a year". A second 'round the world' expedition left England in 1586 and returned in 1588, carrying nautical data on sailing via the Cape of Good Hope. Drake's exploits had already made him a hero in England. But his adventures led the Spanish to brand him a pirate, known to them as El Draque. King Philip II allegedly offered a reward of 20,000 ducats for his capture – alive or dead.[3]

In February 1583, a party of four merchant-travellers set out on their mission, carrying letters from the Queen Elizabeth addressed to Akbar, the Mughal Emperor of India. The party was financed by the Turkey Company. The story of this party has already been narrated in Chapter 1. Ralph Fitch was the lone survivor of the party who returned to England after eight years. During his journey, he had noted the tremendous prosperity of the Eastern countries, when compared to which his own country appeared to him very

iv Elizabeth awarded Drake a knighthood in 1581.

insignificant. He noted that even Pegu was much bigger than London. During his voyage in the East, Fitch also collected a lot of information that was valuable to English merchants. A shrewd observer, he had also noted, for example, about Nanda Bayin, the king of Burma, who had conquered Siam, that, "*This king hath little force by sea, because he hath but very few ships*". Such comments emphasized the importance of a strong naval power on which the prosperity and final supremacy of these merchant companies would ultimately depend.

In the same year, Linschoten had returned to Holland, his native country. The English merchants found that his experiences confirmed that of Fitch. Readers would remember Linschoten as the one whom Fitch had met in Goa as the servant of the Archbishop. In 1596, Linschoten published a book, *Itinerario,* which graphically presented for the first time in Europe, the detailed maps of voyages to the East Indies, particularly India. This book was later published in an English edition as 'Discourse of Voyages into Ye East & West Indies'. During his stay in Goa, abusing the trust put in him by the Portuguese Viceroy, Linschoten had meticulously copied the top-secret nautical charts page-by-page. More crucially, his book provided nautical data like currents, deeps, islands and sandbanks, which was absolutely vital for safe navigation, along with the coastal depictions to guide the way.

Earlier, in 1593, two Portuguese ships carrying merchandise from India had been captured by the English Privateers. The cargoes of the first ship had "*inflamed the imaginations of the merchants; and the papers which she carried afforded information regarding the traffic in which she was engaged*"; and the second vessel was the largest "*which had ever been seen in England, laden with spices, calicoes, silks, gold, pearls, drugs, porcelain, ebony, etc and stimulated the impatience of the English to be engaged in so opulent a commerce*".

By 1599, the Levant Company fell into difficulties as the Dutch began bringing spices directly from the East Indies, thereby making the purchase of spices at Aleppo unprofitable. On 19 July 1599, a Dutch ship under Admiral Jacob Corneliszoon returned home with 800 tonnes of pepper, 200 tonnes of clove and large quantities of cinnamon and nutmeg. The voyage had made an unprecedented profit of 400 per cent. The Dutch seized the opportunity afforded to them by a scarcity of spices in England by raising the price of pepper from 3s. 6d. to 6s. and later 8s. per lb. It became clear to the English merchants that the time had come to make a fresh effort to open a direct trade to the East Indies via the Cape of Good Hope. In the latter half of the year, preparations became so far advanced that on 24 September 1599, 101 persons had undertaken to adventure £30,133. 6s. 8d for the intended voyage. Of these, as many as 23 were members of the existing Levant Company, a number that might be considerably increased if account be taken of names that were added subsequently. Among these was one Thomas Smythe who later filled the position of Governor in both bodies, the Levant Company and the East India Company.

The first recorded meeting was held on 24 September 1599, in the presence of 57 adventurers. Fifteen of them were elected to serve as committees or directors. It was resolved that neither ships nor goods should be accepted in payment of the amounts adventured, only cash. It was also decided that the minimum subscription should be £200, and that an immediate call of 1s. per cent be made. The committees at once applied to the Privy Council[v] for a

v The Privy Council was a core group of English nobles that acted as Queen Elizabeth's main advisors and key members of the government. The main function of the Privy Council was to provide opinions on the matters at hand and to help the queen make decisions. When the queen had made a decision, it was the responsibility of the Privy Council to carry out the wishes of the queen.

charter of incorporation, since trade to India was so remote that it could not be carried on, but in a joint and united stock.[4] At this time, a proposed peace with Spain was under consideration by the queen, and the Privy Council feared that the sending out of the expedition might lead to a failure of negotiations with Spain. The Charter was thus put on hold.

In view of this, the adventurers decided to proceed no further with the fitting out of any expedition until the Royal Charter was granted. Just a year after the first meeting, the adventurers again assembled. Though no entry had been made in the minute-book from 16 October 1599 to 23 September 1600, much had been accomplished in the interval. An undertaking from the Privy Council had been secured, under which it was provided that the voyage would not be stayed. There was increased support from the merchants of the city. In view of these considerations, it was proposed that preparations be made for the expedition. This motion was carried in the meeting, the vote being taken by a show of hands.

The intended trade costs were astronomically high. The commodities they wished to buy, the spices, were expensive and had to be carried in huge, costly ships. These ships had to be manned by large crews and had to be protected by artillery masters and professional musket-men. And even if everything went according to the plan, there would be no return on investment for several years.

After-thoughts from October 1599 to September 1600 made them realize that a larger capital would be required than what was originally proposed. On 13 October, the committees decided not to refuse any investment of £200 until the whole sum had reached £55,000. Since it was proposed in this instrument that the management of the company was to consist of a Governor and 24 committees, Thomas Smythe was elected Governor, and additional adventurers were nominated for the latter posts in order to complete the number.[5]

The charter was signed on 31 December 1600. It incorporated 218 persons, whose names were given as the Governor and Company of Merchants of London trading into the East Indies, with the usual privileges of a corporation including the right to have a common seal, which *"from tyme to tyme, att their will and pleasuer to breake, change and to make new or alter as to them shall seeme expedient"*. Membership was confined to those mentioned in the charter, their sons at the age of 21, their factors and apprentices, as well as to those who were subsequently admitted. The management was to be in the hands of the Governor and 24 committees. The first four voyages were exempted from customs outwards. In each voyage, the company was allowed to export all the foreign silver it had brought into the country, provided that such export should not exceed £30,000 in any one voyage, and that £6,000 of it had been first coined at the mint. All Englishmen, except the licensees, were forbidden to trade in the area assigned to the company under penalty of the Queen's indignation, and the forfeiture of the ships and cargoes (half the value of these falling to the Crown, the other half to the company). All these privileges were granted for a period of 15 years beginning from Christmas of year 1600, renewable for a like term upon condition that the trade *"be not hurtful, but shall be shown profitable"* to the realm. On the other hand, should the company be found hurtful (to English interests), its privileges might be recalled or modified on two years' notice. Thus, the English East India Company was born.[6]

The Voyages

On 22 April 1601, Captain James Lancaster commanding a fleet of four ships – the Red Dragon, Hector, Ascension and Susan – carrying 1,400 tonnes of merchandise for trade, accompanied by John Middleton and John Davis and a total of 480 men, set off for the East Indies. Lancaster himself was aboard the Red Dragon, a 38-gun ship, bought by the East India Company from the Earl of Cumberland for £3,700. Originally, it was a pirate ship named Scourge of Malice, but had been renamed the Red Dragon to give a civil face to the voyage. This ship was to later become legendary, as it was to stage the first recorded performance of Shakespeare's play *Hamlet* while anchored off the coast of Sierra Leone. The fleet mostly carried the five staple merchandise of England – wool, woolfells, leather, lead and tin. It reached the Cape of Good Hope on 1 November; the Nicobar Islands on 9 April 1602; Achin and other parts of Sumatra on 5 June 1602, and finally anchored at Bantam in Java where the first English East India Company factory was established. A concession was obtained from the king of Achin by which freedom of trade, immunity from the payment of customs and some other privileges were accorded to the English in 1602. At Bantam, the king permitted Lancaster to trade with his kingdom, and a factory was established in 1603. He purchased pepper for return cargo. A pinnace[vi] was despatched to Moluccas and a factory was established there as well, anticipating the arrival of the next shipping from England.

The return voyage was from 20 February to 11 September 1603, and Lancaster, whose success both in trade and diplomacy had been brilliant, was rewarded with a knighthood from the newly-crowned King of England, James I, in October 1603. He carried home no less than 900 tonnes of pepper, cinnamon and cloves. The Second Voyage was on an identical route. Whatever the English thought of this success, it was small fry compared to what the Dutch had been achieving on the other side of the English Channel.

---

vi A pinnace is a small boat with sails and oars.

Moreover, even after two successful voyages, the Indian mainland remained untouched.

However, the times were bad and capital was scarce. The greater part of what was paid promptly consisted of funds temporarily diverted from the Levant trade where it could not be profitably utilized. After some difficulty, the nominal capital for the voyage of 1601 was arrived at, which was £68,373. 6 The initial plan of these merchants was to float a separate stock for the Second Voyage to India in September or October 1601. It was proposed in September 1601 that the minimum subscription should be £100, and that no adventurer should be assessed beyond the amount he had undertaken to provide.[vii] It required some courage for a member to join the new stock, since the returns from the First Voyage were below par. The plan failed. There were hardly any investors for the Second Voyage. The Company merchants finally decided to await the outcome of the First Voyage, compelled by the general feeling of the members of the company. Pending the return of the ships from India, an effort was made to discover an alternative route to the East by the North West passage. Though this expedition only required £3,000, the Company managed to arrange it with great difficulty. From September 1601, till news was received in June 1603 that one of the vessels of the First Voyage might shortly be expected with a rich cargo, the Company devoted itself mainly to streamlining its internal organization.

More misfortune awaited the Company in its infancy. Just when the ships of the First Voyage returned to England, the country was being decimated by the plague, raging most fiercely in August and September 1603. It continued to claim lives till the end of the year. Business came almost to a

vii This meant, one man could have only one vote in meetings, irrespective of the amount he invested beyond £100. This was the usual practice in those days.

standstill and it seemed impossible to sell the cargoes of the ships that had returned from the First Voyage. Sending out the Second Voyage (which should have sailed in 1602) was urgent, and the only way by which the second expedition could be set forth in the spring of 1604 was by applying all the resources from the First Voyage that could be sold off. This meant the continuance of the jointstock, and therefore, the accounts of the first and Second Voyages had to be amalgamated, and the divisions applied to both. According to the statement of the Company, the capital of the Second Voyage was £60,450, which was added to that of the first, and dividends were paid on the total of £1,28,823. It was able to send out in the Second Voyage, goods and bullion to the value of £12,302 only, the rest being required for the repair of the ships.

The Second Voyage was set out under the command of Henry Middleton. It proceeded first to Bantam and then to Moluccas and Banda, touching at Amboyna. At Banda, a factory was established. Permission to enter Amboyna was given by the Portuguese captain only after the conclusion of the Treaty of Peace between Spain and England at London on 18 August 1604. Another factory was opened at Tidore. The first two voyages of the English Company were directed towards the spice Islands – Sumatra, Java and the Moluccas – in order to get a share of the spice trade. These two expeditions proved to be great success, and the profit of the two voyages amounted to 95 per cent upon the capital originally subscribed, clear of all charges.[7]

Meanwhile, the various Dutch East India Companies amalgamated under an umbrella company by the name of VOC in 1602. When all their subscriptions were added up, it was almost ten times the capital base of the English East India Company. With an initial subscription of £550,000, the VOC was immediately in a position to offer its investors

3,600 per cent dividends.[8] While the English Company was struggling to get money, money kept pouring in for VOC.

The result of this inadequate funding was that a smaller company with smaller fleet and fewer guns to protect the fleet, was an easy prey on international waters. It was not that the London merchants were poorer or less inclined to invest – it was just that better investment opportunities existed for them at that time. These were times when 10s. could get them 100 acres of fertile land in Virginia, which seemed a much better option than a share of East India Company for £12.[9] Not only was the English East India Company confronted with financial distress in 1604, but in the same year, its legal position was also seriously endangered by attacks made upon it both by the Crown and in Parliament. James I became the King of England on 24 March 1603. On 18 June 1604, he granted licence to Sir Edward Michelborne to trade with China and other places in the East, notwithstanding any grant or charter to the contrary.[10] On the strength of this licence, Michelborne's syndicate sent out an expedition which is said *"to have made the English name abhorred in the Eastern seas"* due to several acts of piracies.[11] While Michelborne's ships escaped with their plunder, the East India Company was left to bear the odium of their misdeeds. To these anxieties were added fears as to the safety of the ships of the Second Voyage, which became considerably overdue. At one time, many of the merchant-adventurers had become so discouraged that they were inclined to abandon the whole enterprise.[12]

At length, in 1606, the Second Voyage returned, and it became known that a considerable profit had been obtained. Steps were taken to begin the winding up of the stock by clearing accounts and making divisions (on account of principal and profit) to the members. It was only in 1609 that the liquidation could be completed, and the total divisions came to 195 per cent. The success of the first and Second

Voyages had the important result of establishing the trade, and the company at once began to take subscriptions for a Third Voyage which sailed in 1607. From this date onwards, vessels were sent every year. The whole capital raised was £53,500, out of which £6,000 was paid to the former stock for certain assets purchased from it. As early as 13 May 1607, plans were under consideration for the preparation of another voyage, which was to be ready by early 1608.

The success obtained was not without its penalty, nor was the King James I entirely pleased with the proceedings. On 9 January 1607, Richard Penkevell and his associates obtained a grant, under the title of 'The Colleagues for the Discovery of a Northern Passage to China, Cathay, and other parts of the East Indies'. This patent was for a period of seven years, and conferred the absolute possession of all lands not previously occupied by any Christian power, discovered by the agents of 'The Colleagues'. While this instrument was less injurious to the company than the licence to Michelborne in 1604, the two in conjunction were sufficient to show that King James I might modify the original charter of Elizabeth. When a favourable opportunity presented itself, a new charter was obtained by the East India Company at considerable expense, in which James I bound himself and his successors "not to grant any license contrary to the tenor of this present patent". In order to meet the Parliamentary objection that the Company was hindering the progress of geographical discovery, it joined hands with the Russian Company to finance Henry Hudson's expedition in search of the North West passage. On 26 July 1612, the shareholders in this venture were incorporated as 'The Governor and Company of the Merchants of London, Discoverers of the North-West Passage'.[13]

The Third Voyage was commanded by Captain William Keeling, who was accompanied by William Hawkins and David Middleton. It was decided to leave Hawkins at

Surat for his mission to Agra. The expedition started on 12 March 1607, directly to India touching Madagascar, Zanzibar, Socotra and Aden. Hawkins had disembarked from the ship at Surat on 4 August 1608, and proceeded to the Mughal Court at Agra bearing letters from the English Crown to Jahangir, seeking certain concessions for the English. Hawkins was received favourably at the court and permission was given to the English to settle at Surat. But unfortunately, the concession was revoked because of the Portuguese influence at the Mughal court. The Portuguese did all they could to nullify the success of Hawkins' mission. Hawkins waited in vain for two years at Agra, but had to return without any reply. On reaching Surat, he embarked on board with Henry Middleton on 18 January 1612. Then he proceeded to Bantam and Moluccas, took in a full cargo of spices at Bantam, and returned to England. The profits realized by the Third Voyage accounted to not less than 234 per cent upon the subscribed capital.

Meanwhile, trade with India had been subject to considerable fluctuations. The Third Voyage of 1607 had left England before all the money necessary had been paid by the adventurers. Those who had promised to support the next two expeditions refused to provide capital for more than one. Accordingly, the Fourth Voyage of 1608 was set out with a stock of its own, amounting to £33,000. In June 1608, there was a debt on both these voyages, and it was proposed to unite them in one. But this scheme suffered a setback by the loss of the ships belonging to the Fourth Voyage. This misfortune diminished subscriptions for the fifth expedition, which was due to sail in 1609.

Though efforts were made to secure the support of adventurers, the total capital obtained was only £13,700. It was decided to amalgamate this capital with that of the Third Voyage, and to continue to trade upon the united stock of both. When the accounts were finally made up, there were assets available for distribution which enabled a distribution of 334 percent to be paid, yielding a profit of 234 percent, which was the largest in the history of the early terminable stocks of the company.

Beginning with 1610, there were seven independent voyages, each with a separate capital, and which were sent out till January 1613. The largest stock was that of the sixth, for which £80,163 had been paid in, while the smallest belonged to the twelfth, which had only £7,142. The most profitable was the eleventh in 1612, which gave its shareholders a profit of 320 per cent. Even the sixth, which was the least successful, returned divisions of 221. 67 per cent.[14] For a company in its infancy, which was facing formidable opposition from the king at home, and from the Portuguese and the Dutch in the Eastern Waters, the initial ventures did not pay badly. The average profit for the period, making allowance for losses caused by delay in winding up, was about 20 per cent per annum. How big this profit was per voyage undertaken would be evident from the fact that between 1603 and 1613, a total of eight voyages were carried out, of which the one in 1607 (the Fourth Voyage) fetched nothing, as all the vessels were lost. However, the remaining seven voyages were so prosperous that the clear profits were hardly ever below 100 per cent, being in general more than 200 on the capital of the voyage. In 1617, the Company made a profit of £1,000,000 on a capital of £200,000. The East India Company had become the most important jointstock company in England. In the whole of 17th century, it averaged a rate of profit of over 100 per cent.

Product Diversification

To begin with, the East India Company ships brought its five staple items – wool, woolfells, leather, lead and tin to Asia and took spices back. All the items it brought with it had a very low demand in Asia and the Company ended up buying all its spices for hard cash in silver. Its factors stationed in the Spice Islands pointed out to the Court of Committees at London about the cloths and calicoes imported by the Dutch from the Coromandel Coast in India, which enjoyed considerable demand in Spice Islands. They pointed out that if they were supplied with these goods, the latter could be profitably exchanged for pepper and other finer spices, thereby saving precious silver from England.[15]

In other words, they wanted to use English silver to buy cloth and calicoes in the Coromandel Coast and use them to get spices from Spice Islands, as the Dutch had been doing. Therefore, the factors recommended that trade with the Coromandel Coast should be attempted. The locals in the Coromandel Coast were gifted with the art of painting on calicoes to the highest pitch of perfection, and their products were in great demand in Europe and the countries in the South East Asian region. The Company decided to purchase textiles from the Coromandel Coast to send them to Bantam and Moluccas, and to expand the pepper trade by establishing a permanent factory at Sumatra. A part of the textile purchased was also to be brought back to England. The Dutch used the Coromandel textiles to barter for the South East Asian spices. The relative weakness of the Portuguese by the turn of the 17th century, the availability of a wide variety of cotton textiles on the Eastern coast, and its nearness to the South East Asian region (the Spice Islands), which was the centre of the spice trade, and the geographical advantages, viz., the existence of sea-ports surrounded by a good number of production centres, could be counted as important considerations. The other idea of the English Company was that the textiles of the Coromandel could be used for bartering the spices of South East Asia, or for enhancing their purchasing power through the Asiatic trade, thereby ensuring the doubling or tripling of their investments.

As Hawkins had failed to get permission to establish a factory at Surat, the Company decided to establish a direct trade relationship with the Coromandel Coast. On 8 August 1611, Globe, one of the Company's ships commanded by Captain Anthony Hippon, accompanied by Peter Floris and Robert Brown, arrived at Petapoli on the coast. They came with the intention of selecting a site where a permanent settlement could be founded. The local Governor at Petapoli asked them to pay the customs at the rate of three-and-a-half per cent for their trading activities. So, they left Robert Brown with some capital to invest there. Then they arrived at Masulipatnam, the port of the Golconda kingdom which was famous for the manufacture of large quantities of locally-woven piece-goods named chintz, and calico of diverse colours and artistic works.[16] After long parleys, the Sultan of Golconda permitted the English merchants to trade at Masulipatnam and collected the customs at four per cent for both incoming and outgoing goods from the English. These goods were being exported to Persia and Bantam by the local merchants for centuries. A small English agency at Masulipatnam was put under a chief called an Agent. A factory was established at Masulipatnam on 10 September 1611. For the benefit of South East Asian trade, the Masulipatnam factory was placed under the superintendence of the President at Bantam. English goods and bullion were invested to procure the calico, chintz and other varieties of cloth. This was the first English settlement on the eastern coast of India.

Criticism back Home

In 1615, a book titled *The Trade's Increase* appeared in London. This book surveyed the commerce of the time, stating that the trade of the East India Company had greatly developed mercantile, marine, as well as shipping in England. It went on to state that out of 21 ships used by the Company, four had been totally lost, and the remainder returned home broken. The mortality amongst the crews was lamentably great. The total number of men who sailed from England in the service of the company was given as 3,000, two-thirds of whom never returned. Of the one-third that returned, most suffered from disease. The book argued that the trade and the commodities it brought to the English household were at a far dearer cost than was being realized, being bought with so many men's lives. Moreover, the company was described as resembling the enemies of Christendom, for they carried away the treasure of Europe to enrich the heathen by the purchase of unnecessary commodities. Finally, the book boldly claimed that no subjects of the Crown should be debarred "from trading equally in all places".[17] In those days, it was almost impossible for sailors to return from a long voyage without contracting a disease. The universal one was scurvy. Scurvy is a disease caused by a deficiency of vitamin C. When the sailors began their voyage, they stocked fresh fruits and vegetables on their ship. If the sailors were at sea for many months, they would not have fruits and vegetables for most of this time, thereby causing scurvy. Sometimes it got mingled with other ailments, like beriberi. Sailors would get large concentrations of fluid in their legs, a sign of beriberi. Both beriberi and pellagra caused mental instability and personality changes.

Application was made to the Archbishop of Canterbury for the suppression of the offending publication as being treasonable and dangerous. However, on further reflection, Sir Dudley Digges, a member of Parliament and co-adventurer, was able to convince his fellow-adventurers that the case was one for a reply in defence of the East India trade rather than any penal measures.[18] The answer to the book appeared soon afterwards under the name of Digges, who was able to dispose of many of the exaggerations of his opponent. He pointed out that considering the length and dangers of the voyage, a loss of only four ships was not excessive in fifteen years. The large cost of repairs was shown to be a temporary, not a permanent condition of the trade. It arose from the fact that the vessels first used were purchased from others, and had not been designed for use in the tropics. He claimed that now the company had begun to build its own ships, and that the expenditure under this head had been greatly reduced. As to the export of treasure, Digges was able to show that the reduction in the price of spices as a result of trade had saved public money.

The period till 1620 was one of considerable prosperity for the Company. It had established itself against the opposition of the Portuguese. A foothold in the Moluccas or Spice Islands had been secured. In addition, as early as 1613, a factory and a valuable trading concession on the Indian mainland at Surat had been procured. In 1614 and 1615, there were negotiations with the Dutch company to establish a working agreement between the two. But the Company's problem with James I was not over yet. The charter of 1609 by which James I had bound himself and his successors not to issue any licences or other patents contrary to that grant, was again violated. Some rapacious courtiers found a method by which, while the letter of this engagement was observed, its spirit was broken. This consisted of the grant of a royal licence covering the limits assigned to the Company, but issued under the seal of Scotland[viii]. Accordingly on 24 May 1617, Sir James Cunningham, his heirs and associates, constituting the Scottish East India Company, were authorized to trade in the East Indies, the Levant, Greenland, Muscovy, and all other countries and islands in the north, North West and North Eastern seas. This grant in reality, invaded the charters of the East India, Levant and Russia companies. It was the latter

viii James I was King of England as well as of Scotland.

which was chiefly affected, since it was to whaling activities in Russian waters that the new company proposed to direct its energies in the beginning. Accordingly, the East India Company assisted the Russia Company, and eventually the licence to Cunningham's Company was purchased from him at a considerable expense.[19]

Just when the company was endeavouring to rehabilitate its finances and to avoid giving offence to a hostile House of Commons, it received news of the massacre of Amboyna, where ten English East India Company employees were killed along with the Japanese and Portuguese, by the Dutch in 1623. But the incident became known in England only in May 1624. At first, the adventurers were buoyed up by expectations of obtaining help from the king. But when none came, the courts of the Company were scenes of deep depression. Many of the members complained of the injuries the Company had sustained through false friends abroad and at home. They expressed the opinion that the best course would be to wind up the stock and retire from the trade, unless the enterprise was supported by the State, like those of the Dutch. This was the second instance when the adventurers gave serious thought to winding up the Company. At this juncture, James I offered to himself become an adventurer, and to send out the Company's ships under royal patronage. But the governor and committees discreetly replied that it was found, on taking the opinion of counsel, that the effect of the proposed arrangement would be that the whole undertaking would revert to the Crown, since there could be no partnership with the king.

Even before news of the massacre had been received, there had been dissensions within the company, though of a temporary nature. In 1623, there had been a scene at a Court meeting, when some members had demanded the return of the money they had invested in the Second Joint Stock. There were also charges of corruption in the administration.

From 1625 onwards, these contentions, charges and counter-charges that had previously been rare, became frequent. The smaller adventurers who should have been content to recover what they could, provided they were not required to furnish more capital, suddenly began lamenting their decision to invest. The practice of dividing commodities also caused a considerable amount of friction[ix]. Persons who were not in trade and whose dividend consisted of pepper or calico, found it difficult to sell them off profitably. On the other hand, adventurers who were merchants themselves, obtained in addition to the nominal return on their capital expressed in terms of the price at which the commodities were rated, a further profit in retailing them. In 1629, there was a long discussion lasting three hours, and it was proposed that the dividend be paid in cash only.

Bullion Problem and Asiatic Trade

Nationalists and economists of the period severely criticised the export of bullion by the English Company to the East. They identified bullion with the wealth of nation and considered that *"the exportation of the same for the procurement of Oriental goods as national loss"*. The Company was condemned in many ways. The English merchants were accused of carrying away the treasures of Europe to enrich heathens. Efforts were made to make common people understand that eastern commodities were unnecessary. The East India merchants were branded as enemies of Christendom because of the export of bullion to the East. The Company was also attacked for the employment of hundreds of men in the dangerous voyages. The manufacture of the Company's ships involved the cutting down of trees, a cause for the loss of national resources.[20]

---

ix The prevalent practice of giving dividend was to give it in kind, with items brought from Asia, rather than in cash or money.

On the other hand, writers like Thomas Mun came forward advocating overseas trade. Mun claimed that the drain of precious metals to the East was balanced by the Company's re-exports to the Continent[x], an important earner of precious metals. Further, the Company justified its existence as the supplier of necessary commodities for domestic consumption, and there was benefit derived by the nation from the employment of men, the construction of ships and the increase of customs duty. In the initial stages, Queen Elizabeth's charter permitted the Company to export from England to the East only £30,000 in the form of bullion[xi] per annum. Therefore, the Company was left with two options. First, to continue its commercial activities in the East, money had to be borrowed at exorbitant rates of interest either at home or abroad to meet financial scarcity. But it was totally harmful for the Company to get involved in such a practice in its incipient stage. The second option was to generate some money in Asia to continue its commercial activities. This second method, called Asiatic trade, was decided upon.

In the Asiatic trade, the Company bought goods in India that had demand in South East Asia, and the profit was used to buy spices to be taken back to England. This leg of their commerce, which they called the country trade, was no innovation. Earlier, the Portuguese used to export Indian fabrics to Japan and brought cheap silver from there. With this silver, they purchased porcelain, silk and tea from China. Against these commodities, they procured all sorts of spices in the Moluccas Islands for shipment to Europe. Following the practice of the Portuguese, the English factors in the East thought that the Company could be free from the necessity of importing money or bullion from England as the money generated through this Asiatic trade should be

x The European mainland.

xi Spanish or other foreign silver.

enough for the purchase of items that had a good demand in other parts of Asia – like the export of Indian cotton textiles to the South East Asian islands to barter for pepper and other spices, and in turn to export the spices for West Asian and European markets, to double or triple the investments.

Even the Dutch, who came to that region prior to the English, followed the same practice. Sir Thomas Roe had also constantly put forward this suggestion to the Company in London.[21] In the First Voyage of James Lancaster, it was found that the Portuguese ship captured by him was loaded with a large quantity of calicoes, which he successfully exchanged for pepper at Bantam. It also proved how useful that commodity was to procure pepper and other spices.[22]

The fundamental idea of the Asiatic trade was to supplement the inadequate European cargoes and available treasure, by increasing its purchasing power. This was considered feasible only by regularly carrying all sorts of merchandise from surplus areas to the areas of demand, and dealing mostly in markets favourable for Asiatic trade. Thomas Roe had already suggested that only the profit of 'Asiatic trade' should be remitted to Europe in the form of spices or cloths, but not the capital itself. "*The cargoes sent out from England would never drive this trade. You must succour it by change.*" He calculated that the trade with the Red Sea would suffice to finance the whole of the Company's business in India.[23]

Some of the islands such as Sumatra and Borneo yielded small amounts of gold, and the locals were ready to exchange them for Indian commodities. Further, the English invested Indian (mostly hides and leather) and Chinese goods (silk and velvets) as well as South East Asian spices in Japan, to get local silver and copper that were available in abundance. In exchange for Indian and South East Asian commodities with the Chinese merchants at Siam, the English bought silk, porcelain and later, tea. They sold these items in the

East Indies, and in return, all sorts of spices were bartered for shipment to Europe or West Asia[xii], where they sold them for gold and silver to invest in India. Additionally, they procured silk from Persia for European consumption.

The reason the English Company established a network of trading centres from the Red Sea in West Asia to Japan in the Far East, was to create a chain of supply points for its commercial operations. They developed the factory system, by which factors or agents of the Company who were left behind by the ships from Europe, sold their goods and made provision for the return cargo well in advance of the arrival of the next year's shipping. This helped the speedy disposal and acquisition of the goods, whereby they attempted to prevent any hike in prices created by the sellers' market.[24]

Once the Company established its trading links, it started to expand its commercial operations. Apart from the factories in the South East Asian region for the purchase of pepper and spices, its commercial enterprises were extended up to Hirado in Japan in 1613, Borneo Moluccas, Banda, etc. in the further South; Ayuthya in Siam; and to Persia in 1616, followed by the Red Sea region in 1618. Thus, direct contact was established between London-Surat-Bantam-West Asia, for supplying calicoes and indigo on one side and spices and silk on the other.

In addition to the coastal trade, the Company was also engaged in port-to-port trade on the Indian coastline. For this trade, the Company used a fleet of small country-built vessels to supply to the various factories on the coast, and collect goods from them to be transported to England. The region around Madras imported rice from the Godavari delta, Ganjam and Bengal. For southern Coromandel, the centre was Madras, which supplied its famous muris rice from the Cauvery delta, pearls from Tuticorin and Ceylon, to factories at Masulipatnam and Armagon. In return, ginger,

xii Red Sea and Persian Gulf regions.

chillies and mangoes from the Golconda region were taken to southern Coromandel.

As for China, there was no direct trade relationship initially. Instead, the English factors had commercial contacts with the Chinese merchants who traded at Siam, Patani and Bantam. Indian and English commodities were exchanged for Chinese goods. After the conclusion of the Anglo-Portuguese accord in 1635, English ships started plying to Macao from Goa, and regularly carried freight goods. In March 1635, the London, one of the Company's ships, sailed for Macao with some cargo, the first direct attempt of the Company. The Chinese traders were willing to supply commodities such as silk, sugar, porcelain, herbs, coloured dyes, tea, copper, quicksilver and other diverse Chinese products. The commodities that were in great demand in China were 'pucho'[xiii], incense, myrrh, resamalis or selases, elephant teeth, red sandalwood, coral in large quantities[xiv], pepper from Bantam, camphor, fish skins, gantee[xv], dyed wood, and red wood. Besides, a wide variety of consumer articles like nutmegs, cloves, cardamom, cinnamon, coconuts and mace were taken by the Chinese traders from South East Asia.

Initially, indigo and saltpetre were the only Indian commodities taken for European consumption by the Company. The textiles of India were mostly intended for Asiatic trade, but occasionally, they were taken to Europe as well. The most valuable articles of commerce from the sale of which the Company expected to gain maximum profit were the products not of India, but of the Islands of the South East Asia, i.e. pepper and other spices. Only the realisation that the products of the islands could be

---

xiii The pachak or costus root was obtained from Kashmir and used in China for incense.

xiv Coral commanded a payment in an equivalent weight of silver.

xv Its roots are largely used for medicinal purposes.

profitably exchanged for the textiles of India, turned the Company's attention on the development of trade with India. It was stated that the investment of the Company on cloves brought into England on the occasion of the Third Voyage in December 1608, was £2,948, and the consignment was sold for £36,387 in England.

The main Indian commodity purchased directly for the European markets were indigo and saltpetre. The export of saltpetre was a new development in the history of the English Company's maritime trade, since there was an ever-increasing demand for it in Europe. It was an essential commodity for the manufacture of gunpowder. Though it was prohibitive because of its weight, the growth of an extensive munitions industry in Europe, and the use of artillery, made Indian saltpetre a strategic raw material, and a profitable article of commerce. In England, the demand for saltpetre was closely connected with national, political and military considerations, especially during the civil war between King Charles and the Parliament. In the year 1639, the Company despatched 33 tonnes of saltpetre to England. From 1643 to 1648, on an average, the Company sent 40 tonnes (300-400 bales) of saltpetre. Sometimes, it was re-exported to mainland Europe, mostly to Amsterdam. It was also used as ballast for ships. However, in 1646, Aurangzeb prohibited its sale to Europeans, who could also use it against the Muslims. But the English factory records show that they were still successful in procuring this commodity to the desired quantity. There was a gradual expansion of saltpetre trade after the establishment of an English factory at Patna. In 1653, the Company exported 200 tonnes of saltpetre from India. After the restoration of the Company's monopoly in 1661, the annual volume shipped from Bengal and Bihar was fixed at 800 tonnes. In the second half of the 17th century, saltpetre ranked as an important object of commerce. Its production for export was localised to Bihar, because of the low price and high quality.

The cotton fabrics procured by the English East India Company in India were very useful in two different ways: (1) In the early stages, the textiles of India were used to barter for the spices of the South East Asian Islands, which in turn were exported for West Asian and European consumption. (2) Later, the discovery of the existence of a market for Indian textiles in Europe initiated direct export from India to Europe. Cotton goods, both plain and designed, found a favourable demand in England. The plain textiles of India replaced the more expensive linens imported from Holland and Germany for household use in England. The patterned or designed varieties were popularly used for wall hangings and decorative purposes. So much so that in 1624, the Company declared that England saved a quarter of a million sterling annually by the substitution of Indian calicoes for foreign linens through the Eastern trade. The available records show that the first successful attempt of the Company to sell calicoes in England, in 1613, was just over 5,000 pieces. By 1614, the Company had decided to increase the supply. The Surat factory alone was trying to buy some 12,500 pieces of calicoes suitable for England. It invested some £2,800 in calicoes alone. Since then, the export of calico went up gradually. In 1619, 26,000 pieces of calico were sent to England from India. The English Company sent home nearly 100,000 pieces from Surat for the year 1620. Calico export by the Company from India increased to 1,23,000 pieces in 1621, and 2,21,500 pieces in 1625. In 1628, the total volume of textiles sent to England by the Company was 1,000 bales, which would represent 1,50,000 pieces.[25]

Diamonds from the newly-discovered mines in the neighbourhood of Masulipatnam were in great demand in England, and were also exported to Europe. The English East India Company made special arrangements to procure as many diamonds as possible from the Golconda region. Middlemen were employed to procure diamonds and pearls in abundance. Sometimes, a large sum of money was sent to Masulipatnam by the adventurers in individual capacities, specifically for procuring diamonds. On 12 November 1645, one large diamond was sold for £61, and one ring with five diamonds for £55. 1s., and a ring with one diamond for £16. 5s. This account clearly brings out the diamond trade of the Company and its earnings.[26]

More Trouble at Home with the New King

Charles I was the King of England, King of Scotland, and King of Ireland from 27 March 1625 until his execution in 1649. His relations with the East India Company were no better than that of James I. Between 1627 and 1629, Charles I had several causes of complaint against the Governor and committees. They had refused to lend him £10,000 when required, nor would they admit him as an adventurer gratis (i.e., a shareholder). Moreover, an appeal had been made to the Parliament in 1628, in which Thomas Mun, a prominent economist of the period, and later, Director of the East India Company, made a strongly-worded protest against the lack of support the Company had received when it was confronted by the aggression of the Dutch during the massacre at Amboyna in 1623.

In 1635, Endymion Porter, a prominent courtier, obtained a licence to fit out two ships as privateers. The funds necessary were obtained by taking few London merchants into partnership, amongst whom were Thomas Kynaston and Samuel Bonnell, the latter being closely connected with Sir William Courten, one of the biggest London merchants of the period. The two vessels sailed in April 1635 and intended to take on ships of any nation not in amity with the King of England, as prize. They proposed to cruise in the Red Sea. A new company was formed for this adventure in secrecy. Charles I was to be credited with stock to the extent of £10,000 without payment, but when the profits came to be divided, interest and insurance were to be deducted from the division on these amounts. Similarly, Sir Francis Windebank, the Secretary of State, was to be an adventurer for £1,000 on exactly the same conditions.

The ships of this rival company floated by Sir William Courten, called Courten Association, began full-scale piracy in the Indian Ocean and the Arabian Sea. There were attacks on few ships of prominent Indian merchants close to the Mughals. Consequently, the Mughal Governor at Surat seized all the goods at the English East India Company factory at Surat, and imprisoned every factor there, including the President. The value of shares of the East India Company fell, and by the end of 1635, it was in debt to the extent of £100,000. To further bleed the Company, Charles I raised the duty on pepper, one of the major trade items of the East India Company, to as much as 70 per cent.

There was a deep sense of depression amongst the members of the company, and many of them were determined to wind up the current stock and abandon the trade itself. This was the third instance since its inception, that the East India Company was almost on its deathbed.

However, the adventures of Courtens Association did not last long. Sir William Courten passed away in June 1636. His son tried to run things for a while, but in 1638, the Dutch attacked and destroyed or captured all the ships of the Courten Association. However, enmity between the two trading organisations continued until a settlement was ordered by Oliver Cromwell, the 'Lord Protector of the Commonwealth of England, Scotland, and Ireland', and the two were merged in 1657. Oliver Cromwell was the General of the New Model Army of the English Parliament that fought the English Civil war against the forces of King

Charles I, and defeated them. Charles I was tried, convicted, and executed for high treason in January 1649.

The charter granted by Cromwell to the East India Company restored its privilege of exclusive trade within the same limits as before. The company became more prudent. In 1660, when Charles II ascended the throne, it built a relationship with him. The Cromwellian charter was suppressed. The company was one of the first bodies to offer its address to Charles II, presenting him with a service of plate worth £3,000. It also gave a gift of £1,000 in cash to the Duke of York. This was followed up on 27 November 1660, by a petition to the Council of Trade, which reported on 3 January 1661, recommending the Company to royal protection. Accordingly, on 3 April 1661, a charter was signed by Charles II, repeating almost word for word, the grant of James I. When the Crown had performed its part in recognizing the legal status of the Company, it was expected that the body so established would make a suitable return for the royal favour shown to it. In May 1662, when Charles II asked for a loan of £20,000 at 6 percent, the company responded by lending £10,000. This association with the Crown was satisfactory to both the parties. By the end of the year 1664, the net assets of the East India Company were worth almost £500,000.

References

[1] Haklyut, Richard, *The Principal Navigations, Voyages, Traffiques and Discoveries of the English Nation* (Glasgow, 1903), ii. p. 240.

[2] "The Charter of the Russia Company", in Hakluyt, *Voyages et supra,* ii. pp. 304-16.

[3] Mark G. Hanna (22 October 2015). *Pirate Nests and the Rise of the British Empire,* 1570-1740. UNC Press Books. p. 46.

[4] Court Book, I., Sept. 24, 1599, Stevens, pp. 4-7.

[5] Court Book, I., Oct. 28, 1600, Stevens, p. 62. The number of committees had been increased from the original 15 to 17 by October 30, 1630, so that only seven names were to be added on this occasion.

[6] Court Book, I., March 29, 1602, Stevens, p. 207.

[7] Bruce, John. *Annals of the East India Company*, Vol. 1, p. 153; w., Vol. 1 (1602-1613), pp. XXIII- XXVIII.

[8] Furber, *Rival Empires of Trade in the Orient*.

[9] Marshall, *The English in Asia till 1700*.

[10] Court Book, I., July 6, 1601, Stevens, p. 178.

[11] Hunter, *History of British India*, I. p. 284.

[12] Macphereon, David. *History of the European Commerce with India*, London, 1812, p. 84.

[13] Charters granted to the East India Company, I. pp. 27-53.

[14] Cf. "Summary of Capital", infra, p. 123.

[15] *Letters*. Voi. 1 (1602-1613), p. XXVIII – XXX.

[16] T. Wheeler, *Early Records of British India – A History of the English Settlements in India*, Delhi (reprint), 1972, p. 47.

[17] "The Trade's Increase" by J. R., London, 1615, in Harleian Miscellany, w. p. 207-11, 219, 220.

[18] Court Book, III., Feb. 17, 22, 1615.

[19] State Papers, East Indies, I. 65; partly printed by Bruce, *Annals of the East India Company*, I. pp. 193-194.

[20] P. J. Thomas, *Mercantilism and the East India Trade: An early Phase of the Protection Vs Free Trade Controversy*, London, 1926, p. 11.

[21] Foster, *The Embassy of Sir Thomas Roe*, p. 308, 338.

[22] The Voyages of Sir James Lancaster to Brazil and East, 1591-1603, p. 107.

[23] Foster, *The Embassy of Roe*, pp. 255-256, 338.

[24] Chaudhuri, *The English East India Company*, p. 15, 17.

[25] Chaudhuri, *The English East India Company*, p. 192, Letters., Vol. 11 (1613-1615), p. 125.

[26] *Letters*., Vol. VI (1617), p. 55; EFI Vol. VIII 1646- 1650 p. 75.

Chapter 3
The First English Factory in India

The first two voyages of the East India Company did not even touch the Indian mainland. However, the idea as had been suggested by Ralph Fitch had not been forgotten. In 1599, an embassy was sent to the court of Akbar, the Mughal emperor at Agra. This was to be followed by a voyage. John Mildenhall was chosen for this task by the East India Company. He was already in the services of Richard Stapers, one of its directors, in some fiduciary capacity. His assignment was to try to negotiate some kind of commercial treaty or arrangement with Akbar, which would be basis for the future English trade. John Mildenhall went by sea to Aleppo and travelled overland through Armenia, Kurdistan, Persia and Afghanistan, and finally, through Kandahar and Lahore, reached Agra in 1603. On the third day of his arrival, Mildenhall was presented before Akbar and made him a present of 29 horses and some jewels. A few days later, a second audience being granted, he stated his requests – firstly, friendship between Akbar and the Queen of England; secondly, permission for the English to trade in his dominions; and lastly, his neutrality in case of English and Portuguese ships ended up fighting in his seas. Akbar ordered these requests to be put down in writing and promised a speedy answer. In the meantime, he began to enquire about the power and the character of the nation to which this new visitor belonged. The Portuguese Jesuit mission at his court, perceiving the dangers of a Protestant rivalry to the ascendancy they had gained at the Mughal court, began to oppose Mildenhall. Mildenhall later informed Stapers that upon being asked by Akbar what the Jesuits knew about the English, they flatly answered that England was a nation of thieves. They told the emperor that

Mildenhall was a spy sent there to befriend His Majesty, but that afterwards, they would send men and get some of his ports, and will put His Majesty to much trouble.[1] They further hindered his negotiations with the emperor by bribing his interpreter to abscond. The influential men at Akbar's court whom Mildenhall might have bribed to favourably put the English case before Akbar, had already been over-bribed by the Jesuits. But Mildenhall claimed in his letter to his employer that he learnt Persian in six months, and according to his own story, scored a brilliant diplomatic victory, *"to my own great contentment, and as I hope, to the profit of my nation"*. Accordingly, Akbar ordered that *"whatever privileges or commandments he would have, should be presently written, sealed and given, without any more delay or question"*. On 21 June 1608, some two-and-a-half years later, he had still not arrived in England, but his letters reached London. His letters detailing the privileges he had obtained from Akbar were read to the Committees of the East India Company, with an offer that these could be theirs for a payment of £1,500. The Company decided to await Mildenhall's arrival before committing themselves.

When he made his petition in person in May 1609, Mildenhall had been away for more than a decade. He had lingered too long. More than two years before that day, the Company had already sent William Hawkins with letters for the Mughal emperor from King James I, and they now preferred to await the outcome of this more official voyage. In disgust, Mildenhall appealed to James I, arguing that given his expenditure of time and treasure, he should be permitted to capitalize on Akbar's grant in a personal capacity. After some debate, this idea was rejected. In October, perhaps by way of compensation, the Company suggested a post as a factor, but terms could not be agreed and in the end, the offer was rescinded, Mildenhall being judged *"for divers respects ... not fittinge to be ymployed in the service of the Companie"*.[2]

Unfortunately, the firman never came, and it was difficult to avoid the conclusion that Mildenhall was a bluff who did not scruple to invent whatever he thought might please his employers. Staper apparently thought the same, for a note in the Company's minutes for 18 November 1609, states that his application for further employment was rejected as he was "not thought fit to be engaged". Mildenhall later managed to find employment with three young English traders to accompany them to India by land. He poisoned them in Persia and took their goods, but in the process, he was himself poisoned. Yet, by medical supervision, he survived for a few months after. He finally reached Agra with goods worth 20,000 dollars.[3] At Agra, he died early in 1614. In the Court Minutes entry dated 20 September 1614, it seems the Company was able to recover half of that amount from his illegitimate children.[4]

When the third fleet of the East India Company was ready to sail, it was decided that one vessel from the fleet be sent to Surat to establish a factory there, by treaty with the Mughal Court, to buy calicoes, and re-join the rest at Bantam.[5] Surat was chosen for many reasons. As the great entrepot of the Mughal Empire on the western coast of India, it was, in the words of a contemporary traveller, "*a city of very great trade in all classes of merchandize, a very important sea-port, yielding a large revenue to the king and frequented by many ships from Malabar and all parts*". The Portuguese had recognized the importance of Surat in 1530-31 itself and tried to capture it. Antonio de Silveira had burnt the ships in the harbour and raided the town. Since the conquest of Gujarat by Akbar in 1573, they had left it alone. Hence, it did not come under the Company's agreement not to trade with any place "in lawful and actual possession of any Christian prince at amity with England, who would not accept of such trade".

The ambassador selected for this mission was William Hawkins, a nephew of the great Sir John Hawkins, the terror of Spain. He was one of eleven children, two of whom, besides himself, were associated with the East India Company.[6] He had been fighting under Fenton off Brazil, and had been in the Levant where he learnt Turkish.[7] Hawkins sailed as master of the Hector from Erith on 8 March 1607. Captain Keeling, on the Red Dragon accompanied him as General. A third ship, the Consent, under Captain David Middleton, sailed independently,[8] and reached the Cape of Good Hope on 27 July, whereas Keeling and Hawkins did not make it until 17 December.[9] Keeling had been blown right off his course to the Brazil coast, and owing to scurvy and lack of water, was forced to land at Sierra Leone. Here, an interesting event is recorded by Keeling. On 5 September, the crew of the Hector enacted Shakespeare's tragedy, *Hamlet*. On the 30 September, Captain Keeling asked Hawkins for dinner, "where my companions acted King Richard II"; and on the following day, he again invited Captain Hawkins to a fish dinner, and had *Hamlet* enacted *"which I permitt to keepe my people from idleness and unlawful games, or sleepe"*.[10]

Hawkins arrived at Surat on 4 August. As the first impression, he gave the following interesting description of Surat:[11]

> *"The city is of good quantity, with many fair Merchants' houses therein, standing twenty miles within the land upon a fair river. Some three miles from the south of the river, (where on the south side lieth a small low island overflowed in time of rain), is the bar, where ships trade and unlade, whereon at springtide is three fathom water. The river runs to Bramport (Burhanpur), others say to Musselpatan. As you come up to the river, on the right hand stands the Castle, well walled and ditched, reasonable great and fair, with a number of fair pieces, some of them of exceeding greatness. It hath one gate to the Greenward,*

with a drawbridge and a small port on the river-side. The captain hath in command two hundred horse. Before this lieth the Medon (Maidan), which is a pleasant green, in the midst whereof is a May pole to hang lights on and for other pastimes on great Festivals. Near to the Castle is the Alphandica (alphandega, customs house), where is a pair of stairs for lading and unlading of goods: within are rooms for keeping goods till they are cleared, the custom being two and half for goods, three for victuals, and two for money. Without the gate is a great Gondoree or Bazaar. Right before this gate stands a tree within an arbour, whereon the Fokeers (fakirs), which are Indian holy men, sit in state. Betwixt this and the Castle, on the entrance of the Green, is the market for horse and cattle. A little lower, on the right over the river, is a little pleasant town, Ranele, [Rander (called Ranel by Barbosa)] inhabited by a people called Naites,[Nayata, Arab merchants and sailors who settled there in 1225. Cf. Stanley's Barbosa, p. 67.] speaking another language, and for the most part seamen: the houses are fair therein, with fair steps to each man's door, the streets narrow. They are very friendly to the English."

Hawkins landed and was politely received by the local authorities, who, however, referred his case to 'Mocreb chan', or Mukarrab Khan, the Governor of Cambay and Surat, afterwards known to the English as their most relentless opponent, perhaps under Portuguese influence. The messenger to Cambay was delayed due to rain. At Surat, Hawkins soon found himself in an awkward plight, surrounded by enemies. Mukarrab Khan, instigated by the Portuguese, tried to kidnap him and steal his goods. Hawkins decided that his best course was to lay his case before the emperor at Agra, and on 1 February 1609, he set out for the capital, leaving William Finch, who was down with dysentery, to look after his goods at Surat. After sundry attempts had been made to murder him *en route* (or so did he claim in his letters), Hawkins managed to present himself before Jahangir on 16 April 1609, at Agra. The emperor was pleased to see him, and Hawkins found that he could make himself understood in Turkish, which is not far removed from Turki, the ancestral tongue of the descendants of Babur.[i] Jahangir was a man of curiosities. He had been presented with a turkey only few days back by the Portuguese at Goa[ii] and Jahangir spent exactly the same amount of time examining the new bird as he did examining Hawkins. Interestingly, the bird could make enough of an impression upon Jahangir to find a mention in his autobiography 'Tuzuk-i-Jahangiri', while Hawkins could not. But gradually, the emperor developed a liking for this fellow from a distant foggy island.

Jahangir liked new acquaintances, especially good fellows who could hold their liquor, and Hawkins entertained him vastly with stories of his travels. No wonder the Portuguese, who since the time of Akbar had held a distinguished position at the court, became like *"madde dogges"*. Hawkins, his staff Nicholas Ufflet and his orderly, Stephen Gravener, became mysteriously ill, perhaps poisoned. After a few days, Gravener died. Concerned at this, Jahangir gave his new friend a wife out of the royal harem to cook his food and to avoid untoward accidents in the future. This lady was a daughter of Mubarik Shah, an Armenian Christian who had risen to distinction in Akbar's service. The marriage service was read by Nicholas

---

i What Jahangir spoke was not Constantinopolitan Turkish but Turki, and though the two are by no means identical, sufficient resemblance exists between them to make it probable that Jahangir had little more trouble in understanding Hawkins than two provincials from widely-sundered parts of England have in grasping each other's meaning.

ii The Portuguese had got the bird from America.

Ufflet, Hawkins' staff, until such time as a more formal ceremony could be performed by a regular chaplain. The emperor gave Hawkins his commission written under his Golden Seal, to be sent to Surat, together with a stinging reproof to Mukarrab Khan for his bad behaviour towards Hawkins. Jahangir, in an outburst of friendship went so far as to offer him, if he would stay at the court, a pension of £3,200 a year, a troop of horse, and any concessions for the factory that he liked to ask. Finding Hawkins' a difficult name to pronounce, Jahangir gave him the title of 'Inglis Khan', which in Persia, was the title for a Duke, as Hawkins parenthetically explained when he wrote to his employers.

This triumph, however, was destined to be short-lived. The nobles and the Portuguese were consumed with jealousy. De Mendosa, the Viceroy of Goa, sent a letter accompanied by a handsome present, warning Jahangir that if the English got a footing in the country, he would eventually lose his harbours and his trade altogether. He treated Jahangir's concession as an act of war. Father Pinheiro, one of the Jesuit missionaries at Agra, finally got the concessions reversed.[12] This, according to Hawkins, was the cause of his downfall. *"The king went from his word, esteeming a few toys which the Fathers had promised him more than his honour."*

Unfortunately for Hawkins, there was another Englishman at Agra who kept a journal, and he supplements the story in a very different fashion, though, as there was no love lost between the two, we must, perhaps, allow something for the writer's malice. This was John Jourdain[13] who had set out in 1608 on the Company's Fourth Voyage, and had been wrecked on the shoals in the Gulf of Cambay. The survivors, Jourdain and others, had found their way to Surat, where, owing to the lack of control exercised by Captain Sharpeigh, they had been involved in various broils. One Tom Tucker had got drunk and killed a calf. This enraged the local baniya community, who used to pay a handsome sum to the authorities every year to stop cow-killing. Jourdain and all others of the party were asked to leave Surat, and so he had finally set out for Agra. Jourdain wrote that Hawkins had at first acquired popularity at court by winning the favour of Asaf Khan, a powerful nobleman, whose sister was the famous Nur Jahan, afterwards Jahangir's wife. After a while, however, by trying to drive a hard bargain in trade, Hawkins offended the Queen Mother and Khwaja Abul Hassan, the Chief Secretary. Abul Hassan took his revenge in an amusing fashion. The king was a great drinker, but was ashamed of his vice and cruelly punished those who talked of his orgies or of the part they took in them. "*The king,*" says Jourdain, "*was informed that some of his great men were bibbers of wine and that before they came to the Court daily, they filled their heads with strong drink, and commanded that upon pain of his displeasure, none of his nobles that came to his court should drink any strong drink before coming. Now Abdelhasan (Khwaja Abul Hassan), knowing that Hawkins was a great drinker, feed the porter (as is supposed) to smell if he had drunk any strong drink, which is easily discerned by one that is fasting. So the chief porter finding that Hawkins had drunk, he presently carried him before the king in presence of the whole Court, where, by the mouth of Abdelhasan, being Secretary, it was told to the king he had drunk strong drink. Whereat the king paused a little space, and considering that he was a stranger, he bid him go to his house, and when he came next he should not drink. So being disgraced in public, he could not be suffered to come into his accustomed place near the king, which was the cause why he went not so often to Court.*"[14]

Whether this was true or not, Hawkins was now out of favour. "*Stay I would not, among these worthless infidels,*" he wrote. But unfortunately, Mrs Hawkins' relatives objected to her leaving India. At first, he thought of asking the Portuguese Jesuits, who were ready to do anything to get rid of him, to give him a passport to settle in Goa with full liberty of conscience, and eventually return to England when the opportunity offered. Jourdain, however, pointed out the dangers of this. *"I told him,"* he writes, *"if he went to Goa his life would not be long, because he had much disputed against the Pope and their religion, and was apt to do the like again there, which would cost him his life."* News had come of the appearance of a fresh English fleet off the coast of Cambay, and Jourdain proposed to join it. With this, Jourdain parted from Hawkins on 28 July 1611, and reached Surat in October.

The Sixth Voyage

In 1609, the Company, after a period of deep depression at the loss of the Ascension and the Union in the Fourth Voyage, had recovered its spirits owing to the success of Captain Middleton's voyage in the Consent in the fifth one. In 1609, they equipped the Sixth Voyage on a scale which they had not yet attempted. £82,000 was subscribed, and they built at Deptford a splendid new vessel of 1,100 tonnes, naming it the Trades Increase. The king himself launched it, and gave Sir Thomas Smythe a medal in honour of the occasion.[15] Trades Increase was put in charge of Sir Henry Middleton, the other vessels being the Peppercome, Captain Downton, and the Darling.[16] Besides Middleton, the Trades Increase carried one Lawrence Femmel as chief factor for the Surat factory. Middleton and Femmel had detailed orders as to their procedure. Journals were to be kept, giving details about trade, coinage, weights and measures, and the character of the inhabitants of the various ports. 'Civil behaviour' to natives on the part of the crew was emphasised. Blasphemy, swearing, drunkenness and gambling were to be punished. The captains were to be *"very careful to assemble together their whole family every morning and evening, and to join together in all humility with hearty prayer to Almighty God for His merciful protection and favour"*. They were to go to Socotra Aden, and Mocha, and then to Surat, where they were to get into touch with Hawkins and ascertain what privileges he had obtained from the Mughals. At Surat, they were to do their best to establish a factory and obtain the privilege of trading free of duty. In all things, they were to uphold *"the honour of our King and the reputation of our traffick"*. Strict economy was to be observed in firing salutes, wages were not to be raised, there was to be no private trade and no carrying of passengers. Their cargo consisted of cloth, lead, red lead, tin, quicksilver, vermillion, sword blades, kerseys and red caps. They were to load up with indigo, calico, cotton yarn, cinnamon, sandal, ginger, opium, gum benjamin, olibanum, aloes and lac. They were to sell their iron, lead, calico and cloth at Bantam where silk, gold, and, above all, pepper (400 tonnes if they could), were to be loaded; but too much anxiety for pepper was not to be displayed for fear of raising the price. Rare birds and beasts for the Company's patrons were to be bought.

The voyage began on 1 April 1610. They reached the Cape of Good Hope by the end of July. At St. Augustine's Bay, they met the ill-fated Union of the Fourth Voyage, and gave her much-needed food and other supplies. Socotra was reached in October and Aden on 7 November. Here the conduct of the Arabs was suspicious, but Middleton pressed on to Mocha, leaving behind Captain Downton with the Peppercorne. The Turkish Governor of Aden refused to trade and imprisoned two parties which had gone ashore, upon which Downton went to Mocha to join his chief. Here he found that Middleton had been treacherously captured by the local Turkish Governor with 58 of his crew, and it was not until May that making their guards drunk, they managed to escape. Middleton was furious at the Turkish Governor, but could do nothing. So, he went on to Surat, where more bad luck awaited him. The coast was blockaded by Don Francisco da Soto, the Portuguese Captain Major, with eighteen frigates, and he refused to allow the English to go any further. Letters from Hawkins were, however, smuggled aboard.

On 26 January of the following year (1612), Hawkins appeared, having taken Jourdain's advice. He had outwitted his wife's relatives in an amusing way. He persuaded the Jesuits to make him duplicate passports, first an open one licensing him to settle down as a trader in Goa, the other, a secret permit to return to England, *"and what agreements I made with them to be void and of none effect, but I should stay and go when I pleased"*. Hawkins, his wife, and the other Englishman were taken on board one of the ships of the Sixth Voyage under an armed escort. Mukarrab Khan, the governor, overawed by the Portuguese fleet, peremptorily refused to allow a factory to be opened, or any English traders to be left behind at Surat.

Middleton too, who was to leave India with the fleet of the Sixth Voyage, made a most valuable discovery, acting on information supplied by Jourdain from local sources. He 'discovered' Swally. This was the location of the famous Swally Hole, a roadstead seven miles long and a mile broad, protected from the sea by a long sandbar. Here, a fleet could ride at anchor much more safely than among the shifting shoals of the Tapti. Swally became the port of Surat and became famous later.[17] Other than this, Middleton had accomplished nothing during a stay of 138 days.

The Portuguese blockade was lifted upon the arrival of Captain John Saris with the Eighth Voyage. As usual, the rival commanders could not agree on their mutual seniority and unfortunate squabbles about precedence made co-operation between the two fleets impossible. Hawkins had left Agra in November 1611, and three months later arrived at Surat, where he found Sir Henry Middleton, with whom he went to the Red Sea, and afterward to Java. At Bantam, he went on board the Thomas, part of the fleet under the overall command of John Saris, and sailed for England. The fleet reached the Cape of Good Hope in April 1613, and on the passage home, probably near the end of it, Hawkins died. His remains were brought to Ireland and buried there. Finch, who had started by the overland route after having been badly treated by Hawkins, if Jourdain is to be believed, died at Baghdad. Middleton went on to Bantam, and on the way, the Trades Increase ran on to a coral reef and was damaged. While being careened for repairs, it was fired at and destroyed by the Javanese.[18] The dangers of sea voyage in those days were great and the casualties high. Besides the Ascension, Union and Trades Increase, the Darling, Thomasine, Hector and Hosiander, were all lost before 1616. Middleton, Hawkins, Downton, Aldworth, and countless other sailors, died of disease.[19] Downton struggled home in the Peppercorne, his men dying like flies of scurvy and his timbers strained and leaking. But he had a rich cargo of spices, and the Sixth Voyage for all its disasters, paid over 121 per cent, in dividends.

Two Battles that Changed the Course of History

Hawkins' mission was a failure. He had failed to obtain from Jahangir even those worthless firmans that the emperor bestowed upon the other English ambassadors. Jahangir, convinced by the Jesuit Fathers that the English were a paltry and distant race who wanted to rob him of his trade, took no notice of Hawkins when he had exhausted his stock of novelties and good stories. The English are mentioned only once in Jahangir's voluminous memoirs.[20] Nor was any change likely to come about while the Portuguese fleet could blockade the coast at will. A decisive victory at sea was supremely necessary for English prestige. In spite of his apparent failure, Hawkins had thoroughly explored the resources of the Mughal Empire of which he wrote a very able account. He had also investigated the possibilities of Surat as the site for a factory.

The Struggle with the Portuguese at Sea – 1612-33

Hawkins left Surat in February 1612. The next Englishman to come to the Surat port was Captain Thomas Best with the Tenth Voyage, which consisted of the Dragon and the Hosiander. They cast anchor off the Swally Hole on 5 September, and were met by Jadu, Hawkins' old broker. Thomas Kerridge, also on the voyage, was sent ashore and received a hearty welcome from the Governor, who was no doubt overawed by Middleton's peremptory dealings with his opponents. On the 13th morning, 16 Portuguese frigates[iii] appeared, and took Mr Canning, the purser and another Englishman who had landed, as prisoners. Best replied by capturing ten locals from the crew aboard a large Gujarati ship anchored near him as hostages. He then moved his fleet out of the Tapti, round to Swally Road, where there was more sea-room in case of an attack, especially by light craft. The Governor of Ahmedabad, who was probably desirous of good terms with both sides, came to visit him, asking to release the locals who had been held as hostages. Best went ashore to greet him, still keeping his hostages on board. He then drew up thirteen 'Articles of Trade' with the Governor, of which the principal were:

1. Compensation for the attack on Sir Henry Middleton and a promise not to repeat the offence.
2. The Mughal emperor was to receive a permanent English Envoy at Agra.
3. The arrival of each English Fleet was to be publicly proclaimed, and the country people to be allowed to trade freely with it.
4. Customs duty not to exceed three-and-a-half per cent, and cartage from Swally to Surat to be provided

iii Light galleys, a gun mounted in the bows, used for river and coastal work. They usually had about twenty soldiers aboard and eighteen oars on each side.

by the local Muqaddam[iv] at a fixed rate. Provisions up to Rs 1,000 to be sold to ships without duty.

5. If an Englishman died, his belongings were to be invoiced and returned intact.[v]
6. The Mughal authorities were to be responsible for any molestation on the part of the Portuguese in their territory.
7. The English Company was not to be held responsible for the misdeeds of pirates and interlopers, though it would do its best to suppress them.
8. Speedy redress was to be given for wrongs and injuries.
9. The articles of the treaty were to be confirmed by the Royal Seal.

Best also refused to send the Mughal Emperor any present until the treaty was signed. Just then, Canning came on board with news that a Portuguese fleet was coming from Goa. Canning had been taken by the Portuguese, but the viceroy had commanded to set him ashore at Surat, saying, "Let him go help his countrymen to fight, and then we will take their ship and the rest of them altogether." Sure enough, on 29 November, four big galleons and around twenty to thirty frigates appeared under the command of Admiral Nunes de Cunha. The Portuguese showed their usual arrogance, assuring the Surat officials that they would force the English to yield in an hour. Best weighed anchor and stood out to meet them, but soon found himself alone. The Hosiander, having damaged her cable, could not join. But this did not daunt him. After a few words to the crew, he laid the old Dragon two cables' length from the enemy. He was unable to go closer due to shoal water. To continue

---

iv Village headman.

v As per the existing law, the goods of a foreigner dying in Mughal territory were liable to confiscation by the government. This was a constant source of friction.

the story in his own words, *"began to play upon the Vice Admiral both with great and small shot, that by an hour we had well peppered him with some fifty-six great shot. From him, we received one small shot, saker or minion, into our mainmast, and with another he sunk our longboat: now being night we anchored, and saved our boat but lost many things out of it. The thirtieth, as soon as the day gave light, I set sail and steered between them, bestirring ourselves with our best endeavours, putting three of their four ships on the sands thwart of the Bar of Surat"*.

The next morning the battle resumed and the Hosiander, making up for her inaction on the previous day, *"danced the hay upon them, so that they durst not show a man above the hatches"*.

Best then held a council of war. As the bay was shallow and the Dragon drew much water, he decided to run up to the coast. Here they anchored off 'Mendafrobay'[vi] where all that time, Sardar Cham (Sardar Khan), or Khwaja Yadgar[21] a noble of the Mughals, having a mansab of two thousand horses, was besieging a fort. This was on the Kathiawar coast, about ten leagues east of Diu. Sardar Khan and Best exchanged compliments and presents. This was a chance for the English to show the Mughals their naval strength. This fight did much to enhance the English prestige, and proportionately lowered that of the Portuguese.

By 27 December, Best was back in Swally. He had lost only three sailors in the entire action, while the enemy's casualties had been very heavy – at least 160 killed. The Dragon had fired 680 'great shot', 3,000 'small shot', and 60 barrels of powder. On 6 February, the royal firman arrived, but Best refused to receive it unless it was formally delivered. Unfortunately, it was hardly worth the paper on which it was written. The articles agreed upon by Captain Best were never signed by Jahangir. It was *"otherwise a general firman*

---

vi Muzaffarabad or Jaffarabad on the Kathiawar coast thirty miles east of Diu.

without knowledge of particulars, and are of small validity", as Kerridge wrote to Roe in 1615.[22] Nonetheless, the first factory of the East India Company at Surat had come up.

On 17 February, Best hoisted sail for Bantam. He passed the Portuguese fleet as he sailed down the coast, but they did not fire at him and allowed him to take an Indian vessel under their very eyes.

Disgusted at the perfidy of the local officials and seeing the difficulty of protecting the interests of the factory from their insults and the attacks of the Portuguese during the interval which must necessarily elapse between the departure of one fleet and the arrival of the next, Best had at first been inclined to abandon Surat altogether.[23] He was, however, dissuaded from this by Thomas Aldworth, who was to be in charge, together with his relative, Thomas Kerridge, as well as Withington, Starkey and others. Canning, in accordance with the terms of Best's treaty, went to Agra as the Company's agent to present the letter from James I. Jahangir at first received him well, but when he found out from the Jesuits that he was a mere merchant and not sent directly by the King of England, he contemptuously referred him to Mukarrab Khan. Canning was treated with studied neglect, his servants deserted him and he lived in constant fear of being poisoned. On 22 June, he died, and it was assumed that the Jesuits made away with him.[24] Kerridge, an honest, capable though hot-tempered man, who was a good linguist, took his place. It was, however, impossible to gain much in the face of the unwearied opposition of the Jesuit Mission headed by Jerome Xavier, *"the implacable enemy of the English. We shall never do anything, as long as that witch Xavier liveth,"* as Withington wrote.[25]

An unusually favourable opportunity for opening relations with the Mughal court presented itself when the Portuguese bitterly offended the Mughals by plundering the Hassan, a Surat ship bound for Jeddah, carrying £100,000 worth of treasure. Jahangir was furious. He banished Jerome Xavier from his court, shut down the church at Agra and told Mukarrab Khan to attack Daman. *"Had we now English shipping here,"* wrote Aldworth, *"we might do great good in matter of trade, which is now debarred to people of this country, having none to deal with them. They all here much wish for the coming of our English ships, not only for trade but to help them, for as they say, the coming of our ships will much daunt the Portugals."*[26]

Under these circumstances, the factors prepared to give a warm welcome to the next fleet which anchored in Swally Road on 15 October 1614. This was the Second Voyage of the First Joint Stock, commanded by Captain Downton. The squadron consisted of the New Year's Gift, of 650 tonnes; the old Hector of 500 tonnes; the Merchant's Hope, of 300 tonnes; and the Solomon of 200 tonnes. Downton was determined to assert his authority. He landed with great pomp and placated Mukarrab Khan's rapacity with a number of presents well-suited to the childish humour of the recipient. These included cases of knives and combs, pictures of Moses and of Paris in Judgement, and last but not least, sundry cases of bottles of 'rich and strong waters'. Mukarrab Khan was very anxious that Downton employ his fleet in joint operations against Diu, and was very sulky when Downton replied that he would not be hired to fight against the Portuguese, *"which is contrary to my King's Commission (unless they gave me first cause), not for the world; neither would I be withhold from fighting with them if they provoke me"*.[27]

The factory at Surat was overhauled. Aldworth was left in charge. Edwards was sent to Agra to present a letter from James I to Jahangir, along with some pictures of the Royal Family, a case of 'strong waters', and a hunting dog, an English mastiff. Dodsworth was sent to Ahmedabad to start buying indigo; Steele and Crowther were despatched to Persia to find trade opportunities there. Soon, news came that the Portuguese, enraged at the arrival of a fresh English fleet, were preparing a formidable fleet to crush them once and for all. On 23 December, the anniversary of Best's glorious fight, Portuguese scouting frigates appeared up the Tapti river. This continued over Christmas, and shots were exchanged, after which Downton went out to Swally Road. Here, on 18 January 1615, the Portuguese armada arrived – six great galleons, the largest being 800 tonnes, three other ships, sixty frigates and two galleys; altogether they mounted 234 guns, with 2,600 European, and 6,000 Indian sailors, against Downton's 400 men and 80 guns.[28] In command was no less a person than the Portuguese Viceroy of India, Don Jeronimo de Azevedo, himself. The locals were overawed by this overwhelming display of force and Mukarrab Khan, assuming defeat for the English as inevitable, began to negotiate peace with the presumed victors.

Downton realized the gravity of the situation. The odds were, indeed, terrible. After much thought and silent prayer, he decided to attack. The enemy must be brought to battle. He therefore called a council of officers on his ship and found them all *"to my heart's desire and tractable to whatsoever I would wish"*. Unfortunately, Downton's abilities as a tactician were not equal to his honesty and goodwill. He was only a gallant amateur, and his men were not trained gunners, though their guns were in excellent condition. He ought to, like Best, have gone out into the open where his superior seamanship might tell, instead of being besieged in a fish pond, as Roe wrote later. He decided to anchor the Hope under Captain Molineux, at some distance from the rest of his fleet, in order to tempt the Portuguese to attack in shoal water. He apparently overlooked the danger of separating his small command in the face of overwhelming odds, and forgot that the enemy was well provided with river-craft. *"I put forward the business as it were, baited my hook, and the fish presently ran there at."* The Portuguese attacked the Hope with full force so suddenly that Downton, who was in his cabin writing his diary, had to cut his cables in order to come to the rescue in time. *"They came with three ships and thirty or forty frigates as I imagined,"* he writes, *"with a veaze laid the Hope aboard with the flower of all their gallants: where by the hand of God in their amazed carriage, they received such a blow as few (and they by their extraordinary chance) escaped with safety, and three ships burnt"*. The attack was ruthless. The crew of Hope jumped into the sea, while those who had not been shot or drowned were picked up by the Portuguese light craft. After this, the fight dwindled into an inconclusive cannonade across the bank.

Every morning and evening, the English fired a salvo into the Portuguese lines, hoping to provoke them to attack. The Mughal officials, seeing how the fight was going, began to bring fruit and other supplies for the English, including the items of commerce such as indigo and cotton. News came from Daman that the Portuguese had buried 300 corpses there. On the 5th and 8th, Portuguese attempts to destroy the fleet by fire-ships[vii] were again foiled by the watchfulness and good shooting of the English fleet. Frustrated, the Viceroy shifted his fleet down the coast so as to threaten Surat. But Downton prepared to attack him the moment he started disembarking his force. Soon, the Portuguese admiral, having run out of food and water, took to sea and disappeared. Downton's fleet was crippled by the loss of the Hope, and as a prudent merchant, he did not wish to imperil the Company's ships. So, he did not pursue. *"I wish no occasion to fight,"* he noted, *"for that which I have already paid for. I am already possessed on, and I am so far from the humour to fight for honour, unless for the Honour of my King*

---

vii Small ships of their own fleet set on fire and sent to English lines.

and Country, that I had rather save the life or lives of one of my poorest people than kill a thousand enemies."

There was much rejoicing ashore at the defeat of the Portuguese. Downton and the Mughal governor exchanged swords and paid one another complimentary visits. On 3 March, the fleet weighed anchor for Bantam. The Viceroy's fleet appeared again on the horizon and followed Downton down the coast, but did not dare to attack. Downton's achievement had been indeed a notable one. He sailed to Bantam but died there soon after – the fatal climate which had undermined the health of Middleton, Hawkins and a number of merchants before him took him as well.

The Portuguese power in the East was now on the downward path. Beyond Indian waters also, they were being humbled. In 1615, Captain Benjamin Joseph's fleet, with Parson Terry aboard, encountered off Madagascar, a Goa carrack commanded by Don Emmanuel de Menezes. "*She was a ship of exceeding great bulk and burthen, our Charles, though a ship of 1,000 tonnes, looking like a pinnace when she was beside her,*" says Terry.[29] Don Emmanuel gallantly refused to surrender when challenged, and kept up a running fight, hanging out a lantern at night lest his pursuer should miss him. The battle was a severe one. Captain Joseph was killed and his successor, Captain Pepwell, severely wounded. Finally, the Portuguese commander, having lost his mainmast, beached his ship on the island of Comoro and burnt it. This victory not only damaged Portuguese prestige, but put Goa itself in jeopardy, for it demonstrated that communications with Portugal were in danger of being cut.[30]

In 1621, the English, emboldened by their striking successes, decided to take the offensive. The key to the Persian Gulf was the frowning citadel of Ormuz. Shah Abbas, the ruler of Persia, enraged at Portuguese pretensions, had attacked the town from the land side, but was unable to make progress while the sea lay open. Monnox, the chief of the English factory in Persia, was eager that the Company's ships should co-operate with the Shah to oust the Portuguese from Ormuz. He was approached by Imam-Quli Khan, military general and governor of Fars, Lar and Bahrain, on behalf of Shah Abbas, seeking English support against the Portuguese. Captain John Weddell, with a fleet of five ships, was sent for the job. Meanwhile, an Anglo-Dutch fleet blockaded Goa and prevented the Portuguese from sending reinforcements.[31] Ormuz was protected by the fortified island of Kishm, the present-day Qeshm island, and the English attacked there first. Ruy Frere, the Portuguese commander at Kishm, tried hard to make terms, but the Persians insisted on an unconditional surrender. Kishm fell after a fierce bombardment in which Baffin, the famous Arctic explorer who was also the master of the ship London, lost his life. While sighting a gun, he received a bullet in the stomach, '*wherewith he gave three leaps and died immediately*'.[32] Ruy Frere and the rest of the garrison were put on board the Lion and taken off in triumph to Surat.

Meanwhile, the fortress of Ormuz was fiercely assailed by land and by sea, and fell on 23 April. Most of the Portuguese garrison, with their women and children, were taken off by the English fleet. The rest were put to the sword by the Persians. The fall of this proud bulwark of Portuguese power in the East echoed all over the world. It struck their prestige a deadly blow from which they never recovered. Assailed by the Dutch on the one hand, and the English on the other, Goa was doomed. Nevertheless, though impoverished by mis-governance and corruption, and paralysed by Spanish neglect at home[viii], they put up a determined fight and continued to trouble all ships in the Persian Gulf. In the autumn of 1625, the English fleet under Captain Weddell arrived at Swally with the veteran Kerridge

---

viii Spain ruled over Portugal in the period 1580-1640.

aboard, to find four Dutch ships about to sail for the Persian Gulf. As the Portuguese were blockading Ormuz and causing much damage to trade, it was decided to combine the squadrons for an attack upon them. On 31 January, they encountered a strong Portuguese fleet under Nuno Alvarez Botelho. Kerridge stepped on to the deck of the flagship and drank to the men, "encouraging all of them to perform with alacrity and boldness".[33] The fight was long and fierce, but by six o'clock in the evening, the Portuguese withdrew themselves.[34] However, Botelho was not one to give up easily. He suddenly appeared off Swally, a challenge to the English to come out and fight again. When the Anglo-Dutch fleet put out to sea in response to the invitation, they found that they had been tricked. Botelho had sailed southward with all speed, and next made his presence known by pouncing upon the outward-bound fleet. He chased half of them northwards to the Persian Gulf, where Ruy Frere lay await. They waylaid the Lion, the vessel which had brought out Sir Thomas Roe, and burnt her at the water's edge under the very walls of Ormuz Castle. Botelho now disappeared once more. Word, however, came to the English authorities that he had "got into a hole called Bombay, where they were fitting themselves up for the war, and look for three more ships from Goa to join forces with them".[35] Accordingly, the Anglo-Dutch fleet hastened towards Bombay, hoping to catch Botelho before he could get reinforcements. But once more, they found that Botelho had bested them. They, however, decided to land at Bombay.

Bombay under the Portuguese was a flourishing port, inferior to Goa, but equipped with storehouses, docks, and the usual complement of monasteries and churches. The Anglo-Dutch forces landed at Bombay and began ransacking and burning all the storehouses and churches. This was on 15 October 1626 – a historic date, as it marks the first landing of the English forces at a spot which their descendants were destined to make famous.[36] A strange story is related of the end of Botelho. During the sack of Bombay, a Dutch captain pillaged the church of 'Our Lady of Pity', tearing down the crucifix and smashing it. Botelho, on his return after the Anglo-Dutch forces had left, swore an oath never to rest until he had chastised the wretched iconoclast, and hung a piece of the sacred symbol round his neck as a reminder. And sure enough, shortly afterwards, he perished in an engagement with a Dutch vessel. His opponent was also slain, and the legend goes that he was none other than the man whom Botelho was seeking.

Desultory fighting between the English and the Portuguese went on till 1630, in which year Captain Morton repeated Downton's exploit by frustrating a landing of the Portuguese at Swally. This little engagement made a great impression on the local people of Surat, including the Mughal officials, and the place where the invaders were repulsed was long after known as Bloody Point.[37] Both sides were now tired of a war which brought no profit, and the English were beginning to doubt the wisdom of an alliance with the Dutch. A truce, which afterwards developed into a regular treaty, brought the long and fruitless struggle to an end in 1633.

The Embassy of Sir Thomas Roe, 1615-18

At first, it appeared that Downton's success had greatly altered the prospects of the English in Western India. The Mughal authorities at Surat seemed inclined to relax the harassing restrictions that they had hitherto imposed. Branch factories were started at Cambay, Broach, Baroda, Ahmedabad and Agra, and the Company's agents went as far as Lahore and Sind to explore and buy items they could profitably trade in. Edwards, the chief of the branch factory at Agra, thanks chiefly to his opportune present of an English Mastiff to Jahangir, caught the attention of the emperor. The gift of the hunter dog from England, which managed to kill a young leopard and tackle a wild boar much to the emperor's amusement, made Edwards the recipient of a firman and a present of 3,000 rupees. Edwards began to give himself mighty airs, posed as if he were an ambassador and treated both Kerridge and Aldworth with scorn. Kerridge had stayed on at Agra to act as linguist or interpreter, but found himself relegated to the background. He was even accused of purposely delaying an answer to James I's letter. On a proposal being made to sell certain items worth £10,000 at Surat, Edwards wrote that *"Mr Aldworth should do nothing without his order, which if he withstood, he would let him know his strength"*. Contrary to the Company's rules, he kept Jahangir's present for himself and spent it on a lavish lifestyle. Edwards even had trouble with Downton and both of them wrote letters to Thomas Smythe complaining against each other.[38]

Edwards' conduct at Agra finally led to his dismissal. He was ordered by Captain Keeling and his Council to report back to Surat to answer for his acts. Unable to justify his acts, by the joint consent of the Governor and his Council, Edwards was ordered to return to England. This was the first reported dismissal from service of a senior official of the Company in India.[39] This roused the wrath of Joseph Salbanke, a worthy and religious-minded factor, who had several grievances of his own as well. Salbanke had carried himself 'very genteelly' to Keeling, but had been forced to work under 'punies and younglings' who might have passed for his grandchildren.[40] Salbanke wrote to the Company very strongly in Edwards's favour.[41]

Bickerings like these fill the records of the period. The anxious life got upon the nerves of the factors. Their position was not enviable. The climate was trying for the young factors who had not yet learnt how to adapt themselves to Indian ways of life. Mortality was high, and between the departure of one fleet and the arrival of the next, which occurred at uncertain intervals, they were practically cut off from the outer world. They were harassed by the avarice and caprice of the local officials and by the constant menace of the Portuguese. All things considered, Aldworth's task was not an enviable one. Added to his other anxieties was the friction, sometimes threatening serious results, caused by unruly and drunken sailors and others, ignorant of native prejudices. The English love for beef gave great offence to the Hindus who paid the Mughal officials an annual sum to stop cow-killing. A curious sailor peeps into a litter containing a purdah lady, another pokes his finger into a Brahmin's food! Parson Terry has an amusing tale of a cook who got drunk, and swaggering down the street, met the Mughal Governor's brother and his attendants.[42] A serious riot broke out over another trivial issue which nearly cost Kerridge his life. A small belfry had been erected outside the English factory, surmounted by a vane. The mob attacked the building, declaring that the vane was a cross, 'a sign of victory and winning over the town', and the bell a 'watchword to give the alarm'. It was only with the greatest difficulty that they were pacified.

Jahangir, as capricious as ever, got tired of the English when they had no more presents to offer, and turned once again to the Portuguese. Edwards had been found out, and like Canning before him, fell into disgrace. Kerridge himself had been beaten and fined by the authorities at Ahmedabad, owing to some dispute over indigo. Worst of all, Jahangir handed over the charge of Surat to the haughty Prince Khurram, the future Shah Jahan. Khurram hated foreigners and left the transaction of his business to his favourite, Zulfikar Khan, who was no better disposed towards the English than had been the last Governor, Mukarrab Khan. A treaty was actually being negotiated by the latter with the Viceroy of Goa for the landing of a Portuguese force at

Swally to expel the English from Surat, and permanently exclude them from the country.[43]

The English realized that something had to be done, especially as the Dutch were threatening to drive them out of the Malay Archipelago at the same time. The Company had decided to accept the advice of its factors and send out a representative who should really be an ambassador, and who should 'breed regard' in the Mughal Court. King James I was quite agreeable to this. In 1609, he had been present with the Royal Family at the launching of the unlucky Trades Increase of the Sixth Voyage. Hence, he readily acquiesced in the project of sending Sir Thomas Roe as his representative to the Mughal Court. Sir Thomas had instructions to act as the official representative of the English nation in order to obtain a permanent treaty with the Mughal monarch, authorizing the opening of factories on the coast and at other places of commercial importance. Sir Thomas, selected by Sir Thomas Smythe, was eminently suited for the post. He belonged to an old city family, and was able to sympathize with the Company's mercantile aspirations. He had been a Member of Parliament from Tamworth. He had already been on an important voyage to South America and up the Amazon. However, some members of the Company regarded him with suspicion. In general, they disliked gentlemen, and they were afraid that the king might force upon them some courtier who would pry into their profits, and perhaps try to overthrow their coveted monopoly. It was only when Sir Thomas, by his tact and firmness alike in dealing with the Mughal authorities and the unruly English factors, and by his excellent advice on the subject of reorganizing the Company's factories, had shown how much he had their interests at heart, that they really took him into their confidence. As per the Company's employment clause, Sir Thomas was to keep a strict account of all his expenses, and to deduct from them any allowance made by the Mughal. He had to promise not to engage in private trade, directly or indirectly, and to report to the Company any offenders whom he should detect infringing this rule. He was on no account to meddle with the Company's investments in India, but to leave them entirely to the management of the local factors. He was not to ask for an advance of over £100. On their part, the Company was to pay Sir Thomas £600 per annum, half to be invested in the Company's stock, plus £100 for servants' wages, £100 to buy plate for his table and to be returned when the contract ends, a preacher at £50, and a surgeon at £25 per annum.[44]

The king's commission to Roe, after stating that the object of his mission was *"to maintain the intercourse and traffic which hath so happily been begun"*, gave him full powers and authority to sign a treaty with the Mughal emperor and his representatives at his discretion, *"concerning the maintenance and continuance of the amity and course of merchandize between us, our realms and dominions, and the realms and dominions of the said Great Mughal"*. In the event of his being unable to negotiate a treaty with the Mughal Empire, Roe might be employed in exploring the Red Sea or any other places likely to be of service. The Commission concluded with the usual caution against fighting with Spain or any other nation at peace with England, except in defence of his rights. In the private instructions issued to Roe, James exhorted him *"in his carriage to be careful of the preservation of Our honour and dignity"*, and to do all he could to advance the Company's interests and to carry out their instructions.

Roe sailed with the Third Voyage of the First Joint Stock. It was a noble fleet. The flagship, the Lion, was commanded by the veteran Captain Keeling, General of the voyage, the other vessels being the Dragon, the Peppercorne and the Expedition. They set sail on 24 January 1615, and reached Swally on 18 September. The voyage was a dull one, especially for Roe, who was looked upon with some suspicion as an outsider who wanted to interfere in the Company's affairs. At the Cape, they met the Hope, with news of Downton's victory and death. On 27 September, Roe landed at Swally Hole with a salute of forty-eight guns, the fleet being decorated with ensigns, flags, pendants and streamers. He was, however, rudely received by Zulfikar Khan, who wished to search him and his servants, and overhaul his goods at the Customs House. Roe politely but firmly refused to submit to this violation of the privileges of an ambassador, and plainly intimated that he intended to be treated with respect. A month passed in weary wrangling with rapacious officials whose manifest object was to extract presents, which Roe ultimately had to give. Meanwhile, the Company had received a serious blow. The heroic Aldworth who was lying desperately ill at Ahmedabad, tried hard to come down to Surat to meet Roe. But he died at Nadiad, a few miles outside that town on 4 October. Roe and his party set out for Agra on 1 November. They halted at Burhanpur, then an important fort and the headquarters of Prince Parviz, who had made it the base for his operations in the Deccan. Here, Roe obtained permission to establish an English factory.

The Portuguese were still in bad odour at the Mughal Court, though a strong group, including Mukarrab Khan and Prince Khurram were trying to negotiate a treaty with them for the expulsion of the English from Mughal territory. Roe recommended a vigorous offensive as 'the nobler and safer part', and the most likely to impress the Mughal emperor. Roe thought Surat to be a bad port, always susceptible to Portuguese attack, and recommended Muzaffarabad on the opposite coast of Kathiawar as a possible alternative; but this opinion he subsequently retracted. He was initially impressed by the courtesy of Mahabat Khan as compared to the 'cruel griping' Governor of Surat, and wanted to take the port of Broach *"where we may safely land all our goods whatsoever, faithfully promising that we should be absolutely exempted from all such exactions and injuries as we were subject unto in Surat*".[45] He also urged the opening of trading stations on the Indus, at Jask, and on the Bengal coast. Roe went on to point out that the parsimony of the Company about presents had made him utterly discredited. He had carried gifts of burning glasses, telescopes, tawdry pictures and knives, a case of virginals and a coach, the cheap velvet lining of which had faded on the voyage. He urged that the unworthy suspicion and secrecy with which he was received by the factors made it impossible for him to examine the state of their finances or offer any further advice.

Since Jahangir was camping at Ajmer at that time, Roe travelled and reached there on 23 December. He contracted fever on the way. On 10 January he was admitted to the court of Jahangir. The courtiers tried to induce him to make the oriental salaam, touching his forehead upon the ground, but in vain. Roe had long seen that it was necessary to uphold above all things, English prestige, and insisted upon being treated with the respect due to the ambassador of a great nation. He accordingly walked straight up to the inner railing reserved for the highest nobles, and stepped in. He bowed to the emperor, who returned the salute. He then, to the horror of the court, demanded a chair. "*I was answered,*" says Roe, "*that no man ever sat in that place, but I was desired as a courtesy to ease myself against a pillar covered with silver that held up his canopy*". Jahangir then asked him what he wanted. Roe explained the difficulties being faced by the English traders and asked permission for a factory in the town. Jahangir, his eye no doubt upon the English coach and other presents that Roe had brought, ordered a firman to be drawn up. Upon reading it, Roe found that he was asked in return to allow the Portuguese to come and go as they liked in and out of Surat harbour. After some complicated diplomacy, Roe presented a draft of the treaty he wished to conclude with Jahangir, the following being the chief clauses it contained:

1. *Permission to come and go freely into any Indian port, to land goods, and to hire a house and establish a factory there.*
2. *Facilities to be afforded for trade with the local traders in provisions, and labour and cartage to be provided.*
3. *Goods landed at any port not to be tampered with at the Custom-house; presents for the emperor not to be pilfered or opened; and merchants not to be searched or otherwise insulted upon landing.*
4. *Goods to be sold freely to any one, and at any price, after dues are paid; no presents to be exacted, or unnecessary escorts imposed; and sealed packages brought from inland not to be reopened.*
5. *The Portuguese must either make peace with the English and agree to free and open trade at Indian ports, or in case of refusal it shall be lawful for the latter to chastise the stubbornness of an obstinate enemy to peace, as also to require any robberies made by them, in taking any of their ships, boats, or goods.*

More delays, of course, occurred over this document, as Prince Khurram, an enemy to all Europeans except the Portuguese, demurred at the last clause. He even asked Jahangir why he favoured the English who only gave mean presents such as knives and cloth, instead of the Portuguese with their rubies, pearls, and other costly gifts? The prince consented, however, to grant firmans restricting the local governors from robbing and oppressing the factors at Surat and Ahmedabad. Shortly after this, the Portuguese arrived with a 'Balass Ruby', a ruby-coloured spinelle found in Badakhshan, weighing five ounces. Worse still, a Dutch deputation from Surat also appeared and was granted the same privileges that the English had been asking for.

The months dragged on wearily. At one time, Roe was debarred from the Court, but by Jahangir's birthday, he was back again, amusing the emperor with miniatures and himself, an amused spectator of the intrigues of nobles and courtiers. By this time, Roe finally learnt that the emperor would not sign the treaty and he had to be content with a firman from Prince Khurram authorizing the English to trade in peace at Surat. In the following month, the English fleet arrived with Parson Terry on board, bearing the news of their victory over the Portuguese galleon off the Comoro Isles. Sir Thomas made the most of this and the Portuguese were correspondingly depressed. But little came of it from the emperor beyond an inquiry about novelties in the way of presents. In November, Roe again wrote home to the Company.[46] After some general remarks about his progress in the first year, he retracted his former doubts about the suitability of Surat as a port of trade, tapping as it did the rich country of Gujarat, but was strongly averse to any projects of building a fort or maintaining any armed force. *"A war and traffic are incompatible, and the Portuguese and Dutch have ruined themselves in this way all that is required is a light pinnace of say sixty tons and ten guns to keep off the enemy's frigates."* At sea, on the other hand, Roe always advocated a forward policy. The Portuguese were on the downward slide, and a blockade of Goa by cutting them off from the annual home-fleet would quickly bring them to their senses and make them agree not to molest English traffic.

As regards trade, Roe did not recommend the opening of fresh factories either in Bengal or at the mouth of the Indus. Nor was Roe very eager to start trading with Persia. For the East India Company, the idea of opening up trade with Persia dated from 1608, when the Shah had sent Sir

Robert Shirley[ix] to Europe to open negotiations with the European governments. Shirley returned to Persia in 1613, with Sir Thomas Powell as ambassador from King James I. The party came to a disastrous end. Sir Thomas Powell died, and the same fate befell his brother Michael and his wife, who perished with her new-born infant. This was a time when many young Englishmen tried to make fortune by travelling to India and engaging in some private trade or getting into the services of the Company. One such young man was Richard Steele, who had travelled overland to India through Persia, and had persuaded the factors to send him, along with a factor from Surat named Crowder, on a mission to the Shah of Persia. They reached Ispahan and reported their success in a letter to Aldworth. Aldworth being dead, Roe opened the letter and answered it. Roe himself was very eager to open trade with the Red Sea, which he thought offered greater prospects of profit for the Company.

Roe soon realised the futility of his mission as an ambassador. It was impossible to obtain a regular treaty. Jahangir could not be brought to treat the King of England as an equal. All that could be obtained were a few trading concessions and firmans. These, however, Roe considered sufficient for the purpose. Meanwhile, he thought that all that the English required at the Court was a native consul at 1,000 rupees a year to represent the interests of the English,

---

ix The Shirleys (or Sherleys), Robert and Anthony, were gentleman adventurers who had been employed by Shah Abbas in organizing his army. Robert married a Persian wife who created a sensation in London. After his return to Persia in 1615, he was again sent to Europe on a prolonged mission; but presenting himself once more at the Persian Court in 1628, he was told he was no longer required. He died shortly afterwards and his body was taken by his wife and buried in Rome.

with a subordinate at Surat on half this sum. *"That,"* said Roe, *"will serve you better than ten ambassadors."*

In the winter of 1616, the Mughal Court moved to Mandu, and Roe, with it. An amusing example of Jahangir's childish rapacity was seen, when a fresh set of English presents arrived at the royal camp. The emperor, unable to wait for the servants' arrival, opened the boxes and purloined the contents, even down to some beaver hats intended for Roe's private wear.[x] The summer of 1617 passed, yet nothing was done. Roe was wearily waiting for his recall, when at the end of September arrived the Company's fleet of five vessels, which however, brought an urgent request to Roe to stay for another year. He reluctantly complied.

In February 1618, Roe sat down to write his last report to the Company, though neither this nor his letter to Sir Thomas Smythe adds very much to what he had already told them. He warned his employers to give up hopes of a regular treaty between the two nations and bid them be content with general firmans obtained from time to time when necessary. He saw no real impediment in the way of English progress, since the Portuguese were on the downward path, and as for the Mughals, *"their justice is generally good to strangers; they are not rigorous, except in searching for things to please"*. He promised before leaving to obtain as much as he could, and this promise he was fortunately able to redeem by a clever piece of diplomacy. He got a pearl, shaped like a pear, smuggled – *"beautiful and orient"*. He promised to sell this to Asaf Khan, Hawkins' old friend. Asaf Khan was the brother of the Empress Nur Jahan and had troubles with Prince Khurram. He, therefore, willingly championed Roe's cause in return for the pearl, and obtained for the English a final firman that was far more favourable than anything they had

x Jahangir had a childish love of toys. Roe noted: *"I gave him a small whistle of gold, weighing almost an ounce, set with sparks of rubies, which he took, and whistled therewith almost an hour."*

previously received. The local authorities were to protect the English if attacked by the Portuguese. Free trade was to be allowed, and the factor's goods were not to be detained or plundered at the custom-house. The factors were to live under their own laws and religion, and were to be allowed to lease a house for their factory, though not to buy or build one. And in case of any violation of the foregoing articles by anyone, the Governor of Surat was to '*aid and entreat them as friends, with courtesy and honour*'.[47]

In August, Roe had a narrow escape. Plague had broken out in Ahmedabad. Plague first appeared in the Punjab in 1616 and raged for eight years.[48] But his work was now finished, and in the following month, he returned to Surat, for enjoying a four months' well-earned rest in a pleasant country villa in the suburbs of Surat. The factors who had fiercely opposed him at first as a prying intruder, now acknowledged his good sense and integrity. In February 1619, he sailed on the Anne and arrived in England in September. He was greeted with an ovation. The Company thanked him with a sum of £1,500 and the king received him at Hampton Court. He afterwards served as ambassador at Constantinople, Hamburg and Vienna, and died – it is said, broken-hearted by the Civil War – in 1644. Roe's visit is the turning-point in the history of the British in India. True, he did not obtain a definite treaty, as a formal agreement of this kind was alien to Jahangir's nature.[49] But from Roe's time, we find the English treated with respect, and what is more, replacing the Portuguese by steady steps as the paramount foreign power in the Mughal dominions.

References

[1] See his letter to Staper from Casbin in Persia, dated 3 October 1606 in Purchas, II. P 299. Casbin is to the North West of Teheran, some seventy miles from the southern shore of the Caspian Sea.

[2] For a brief survey of John Mildenhall's career, see William Foster, *Early Travels in India,* p. 48-52.

[3] Purchas, IV. 173. Withington came out with Captain Best in the Tenth Voyage. Purchas repeats a suggestion, which he ascribes to Nicholas Withington, that Mildenhall had learned "the art of poysoning, by which he made away three other Englishmen in Persia, to make himself master of the whole stock, but … himself tasted of the same cup and was exceedingly swelled, but continued his life many moneths with antidotes."

[4] His tomb exists in the old Roman Catholic cemetery at Agra (J. R. A. S. ,1910, p. 495).

[5] Purchas, VI. 59.

[6] Giles Hawkins was a factor at Bantam while Charles Hawkins was a partner in the Sixth Voyage (Markham, The Hawkins Voyages, p. XIII n.).

[7] Ibid., p. XIV.

[8] She left Tilbury on March 12 (Purchas, III. p 51; cf. his marginal note, II. 502).

[9] Reeling's Diary in Purchas, II. p 508.

[10] Rundall, in *Narratives of Voyages to the North-West* (Hakluyt Society), p. 231.

[11] From the pen of William Finch, preserved by Purchas IV. P. 27.

[12] V. A. Smith, *Oxford History of India,* 1919. Pp 379-80.

[13] For details, see his journal, edited by Foster for the Hakluyt Society, Series II, vol. XVI.

[14] Jourdain's Journal, p. 104 ff. Hawkins was lucky. Some unfortunate nobles, after a banquet to welcome the Persian ambassadors, boasted of the 'merry night past'. For this, Jahangir had them flogged almost to death (Embassy of Sir Thos. Roe, ed. Foster, p 303-4).

[15] Calendar of State Papers, 1513-1616, para. 476.

[16] The details of the voyage are given from the original manuscripts in the India Office in the Lancaster Voyages.

[17] "The Road of Swally and the Port of Surat are fittest for you in all the Moghal's country. The Road of Swally is as safe as a pond" (Roe, apud Foster, ii. 345).

[18] Peyton's Journalin Purchas, *Pilgrimage,* IV p. 304.

[19] Quoted in Anderson, *English in Western India,* pp. 17-18.

[20] A casual reference to the battle of Swally Hole (Rogers and Beveridge's transl., i. 274-275.

[21] Blochmann, Am, p. 492; Rogers and Beveridge, *Jahangir's Memoirs*, I. 237; II. 89.

[22] Embassy of Sir. Thos. Roe, ed. Foster, I, p. 62.

[23] Letters Received, II. 157. According to Kerridge, Best quarrelled with Aldworth on the subject, but afterwards took all the credit for the latter's action.

[24] Withington's narrative, Purchas, iv. 165; and Dodsworth's narrative, ibid, p. 257. See also Letters Received, vol. ii. (1613-15), which does not support the story that Canning was poisoned.

[25] Embassy of Sir Thos. Roe, ed. Foster, II. p. 313.

[26] Aldworth to the Company, 19 August 1614 (Letters Received, II. pp 96-97).

[27] Given in First Letterbook, p 449-52. He was not to attack any Christian allies of the King of England unless provoked.

[28] The Portuguese fleet comprised of Galleons: Viceroy on the All Saints, 800 tonnes, 300 men, 28 guns, all brass; St. Benet, Captain M. de Souza, 150 men and 20 guns, 700 tonnes; Lawrence, Captain J. Cayatho, 600 tonnes, 160 men, 18 guns; St. Christopher, 600 tonnes, 160 men, 18 guns; St. Jeronymo, 180 men, 500 tonnes, 16 guns; St. Anthonio, 400 tonnes, 140 men, 14 guns. Ships: three, 200 tonnes and 8 guns each. Gallies: two of 50 men each. Frigates: sixty, 18 oars a side, and 20 soldiers in each. Dodsworth's account (taken from a Portuguese prisoner) in Purchas, IV. 263. Cf. Aldworth in Letters Received, ii. 137; Low, History of the Indian Navy (1877), I. 19.

[29] Voyage (1777 ed.), pp. 34, 47.

[30] Journal of Sir Thos. Roe, ed. Foster, ii. 359.

[31] For the siege of Ormuz, see English Factories, 1622-23.

[32] Purchas, vol. II. p. 1792.

[33] English Factories, 1624-29, p. 46.

[34] English Factories, 1624-9, p. 51-53.

[35] Captain Weddell's report (ibid., p. 112).

[36] English Factories, 1624-29, p. 112.

[37] English Factories, 1630-33, p ix, x; see also Fryer's New Account, ed. Crooke, vol. I, p. 224.

[38] Downton to Smythe, February 28, 1615, in Letters Received, iii. 27. Also videp 14, 72-83, and 89.

[39] Letter of the Factors to the Company, March 10, 1616.

[40] Anderson, English in Western India, p. 20.

[41] Letters Received, IV. 231.
[42] Voyage (1777 ed.), p. 163.
[43] Embassy of Sir Thos. Roe, ed. Foster, I. pp. 95.
[44] Embassy of Sir Thos. Roe, ed. Foster, I. pp. 95.
[45] Letters Received, vol. IV. p. 233.
[46] Embassy of Sir Thos. Roe, ed. Foster, II. p. 342.
[47] Embassy of Sir Thos. Roe, ed. Foster, II. 506.
[48] V. A. Smith, *Oxford History of India,* p. 381-2.
[49] English Factories, 1618-21, p. 59.

Chapter 4
Surat and its Mercantile Community

The Mughal conquest of Gujarat in 1573 had far-reaching consequences for the province as well as the empire. The northern and western regions of India became politically integrated, and this paved the way for a further degree of economic integration. Gujarat, already commercially important, could now exploit a much larger and expanding hinterland. On its part, Gujarat was already the most urbanized area in the entire Mughal Empire, which is evident from the fact that by 1595, approximately 19 per cent of its revenue resources were realized from urban taxation.[1]

The ports of Gujarat were linked to the ports of West Asia such as Aden and Ormuz, as well as to the ports of Malacca and Achin in South East Asia.[2] The ports of Gujarat had, for centuries, served as entrepots for the flow of goods, mainly textiles, silk, cotton, opium and indigo, drawn from their own rich hinterland comprising a large extent of territory in northern and western India, and shipped to ports in the Persian Gulf and the Red Sea. These Gujarati ports were also the procurement points for bullion and horses imported from the Basra, Ormuz and Mokha[i] ports of West Asia. Gujarat had also developed several manufacturing centres like Ahmedabad, Surat, Baroda and Broach. Generally, they produced cotton textiles, while silk-weaving was especially carried on at Ahmedabad. The main indigo-production centre was Sarkhej. Gujarat also had a variety of other handicraft industries.

Surat became established as a modern city towards the end of the 15th century. Voluminous records are available regarding the business activity in Surat during the sixteenth

---

i Present-day Mocha in Yemen

and seventeenth centuries. The English and Dutch factory records of the period give very precious information. The letters of the East India Company's servant from Surat to their employers in England, and from them to their Surat factors, being chiefly devoted to their own commercial activities, are of great value in tracing the trade of the city of Surat. Besides, several European travellers visited Surat and other parts of the country in the 17th century and have given a good account of the socio-economic conditions of the people and their commercial activities. Chief among them are Edward Terry (1615-1625), chaplain to the embassy of Sir Thomas Roe; Pietro Della Valle (1623-1625); Johan Albrecht de Mandelso, the German traveller (1638-39) who reached Surat on 25 April 1638; the French physician François Bernier, who lived in India from 1659-1666; his contemporary, the French traveller Jean-Baptiste Tavernier, the jeweller, who lived in India from 1641 to 1668; the French traveller Jean de Thevenot who reached Surat on 10 January 1666 and lived in the country for about a year; and the Italian traveller Dr Cremelli Careri, who was in India in 1695. Moreover, the persons who served under the East India Company at Surat, the most famous being Dr John Fryer, surgeon of the English Factory at Surat, (1674-1681) and John Ovington (1689-92), the priest sent by the Company, have given an excellent account of Surat in 1689. In 1514, the Portuguese traveller Duarte Barbosa described it as a city of *"very great trade in all classes of merchandise, a very important sea-port yielding a large revenue to the ruler of Ahmedabad"*.[3] In order to protect it from frequent attacks of the Portuguese, the ruler of Ahmedabad had built a fort in 1546.[4]

The entrance into the city was through several gates. The three main gates were the one leading to Cambay and Ahmedabad; another to Burhanpur; the third being the one to Navsari. Sentries were posted at each gate, who kept on eye on all incoming and outgoing persons. The city had very few splendid buildings. European travellers who visited Surat in the 17th century have remarked that the houses of the inhabitants were not in proportion to their wealth, because they were in the habit of hiding their riches. Even the houses of the rich people were not splendid.[5] Finch remarks about the location of Surat that *"the city has many fair merchants houses therein standing twenty miles within the land up a fair river is the Barred, where the ship trade and unload, where on at a spring tide is three fathom water. Over this channel is fair to the city side able to bear vessels of the fifties tuner laden."*[6]

At the time of Mughal conquest, Surat had a vibrant trading and mercantile community. The biggest community was that of the baniyas followed by the Bohras. Both these communities were strictly mercantile-based, heterogeneous, and incorporated within themselves a number of sub-groups belonging to different castes and religious denominations. These baniyas, as referred to in the European literature of the period, belonged to different castes and sub-castes. Similarly, the Bohras were mostly Sunni Islam, while a minority belonged to different sects of Shiite Islam. Besides, there were the West Asian Arabs, the Turks and the Mughals, who were by and large Sunni, while the Khojas and the Persians belonged to the Asna Ashari Shia creed. Traditionally, the Muslim merchants of Gujarat were predominantly engaged in Oceanic commerce – ship-owning and overseas trading were dominant forms of investment by them. There was also a sizeable community of Armenian and Parsee traders.

The Mughals issued their coins from a large number of mints in the empire and worked on the basis of free coinage, i.e. anyone could take bullion to the mint and get it minted into coins upon a payment made to cover minting costs and seigniorage.[ii] The minting charge amounted to five to six per cent of the value of the coin minted. Mahmudi was the chief coin of the Gujarat Sultanate when it was an independent kingdom, and it continued in circulation side by side with the Mughal rupee when it was annexed into the Mughal territory. The normal rate of exchange was five mahmudis for two rupees. Pagodas were the gold coins issued by the Vijayanagar rulers and the Muslim kingdom of Golconda.

The Baniya Merchants

The term 'baniya' has its origin in the Sanskrit word 'vanij', which means a merchant. In Mughal jargon, the word used for the baniya was baqqal. Describing the prevalent view on the baniyas, Abul Fazl writes: *"Open caste of the vaishyas which is designated Banik, is called Baniya in ordinary usage and Baqqal in Arabic. It is divided into 84 sub-castes."*[7] In towns, these baniyas could be found hawking cloth, cowries and even salt. Ovington describes how at the marketplace at Surat, *"It is not very easier to pass through the multitude of Bannians and other Merchants that expose their Goods. For here they stand with their silks and stuffs in their hands, or upon their heads, to invite such as pass by to come and buy them."*[8]

Among the baniya merchants, a process of specialization had led to two distinct lines of commercial activity, those of brokers (dallals) and of sarrafs (sarraf) – bankers and moneychangers. The brokers were the 'middle men' who directed *"the purchaser to the merchandise and the seller to the price"*.[9] To these brokers, the term 'dallal' was generally applied. Sometimes, even the European factors and travellers used this term to identify the brokers.[10] From *Ain-i Akbari*, it appears that a dallal was appointed in each

---

ii Profit made by a government by issuing currency, especially the difference between the face value of coins and their production costs.

quarter (muhalla) of the town to supervise the selling and buying in the local market.[11]

De Buqoi, a Dutchman wrote in 1684 about the brokers of Surat:

"It is crowding here with this kind of people – just as the Jesuits also creep into the church, the council, chamber and the market place. Every merchant has his own broker, except the bazzar brokers who take care of the business of common and smaller folk. So that nobody is without his broker. Yes, a governor or a grandee even has to use one, for it is seen as a disgrace in this country if one pursues one's personal interest. This in only found amongst commoners."[12] It further seems that these dallals were also an essential part of the commercial establishments of the foreign merchants, who depended on their services for business transactions.[13] Tavernier advises his compatriots to select a broker *"who should be a native of the country, an idolator and not a Musalman, because all the workmen with whom he will have to do, are idolators."*[14] The importance of the brokers in trade in Mughal India is graphically brought out by the account of Caeser Fredericke, a merchant of Venice, who had travelled in the East from 1563 to 1581 and was at Cambay. He speaks of the brokers who are *"Gentiles who are men of 'great authority' having under them fifteen or twenty servants. Whenever a fleet of small ships entered the port of Cambay, the brokers assembled on the water front and the merchants embarking from the ship handed over their goods to one of them".*[15]

John Fryer, an English doctor and Fellow of the Royal Society who travelled in India and Persia between 1672 and 1681, was particularly hostile to this community. Writing in 1674, Fryer explains that these baniya dallals were:"… . *expert in all the studies arts of Thriving and Insinuation; so that Lying, Dissembling, cheating are their Masterpiece; Their whole desire is to have Money pass through their fingers, to which a great part is sure to stick: For they well understand the constant turning of cash amounts both to the credit and profit of him that in so occupied; which these baniyas are sensible of otherwise they would not be so industrious to enslave themselves."*[16] The stranglehold of the broker over the merchant was however such that: *"and when as the Merchant thinketh that he cannot sell his goods at the price current, he may as long as he will, but they cannot be sold by any man but by that Broker that hath taken them on land and payed the custom."*[17]

According to Tavernier it was the *"custom throughout Asia that nothing is sold except in the presence of a broker, and each class of goods has its own separate one."*[18] Almost a similar impression regarding the monopolistic attitude of the baniyas and brokers is created by Fryer. His description runs like this:*"... . Such is their policy that without these, neither you nor the Natives themselves shall do any Business, though they are worse Brokers than Jews."*[19]

Fryer (1674-75) is so hostile, he equates them with pests: *"To this place belong two sorts of Vermin, the Fleas and Banyans: the one harbouring in the sand... The other vermin are the Banyans themselves, that hang like Horse-leeches, till they have suck'd both sangidnem & succum (I mean money) from you: As soon as you have set your Foot on Shore, they crowd in their service, interposing between you and all Civil Respect, as if you had no other Business but to be gull'd; so that unless you have some to make your way through them, they will interrupt your going, and never leave till they have drawn out something for their advantage..."*[20]

The foreign merchants' dependence on the brokers was partly due to language constraints. Fryer in 1674-75, writes on the deceitful means of the brokers at Surat:*"It would be too mean to descend to indirect ways, which are chiefly managed by the Banyans the fittest tools for any deceitful. Undertaking; out of whom are made Brokers for the company, and private persons, who are allowed Two percent on all bargains, besides what they squeeze secretly out of the price of things bought; which cannot be well understood for want of knowledge in their language which ignorance is safer, than to hazard being poisoned for prying too nearly into their actions: Though the company, to encourage young men in their service, maintain a master to learn them to write and read the language, and an annuity to be annexed when they gain perfection therein, which few attempt, and fewer attain."*[21]

In spite of all the negative aspersions and fraudulent practices attributed to them, these brokers were quite faithful to the merchants whom they served. One Benjamin Robinson, factor at Surat, wrote to the Company on 26 December 1638, that commonly, when the baniyas are solely entrusted with such a business (of buying and supplying merchandise of good quality), they are not unfaithful. In case of a fraud, they were liable to be punished. However, in the punishment, care was to be taken not to be too harsh to frighten them away or gain their enmity. The President of the English company at Surat, Methwold, advised the factors at Ahmedabad in 1638:[22] *"... Only take care that you fall not too heavy upon theire persons in corporall punishment, we mean chawbucking[chabuk, a whip i. e. whipping] them, least, being guilty and in that respect desperate persons, they may consent to loose themselves that you may find trouble; in which particular wee doe rather approve that you should deliver them over into the Mahumetan power, but therein also wee would not have you to bee to forward, since wee know that nothing will be taken from them in that way which will bee returned for our satisfaction..."*[23]

It is interesting to note that this advice for a moderation in punishment to a broker caught in a fraudulent practice was followed by a censure of the factors at Ahmedabad by the local baniyas, as they apparently did not heed the advice of Methwold and imprisoned an errant broker for three days 'without rice or water'.[24] The brokers for the European companies during the 17th century were entitled to a brokerage of anything ranging from 1 per cent to 3 per cent of the total transaction.[25] According to Fryer, in the

1670s, the brokers were "*allowed two percent on all bargains, besides what they would squeeze secretly out of the price of things bought.*"[26] Tavernier mentions that "*there are certain classes of goods for which the fee due to them is 1 per cent, Other for which it amounts to 1 and 1/2 and even up to 2 per cent.*"[27] The Dutch factor, De Buqoi, noted in Surat in 1684 that the broker, for his services, got 1 per cent from the seller and 1 per cent from the purchaser.[28]

Besides the commission or dasturi, the dallals would also make further demands on the European factors under whom they served. Streynsham Master informs that in December 1679, Hari Charan, the 'house Baniya', demanded Rs 25 per month as wages besides the usual 'dustoore' of 'one anna upon Rs 100'. This broker was finally allowed 2/3 parts of the claimed dasturi.[29] By the 1690s, the share of brokers appears to have risen to 3 per cent of the total transaction. In large transactions, the earnings of the brokers however, could go as high as 10 to 10. 5 per cent.[30]

The Sarraf Moneychangers

The sarrafs played a very important role in the smooth conduct of trade. The Dutch records mention:

> "*They have their bazaar in a special part of town where they assemble daily or at least send a servant to represent them. And it is by and large according to their whims that the course of money is adjusted, and that the batta paid for, when lending pennies on interest is fixed at a high or low rate. There too, everything is dealt with concerning commerce. It is there as well, where one may most easily find out how much capital and credit a merchant has at his disposal and whether one may rely upon a salesman or not.*"[31]

The sarrafs, who were moneychangers or bankers, also belonged to the baniya class. These sarrafs were dealers in bills of exchange, deposit receivers and insurers. Tavernier says: *"In India, a village must be very small indeed if it has no moneychanger, called a sarraf, who acts as a banker to make remittances of money and issues letters of exchange."*[32] No payment could be made or received unless the sarraf was shown the coin to assess its purity. A coin had to be expertly examined for its genuineness or metallic purity, age and weight.[33] The reason was, that a silver coin, by wear and tear, could lose some weight and consequently become lighter.[34] The sarrafs also earned much profit from assaying gold and silver. For his labour, he would receive a commission of 1/16 of a rupee for cent[iii].[35]

These sarrafs were praised for their thrift and enterprise. Their practice of collecting even the gold dust from their assays is commented upon by Tavernier:

> *"... Of all the gold which remains on the touchstone after an assay has been made, and of which we here make no account, far from so small a think to be lost, they collect it with the aid of a ball, made half of black pitch, and half of wax, with which they rub the stone which carries the gold, and at the end of some years they burn the ball and so obtain the gold which it had accumulated."*[36]

Commenting on the expertise of the sarrafs, Tavernier at one place comments:

> *All the Jews who occupy themselves with money and exchange in the empire of the Grand Seigneur pass for being very sharp, but in India they would scarcely be apprentices to these changers..."*[37]

These baniyas had a prominent presence in the Indian Ocean trade during the 17th and 18th centuries. They had a significant presence in settlements in various cities like Bandar Abbas as well as in all major market towns such as Shiraz, Kirman, Kashan, Isfahan, Tabriz and Aradabil,

iii Cent = hundred rupees

where they had their own quarters in bazaars and mainly worked as sarrafs.[38] Their much-commended expertise in arithmetic, accountancy and methods of business was greatly appreciated by the Persian-Muslim merchants. Even in the Spice Islands, the banker (sarraf) of the Dutch was a Hindu baniya.[39]

The Muslim Bohras

The most numerous of all Muslim merchants operating in Gujarat in the Mughal era were the Bohras. They converted to Islam[iv] in the second half of the eleventh century under the influence of the first Ismaili dai who came to Gujarat in 1067-68 from Yemen, a country which had strong trade relations with Gujarat. Interestingly enough, the Bohras in Gujarat, faced no persecution by the local Hindu rulers for centuries and the community grew and flourished especially in Cambay, Patan, Sidhpur and Ahmedabad, the last of which later became their headquarters. It was only in the last decade of the 14th century under the Gujarat Sultanate (1407-1572) that the suppression of the Ismaili Bohras began. During the reign of Sultan Ahmed Shah I (1411-1442), the founder of Ahmedabad, the suppression of Shias including Ismailis, became so severe that Ismailis started converting to the Sunni faith, a process that was further helped by the schism in the Ismaili Bohra community over the issue of wali or leadership.[40]

The Bohras dominated the saltpetre trade based on its extraction at Malapur, near Ahmedabad.[41] The community was also pre-eminently engaged in overseas trade. They were the big ship owners with a large number of vessels by the close of the 17th century. They specialized in the Red Sea trade due to the advantage of combining trade with the hajj pilgrimage.[42] They also had trade contacts with South East Asia. The Bohras combined trade and hajj pilgrimage,

iv The Ismaili sect

thereby dominating the entire Red Sea trade, particularly to the port of Jeddah, which was the gateway to Mecca and Medina and was also the biggest trading port in the Red Sea. Akbar was the first ruler to organise hajj pilgrimage at State expense and provide subsidies to the pilgrims. All this was done through these Bohra traders.

The earliest-noticed leading merchant of the Muslim community of Surat in English accounts was Mir Jaffar, first mentioned in 1612. Then there was Khwaja Nasim, Khwaja Daud, Khwaja Jalaluddin, Taj Khan, Tashrif Khan, Khwaja Nizam, Khan Sharif, Abdul Latif and Mirza Muazzim. All of them had trading interests in Cambay and other parts of Gujarat. Most of them traded with the West as well as South East Asia. In 1628, the English accounts refer to a Mirza Mahmud as the principal Muslim merchant of Surat who sent his goods to Batavia in English ships and had his own agents in Bantam for whom he sent rice and ghee in 1629. Mirza Mahmud traded with the Maldives and with Basra in the Persian Gulf. However, in 1644, the English establishment at Swally harbour complained to London that Mirza Mahmud, together with a *"company of credulous Moors and Banian merchants have pursuaded Mirza Jam Quali Beg, our then Governor, that the English were spreading false scare of French piracy to get Surat freight in their ships"*.

Another prominent Muslim merchant was Haji Zahid Beg. In 1629, he was appointed to the post of Customs and Port Authority, the Shahbunder, who, even while occupying the official position, continued his private trading activities. His ships plied to Aden and Basra. Two of his ships were the Salamati and the Mahmudi. He brought his commodities from Agra, Diu, Cambay, Ahmedabad, Baroda, Bulsar, Gandevi, Chaul and Dabhol on the Konkan coast. He traded extensively with Malaya where he had established considerable influence with the ruling and commercial circles. In 1664, his house, along with that of Virji Vora, another prominent trader, was plundered by the Marathas. Beg's house was located near the sarai meant for Persian and Turkish merchants in the north-western part of the city. In 1666, the Dutch sold their goods to him in preference to Virji Vora, for Zahid Beg had complained to the Batavian authorities that the local Dutch officials were much too friendly with Virji Vora and accepted his bids even though they were lower than that of Zahid's. In 1668, he and Vora procured thousands of maunds (one maund = 36 lbs.) of quicksilver from the English. After his death in 1669, his son Mirza Ma'sum carried on the family business. He made a deal with the English to buy all the copper, quicksilver, vermillion, alum and tin from them. In 1672, he also bought large quantities of broadcloth and ivory from them.

In Surat, a number of Armenian merchants, some Christians among them, also thrived. The most prominent among them was Khwaja Minaz. His ship, St. Michael, sailed to Mocha and other ports in the region. He is described in the English accounts as "an able and well reputed Armenian merchant" who bought large quantities of broadcloth from them. In 1668, he sent a ship named the Hopewell, with a cargo worth £5,000 to the Philippines. In 1670, he and Nanchand Vora, grandson of Virji Vora, bought English cloth, tin and copper in large quantities. In a letter of December 1665, the English describe Minaz as the President of the Armenian merchants, which obviously implies that the Armenian merchants, like the baniyas, had their own organization looking after their mercantile interests, serving as a liaison between them and the other mercantile communities as well as with the government. In 1665, he indicated to the English that he wanted to move to Bombay "with the rest of the merchants of his nation", but this did not materialize. The reason for such a proposed move must have been the better trading prospects in the projected English possession of the island of Bombay, and the governmental oppression at Surat. Of the latter, we find evidence in an incident in 1672, when Minaz was beaten with slippers and staves by the Mughal governor, and he wrote to Aurangzeb about the injustices done to him by the governor.

The richest Muslim merchant of the century was Abdul Ghafur, who began his career in some work associated with a mosque. He is often called Mulla, which may have been because of his association with a mosque. Hamilton says about him: *"Abdul Gafour, a Mahometan that I was acquainted with, drove a trade equal to the English East India Company, for I have known him fit out in a year, above twenty sail of ships between 300 and 400 tuns, and none of them had less of his own stock than 10,000 Pounds, and some of them had 25,000; and after that foreign stock was sent away, he behoved to have as much more of an inland stock for the following year's market,"* Manucci speaks of him as *"the most powerful merchant at Surat, and owns over twenty ships of his own."* Abdul Ghafur, by all accounts, was a great shipping magnate and his family had 34 ships. Of these, one was the Hussaini of 400 tonnes, which mounted 25 guns. He traded extensively with the Red Sea area and Malaya. In February 1701, Sir William Norris, Ambassador of the New English Company, noticed on his way to Aurangzeb's camp at Brahmapuri, several textile workshops at a place called Shawgur, belonging to Abdul Ghafur. An English record at Surat dated 21 September 1700, refers to a ship of Abdul Ghafur arriving at Surat with 5,000 maunds of coffee along with other cargo. Abdul Ghafur figures a great deal in the English records of the 1690s and 1700s in connection with European piracy in the Arabian Sea, and the damage caused to his ships by such piratical acts.

The Parsis began to participate in commerce in a significant way during the second half of the 17th century. A large number of Parsi merchants began to operate in Swally. The leading Parsi merchant of the times was Rustamji

Manekji. He was born in Surat in 1635, and belonged to a priestly family. He was a broker to the Dutch before 1681, and then figured prominently as a broker to the Portuguese and the New English Company. The Portuguese appointed him as their agent in Surat for issuing passports to Indian ships, and to also act as their attorney or vakil in their relations with the Mughal government in the city. He travelled to Daman, Ahmedabad and Goa for his patrons, and seems to have amassed a fortune from his involvement in ship-building and trade. He died in 1721 at the age of 86, and his three sons carried on the family business after him.

Virji Vora of Surat

If there is one figure that dominates the commercial and urban history of Surat in the 17th century, it is Virji Vora. His commercial activities were as ubiquitous as was his power over-arching. The list of commodities he traded in was endless and the amounts of money he handled ran into millions of rupees. His agents roamed through all the major trading areas of India, from Calicut to Agra and Surat to Patna. His commercial interests also extended from Malaya and Sumatra in the south, to Gombroon and Mocha in the north. English records are replete with references to him, reflecting the varying attitudes of frustration, anger and admiration for the man without whose assistance and co-operation the English could scarcely have been able to function in Surat. The English and Dutch records of the period mention him as arguably the richest person in the world at that time.[43]

The name Virji Vora appears for the first time in the English factory records on 22 March 1619, with reference to "*Hacka Parrack, being servant to Virgee Vora merchant of this cities*", who was recommended for courteous usage of all the English ships. Another reference again is of 1619, where the English "*forwarded letters of credit from Virgee Vora [to] his servant Callian Shaggar (Kalyan Shagird)*" at Burhanpur.[44] Being a merchant of vast resources, Virji Vora traded in almost every commodity which was profitable. Specific mention is made of coral, ivory, gold and silver, mace, nutmeg, pepper, opium, copper, tin, quicksilver, vermillion, alum, amber and tea.[45] He was the biggest dealer in cotton and opium. Pepper was imported on a large scale from Malabar and Kanara, and he supplied these places in return with cotton textile and opium, which were then redistributed by the Malabar merchants into the far south.[46]

The strategy and tactics adopted by Virji Vora to control and manipulate the market was remarkable. Encompassing the entire commodity by use of his syndicate was one such stratagem. Once, Virji Vora bought the entire consignment of cloves brought by the Dutch ships from the Spice Islands to Surat, at the rate of Rs 45 per maund[v] and he resold these cloves at the rate of Rs 62 to Rs 65 per maund.[47] In view of the predominance of Virji Vora, no other merchant dared to buy the goods brought by the English or the Dutch at Surat. One of Virji Vora's commercial ventures is recorded by the English factor at Calicut. *"Virji Vora yearly sends down his people to Callicut with cotten and opium by which hee doth not[gain?] less than double his money to those people hee buyeth his pepper off[and] afterwards disposeth of his pepper to us double what it cost him; for I finde pepper to be worth here but 15. 5 and 16 fanams*[vi] *the maund, which is not half the rate he usually valleweth it to our people in Suratt."*[48]

To engross commodities like copper and quicksilver was the usual practice of Virji Vora so that he could dictate the price to the buyers.[49] He also had secretive dealings with

---

v Maund is the anglicized name of mann, the unit of weight current during the Mughal time, nearly 37 kgs.

vi Fanam was coin issued by Travancore state and was current in most of South India.

the English factors by which prices were raised.[50] At one place, his mercantile dominance is described as follows:

> *"Here in Surratt all merchants, as well town dwellers as those that come from abroad, are so overawed by the overgrown greatnesse of Verge Vora that, if it be a commodity which he is accustomed or doth intend to buy, no man dares look upon it nor the broker (even our owne, which have sole dependence upon our business) dare not accompanie such a merchant into our house."*[51]

Vora, it must be emphasized here, was not a broker for the English in the accepted sense of the term, as Mohandas Parekh was for the Dutch. He was a leading merchant and banker in his own right, able to deal freely with the English, Dutch and later, the French as well as other Indian merchants, on his own terms. He acted as a banker, not merely as a sarraf. The English heavily depended on Vora to bail them out of any financial crisis. There were a few cases of disputes over the quality of coral and quicksilver between Virji Vora and the English factors, and every time, the English had to bend to his wishes.[52] In 1641, Virji Vora promised to provide Deccan pepper at Calicut to the English, but when the English factors approached his agent there, he again promised to deliver the said quantity of pepper to them at Ponnani[vii]. Upon the promised supply being at last received, the quantity was found to be less than promised and the quality bad. In spite of the loss, the English thought it prudent not to get into a dispute with him.[53] Vora also quite often obstructed the sale of English goods, or anything brought for sale by the English factors, in order to buy those goods himself at a lower price. The English factors wrote:

> *"The Potency of Virji Vora (who hath been the usual merchant, and is now become the sole monopolist of all*

---

vii Ponnani, a port town, is 35 miles south of Calicut.

European commodities) is observed to bear such a sway amongst the inferior merchants of this town that when they would often tymes buy[and give greater prices] they are still restrayned not daring to betray their intents to his knowledge and their own sufferance, in so much that the tyme and price is still in his will and at his own disposure."[54]

Virji Vohra exerted such influence over the merchants of Surat that the English came to regard him as *"the most injurious man to your trade in all the Mogulls dominions; for what ordinary banian merchant dare come to the English howse to look upon corral or any other commodity, hee by his potency and intimacy with the Governor forgeth somewhat or against the poor man utterly to mine him; so that no merchant in the towne can displease him by coming to our howse to look upon our commodity, except some or other some tyme whome hee sends purposely to bid for a commodity (that he is about) little or nothing openly to make weary of our commodities."*[55] He did not treat the Dutch any better than he did the English. In fact, both these European companies were a big source of income for him.

The East India companies, both the English and the Dutch, were chronically short of funds. Virji Vora extended credit to both. The rate of interest was usually 7 per cent per annum, but sometimes it rose to 12 per cent per annum, or perhaps even more.[56] The Dutch East India Company (VOC) mostly sold all the goods it brought to Surat from Europe or elsewhere, to a syndicate of which the most important buyer was, of course, Virji Vora. In 1646, he was asked to purchase the goods not only for the Indian markets, but also for Persia.[57] He and his partners would usually purchase entire cargoes of VOC ships carrying spice from the Spice Islands and copper, thus establishing a monopoly in a great part of north India in these commodities. Vora was in a position to lay stocks to minimize his risk.[58] He had also been the most important creditor of the Dutch company (VOC) in Mughal India.[59]

And yet, the most profitable business for Virji Vora was the credit or the hundi system, which may be viewed as a form of the modern-day hawala. Hundi was the indigenous bill of exchange for making cashless payments in Mughal India. This document was essentially a binding, written-promise to pay a named person or its presenter a certain sum of money at some future but proximate date, usually in another town. The standing of the sarrafs engaged in the hundi business ranged from relatively small dealers to very large houses with agents or correspondents all over. On the whole, the system worked remarkably efficiently, and large sums of money got transferred. But as far as the party remitting the funds was concerned, the arrangement did involve a certain amount of risk arising from the possibility of the sarraf going bankrupt before the hundi had been encashed. The extensive interlinking of financial enterprises across the houses of sarrafs, made even a chain of bankruptcies a distinct possibility. It is true that such bankruptcies did not happen frequently or on any scale, but the possibility was always there. Indeed, there is evidence available of such chain bankruptcies happening twice in Patna within a period of sixteen years. Six leading houses of sarrafs are known to have collapsed in the city in 1673. Another group bankruptcy of five houses was reported in 1689.[60] In the 17th century, the biggest house dealing in hundis in whole of India was that of Virji Vora, with its headquarters at Surat. By the first half of the 18th century, he was replaced by another sarraf establishment, that of the Jagat Seth family, operating from its headquarters in Murshidabad in Bengal. Among its other extensive activities, this house handled the remittance of the central revenues from Bengal to Delhi, amounting to over 1 crore (10 million) rupees per annum. The heads of both these houses in their respective eras have been recorded as the richest persons in the world.

Both the English and the Dutch company always remitted money through Virji Vora from Surat to Agra, Ahmedabad and other major trade centres in north India where the factors went to buy goods for trade. For them, it was easier and safer than carrying the money physically. Virji had agents in all major trade centres.[61] The letters of exchange between Surat and Ahmedabad were dominated by a limited number of sarrafs. They included Kasi Das, the gumashta or agent of Virji Vora, who handled 36 per cent of the total amount of such exchange; Nathu Kishandas with 22 per cent; and Rupji Raghu, the gumashta of Venmali Das, with 19 per cent had the next share in this important banking business. About three-quarters of the amounts remitted through the hundis went through these three firms.[62] The English were perpetually short of money, which they borrowed locally to buy goods, especially textile, for England. In 1656, the English at Surat were in the debt of Virji Vohra to the amount of seven tonnes of gold (£70,000) and their credit was suffering.[63] One English factor, as early as 1644, confessed, *"I confess him to be a man that hath often supply our wants in Suratt with moneys, for his own ends. Not with standing, I hould him to have bynn the most injurious man. And I concluded that, so long as Virji Vora is so much our credittor, little or no profit[is] to be made upon any goods we can bring to Surratt."*[64]

Apart from credit and hundi, another rich source of revenue for Virji Vohra was the difference in exchange rate at various places, caused by different currency systems. In 1630, the English borrowed Rs 50,000 from Virji Vohra to finance their purchase in Agra. Besides the usual interest rate, Virji Vohra exacted 3 per cent discount or difference in exchange. From Surat, a bill of exchange of Rs 15,000 was drawn upon Virji Vora's agent at Agra. On payment, however, it cost practically 7 per cent more on the account of deduction from the chalani or current rupee.[65] In 1633, the company purchased gold from Virji Vora. He gave the company an option to pay either in mahmudis or rupees, but made it clear that if the payments were made in rupees, he would discount 13 mahmudis per 100 rupees, "according to difference at present between the rupees and mahmudi".[66] In 1632, the English company owed 12,000 rupees to Virji Vora and they were forced to land 26 chests of money to repay their debts to him.[67] In 1642, Virji Vora unexpectedly lent Rs 100,000 to the English factors at Ahmedabad, when they were in dire need of money. Again, in 1650, the English factors report that *"the company's credit has not suffered in the least, and Virji Vora, their chief creditor, has offered in lend Rs 100,000 whenever required"*. In 1650, the company again borrowed 10,000 old pagodas[viii] at Golconda from Virji Vora, who demanded that the rate of exchange would not be less than Rs 470 per 100 old pagodas. The English factors wanted to transfer the credit to Surat at the rate of Rs 455 per old pagodas, but Virji Vohra did not agree to the English proposal.

In 1669, the English company again borrowed from Virji Vora and his family along with other sarrafs in Surat, an amount of Rs 400,000. The English factors seem to have been quite keen to return Virji Vora's money, the moment money was available to them. The English factors insisted that Virji Vora was the first to be considered for repayment. Thus, the repayment of Rs 60,000 was made to him "when he was in great want thereof, hath add much to your reputation".[68] Owing to his vast financial resources and mercantile operations, Virji Vora exerted influence on European companies in non-business activities as well. Some unpleasant experiences with him led the English

viii Pagodas were gold or half-gold coins minted by various rulers in Southern India.

factors to describe him as a "costly creditor". But they could not do anything about it, for they realized that *"none but Virji Vohra hath money to lend or will lend"*.[69] In 1665, the English factors reported that *"our old customer, Virji Vora that left your or rather we him, having found another way to supply your occasions more reasonable"*.[70] But all these aspirations seem to be diluted as again, the English had to borrow 4 lakhs of rupees from him.[71] Thévenot wrote of Virji Vora as a friend supposed to be worth at least eight million. The unit in terms of which is not specified, but the English factory records clearly mention his net worth as 80 lakhs of rupees.[72]

Outside of India, Vora's trading interests extended to Mocha and Gombroon in the Persian Gulf-Red Sea area, and to Malaya and Sumatra in South East Asia. Often, the English had to accommodate him in transporting his goods at the cost of displacing a part of the regular English cargo, and at times, they even had to carry his goods free of freight charges. Vora also used English agencies in these parts for transmission of money between Surat and the two distant trading zones.

He also lent money to individual Englishmen to finance their own private trade, a practice so often denounced by London, as it affected the Company's corporate profits a great deal. Such loans went a long way in establishing close personal relations between prominent English factors and Vora and his agents. An event in 1652 sheds interesting light both on relations between Vora and the English, and the role of the Mahajan organization in the economic life of the city. There arose a dispute between Vora and the Surat factory concerning certain outstanding accounts which Vora had failed to clear. Vora had insisted that the factory make some allowances and rebates, to which the Surat factory objected. The dispute continued through all of 1652 and spilled over into the next two years. At one stage, the English suggested that the dispute be referred for arbitration to the corporate authority of Surat merchants. This was obviously the Surat Mahajan guild, which on this showing, was capable of dealing effectively as an arbitrator between one of its most influential members and foreign traders. Vora did his best in forcing economic sanctions against the English by trying to deter Surat merchants from buying copper brought in by the English ships. He also hindered the sale of their coral. The English were powerless against him for, as far back as 1634, they had learned that the *"potency of Virji Vora (who hath been the usual merchant and now become the sole monopolist of all European commodities) is observed to bear such sway amoungst the inferior merchants of this town that when they would often-times buy (and give greater prices) they are still restrained, not daring to betray their interests to his knowledge and their own sufferance, in so much that the time and price is still in his will and at his own disposal"*. In 1636, the Surat factory wrote to London: *"...in Surat, all merchants, as well town dwellers as those that come from abroad, are so overawed by the over-grown greatness of Virji Vora that if it be a commodity which is accustomed or does intend to buy, no man dares look upon it, for the broker (even our own, which have sole dependance upon your business) dare not accompany such merchant into our house"*. In spite of all such frustrations, the English endeavoured to maintain amicable relations with him practically until his death. In the event the English captured an Indian ship which had Vora's cargo on it, the English quietly restored his goods. They gave their own safe-conduct passes to ships sailing out of Surat harbour only when such action was recommended by Vora. In 1660, London sent Vora a present in appreciation of his aid to its factors in India.

The greatest crisis of Vora's career, however, came in early January 1664, when the Marathas attacked Surat. His home, along with those of other rich merchants, was plundered on 7 January, and Shivaji's men carried away an enormous booty comprising gold, pearls, diamonds, rubies, emeralds and a large amount of cash. Estimates of Vora's loss during this raid vary. Undoubtedly, he lost a large part of his accumulated treasure. But Vora was by no means completely ruined, for an English letter of 27 November 1664, some ten months after the raid, says that *"Haji Zahid Beg and Virji Vora, the two greatest merchants of this town, hold up their heads still and are for great bargains; so that is seems Shivaji hath not carried away all, but left them a competency to carry on their trade"*. It is not difficult to understand this as Vora's liquid assets were not concentrated in Surat alone. They were distributed at a number of centres such as Broach, Baroda, Ahmedabad, Burhanpur and Agra. But Vora's career was past its prime after 1664, when he was close to 70 years of age. His waning strength is reflected in an English report of 12 March 1665: *"Your old customer, Virji Vora, hath now left you, or rather we him, having found another way to supply your occasions more reasonable, though we believe he would now abate you something to have your custom again, for he loses not only the loan of his money, but the carrying away of many a good parcel of goods out of your warehouse, when he found he had got an advantage of you"*. But Vora was not finished yet. In 1669, the English still owed him substantial debts. In 1670, he had enough influence to try to stop the lading of French ships because of their outstanding debts to him. Possibly, the last reference to him is from 1670, when Khawaja Minaz took delivery of some broadcloth on his behalf, and Nanchand, his grandson, bought some tin and copper from the English.

The above data collected about Virji Vora brings out some crucial features of the business activities of the time. First, it emerges that he was both a banker or a sarraf, and a merchant. He invested in credit as well as purchase of merchandise, solely guided by profit. He drew an advantage by exerting pressure on his debtors to sell to him at discount.

He used extension of credit to invest funds obtained by sale of commodities at particular places. Being a banker, he had the further advantage of transferring funds by bills or hundis more easily than ordinary merchants. For purposes of both trade and finance, he had factors or gumashtas at various places, like Ahmedabad, Agra, Golconda, the Malabar ports, and overseas in the Red Sea and the Persian Gulf region. It also transpires that the English East India Company factory at Surat could not have survived without his credit, and consequently, without the influence he wielded with Mughal authorities, both at Surat and in Agra.

Shantidas of Ahmedabad

Shantidas flourished during the reigns of Jahangir, Shah Jahan and Aurangzeb. Being a great financier and a court jeweller, he enjoyed this position at the courts of successive Mughal emperors. As for the reputation of Shantidas as a Jauhari or Zaveri, a series of firmans were issued by successive Mughal emperors. A firman issued by Jahangir in 1622, had 'Jawahari', 'Javeri' or 'Zaveri' added to his name, signifying his association with the jewel business. Similarly, in 1627, the English factor referred to him as the deceased king's (Jahangir's) jeweller. Shantidas was given royal protection by Jahangir, and being a court jeweller, Shantidas supplied gifts and rarities to the Mughal court from time-to-time.[73] On the occasion of the accession of Shah Jahan to the throne, Shantidas presented Arabian horses to the emperor by the way of Peshkash.[ix] Shah Jahan approved of a roan horse[x] amongst them. It was named Nazar-i-Mubarak. Shantidas was rewarded with a gift of an

ix It was a Mughal custom to give gifts called Peshkash to the emperor on important occasions such as coronation or after a victory over an enemy. These gifts were considered as the symbols of respect and honour in diplomatic relations.

x Horse having a mixture of coloured and white hairs on the body.

elephant from the court and a sum of one lakh of rupees as a present. Later, two horses – one Arabian horse with a saddle of gold enamel, and another Iraqi horse with a saddle of simple gold from the royal stable – were sent to him.[74]

He is regarded as the first nagarseth of the city of Ahmedabad. The financial strength of the Gujarat merchant class and the need for its alliance with the State was well perceived by the Mughal rulers. In one of his firmans, Shah Jahan mentioned Shantidas as the 'beopari' or merchant, and a 'loyal Jawahari' or jeweller, of the court. Regarding the immovable assets of Shantidas in the city of Ahmedabad, the firman mentioned his havelis or mansions along with the shops and gardens owned by him. The firman ordered the administrators of the province that none should occupy the assets of Shantidas and instructed that there should be no interference in realizing the rents from the shops. It also warned against any molestation by any official of his property. In yet another firman, Shah Jahan reaffirmed and directed that the entire property possessed by Shantidas should pass on to his heirs without interference, in the case of his death.[75]

These documents clearly indicate the strong position enjoyed by Shantidas at the Mughal court. They also show how the Mughal emperors protected the personal and business interests of Shantidas. Dara Shikoh too issued a firman to the same effect.[76] Being a court jeweller, Shantidas was supposed to send jewels from time to time to the royal court. This is evident from another firman of Shah Jahan, which was issued on 17 September 1642. In this document, Muiz-ul-Mulk at Ahmedabad was asked to secure jewels from Shantidas and other jewellers for the approaching anniversary celebrations of the royal accession, and the same were to be forwarded to the court. As a mark of patronage, the emperor conferred a robe of honour upon Shantidas in 1658.[77] Shantidas maintained smooth relations with the Mughal court through regular supplies of expensive gifts and jewels. Shantidas also traded with the European companies as well as Persian and Arab traders, in commodities such as cloves. In the light of the Mughal firmans, it appears that his main business activities were related to the jewel profession, but there are references to indicate that he acted as a broker as well as a banker. The English factors referred to him as the 'Governor's broker'.[78]

The brokers were employed by all the European merchants for commercial transactions at Ahmedabad during the 17th century. Being a trusted person, Shantidas worked as broker for the provincial governors. The English factors referred to him as a big sarraf in 1640.[79] It seems that Shantidas also invested in English trade and commerce. Once, Shantidas lent Rs 10,000 to the factors of the English East India Company at a very low interest rate of one per cent per month.[80] In September 1635, Shantidas and some other merchants from Surat and Ahmedabad lost their goods to English pirates. He used his influence and political connections to recover his loss from the English.[81] The English were perturbed when the dispute arose for the restitution of the loss, as he was a man of considerable influence at the Mughal Court, whose demand could not be swept under the carpet.[82]

Shantidas, being one of the richest Jain business magnates of his time, served his community and his faith to the best of his ability. In 1621, he built a magnificent Jain temple known as the Chintamani temple in the Bibipura locality in Ahmedabad.[83] The grandeur and imposing structure of this temple has been praised by contemporary European travellers.[84] In 1645, Prince Aurangzeb, during his tenure as the Subahdar of Gujarat, converted this temple into a mosque.[85] According to the French traveller, Jean de Thévenot, Aurangzeb caused a cow to be killed in the temple premises, destroyed the noses of all idols in the temple, and then converted the place into a mosque called Quwwat-ul-islam or the 'Might of Islam'.[86] Shantidas complained to Aurangzeb's father Shah Jahan. In 1648, the emperor issued a firman declaring that the building should be handed back to Shantidas, and a wall be raised between the mihrabs or the niches in the mosque walls, and the rest of the original temple building. It also declared that the Muslim fakirs housed in the mosque premises should be removed, and the materials carried away from the temple should be restored.[87] The firman instructed Ghairat Khan, the naib-subahdar of Gujarat, and other officials of the province, to restore the Chintamani temple. He also ordered them to make complete restitution of the damage.[88]

Thévenot, who arrived at Surat on 10 January 1666, travelled to Ahmedabad. He gives an interesting information about the temple and says:

> *"Ahmedabad being inhabited by a large number of heathens, there are pagods or idol-temples in it. That which was called the pagods of Shantidas was the chief, before Aurangzeb converted into a mosque. When he performed this ceremony, he caused a cow to be killed in the place, knowing very well that, often such an action, the gentiles, according to their law, could worship no more therein. The inside roof of the mosque is pretty enough, and the walls are full of the figures of the men and beasts; but Aurangzeb who hath always made a show of an effected devotion, which all length raised him to the throne, caused the noses of all these figures, which added a great deal of magnificence to that mosque, to be beat of."*[89]

Another French traveller and jeweller, Tavernier, who visited Ahmedabad several times in the17th century, also talks about the conversion of this temple into a mosque by Prince Aurangzeb.

During the war of succession between Aurangzeb and his brothers for the Mughal throne, Shantidas supported Murad Baksh, the youngest son of Shah Jahan and Mumtaz Mahal and gave him financial support to raise his army. In spite of all apprehensions, Aurangzeb, upon becoming Emperor, showed great courtesy to Shantidas and issued a firman on 10 August 1658, directing Rehmat Khan, the diwan, for the repayment of the loan of 5 lakhs and 50 thousand rupees that Murad Baksh had borrowed from Shantidas at Ahmedabad during the war of succession! Additionally, the emperor granted Shantidas a sum of one lakh rupees from the royal treasury. In this connection, a firman was also issued to Shah Nawaz Khan, the subahdar, that a sum of rupees one lakh should be given to Shantidas without delay and hesitation.[90] There is also a firman issued on the same date as the above two, in which Aurangzeb directed the officials of Gujarat to give better treatment to Shantidas as he was "an old servant of the court", and also to assist him in his financial dealings. The firman further asked the mahajans and inhabitants of Ahmedabad to pursue their business as usual, without any fear.[91] The mere fact that the message of goodwill of the emperor was conveyed through the jeweller-merchant, further testifies his high commercial and social position in the city of Ahmedabad.

Bhimji Parekh and Abdul Ghafur were the other big merchants of Surat having considerable influence at Mughal court. They also did trade with both the English and the Dutch Companies.

The advent of the European companies in India in the early part of the 17th century brought the inland production centres and commerce to become involved with the country's overseas trade. The necessity of establishing contacts with such centres of production was felt both by the indigenous and foreign merchants, which in turn, helped the emergence of a well-organised group of merchants as brokers. This group enabled the foreign merchants to free themselves from the problems of procurement of commodities. Since both the English and the Dutch were quite new to this land, they faced language problem while dealing with the local producers for commodities. They found the Indian market system to be different from that in Europe. They were really hampered by the complexities of the monetary system and the varying weights and measures. The lack of knowledge of the market operations led them to seek the support of the indigenous merchants who could procure goods for them. These factors were quite confused about the different ranges of weights and measurements as well as the different currency system prevalent in the different parts of the country. The production centres of different commodities were widely scattered all over India. This necessitated engaging indigenous merchants who would be familiar with the local centres of production, to arrange for the supply of the required items and act as link between the producer and the company. The production capacity of a single centre was very low. So, to procure the goods by moving far and wide, the help of the local merchants was quite indispensable as links for procurement. The primary job of these local merchants appointed by the Company was to procure cloth and other goods from the widespread weaver's settlements at cheap rates for the company, and to dispose of the company's goods at favourable prices. In this role, they acted as a link between the primary producers and the company, as well as between the company and the consumer. They received commission for the services rendered to the company. These local merchants supervised weavers in the production process to maintain standardization of the produce according to the musters and ensured that they worked to the perfection of the pattern. They minimized the company's risks. The supervisory function was important to control quality, to ensure that the goods were free from any adulteration and to check that the measurements were correct and according to the needs of the European markets. If there were any defects in the supplies or a deviation from the sample agreed upon, a discount had to be made on the price agreed upon. The merchants received some remuneration for their supervisory role as well, from the company.

The problem of transporting goods from upcountry to the factory settlements was another major task for the English merchants. The transport system during those days mostly depended on bullock-carts, or were on the backs of camels or oxen. Further, the roads were mere tracks and robbery was a serious threat. The exaction of duties on the way by disorderly local powers, in spite of various imperial firmans, proved a constant source of dispute. To avert all these problems and to bring down consignments to the ports in stipulated quality and quantity, the services of the indigenous merchants was indispensable. It was for these reasons that the English relied heavily on people like Virji Vora for the smooth conduct of their business.

However, there are recorded instances of brokers playing foul in the supplies. For example, finding evidences of fraud on the part of one Deodass, the English company's broker at Broach, the English seized and imprisoned him, until Virji Vora stood as his surety and promised good conduct in future. Though the broker had agreed to pay a fine of 12,000 mahmudis, he was dismissed from the company's service as a salutary warning to the other brokers of the company.[92]

In the initial stages, these brokers also acted as interpreters for the European merchants in procuring supply from the local producers. As the activities of the companies increased, the indigenous merchants directly involved themselves in supplying their needs. Jadu Das is the first mentioned Indian merchant to supply the goods required by the English at Surat, getting commodities for them for more than three decades. In the same way, Tulsidas Parekh was another merchant who looked after the English interests in Agra. He dealt in coral and textiles and lent large amounts of money to the English.[93] Apart from stray incidents, there are no records of Indian merchants being treated unfairly by the English factors. Nor is there any instance of the English failing to pay interest which was agreed upon. This adherence of the English factors to the basic mercantile values, made them a preferred partner for Indian merchants, as compared to other European companies.

Swarms of baniyas frequented the European factories, working as brokers and stewards, responsible for the smooth running of the factory, supervising the weighers, packers, skinners, mazurs or porters, peons and messengers. Each European factory maintained on its staff a number of its own brokers, who performed a variety of essential tasks. They looked after the loading and unloading of ships, the transport of goods from Swally to Surat and back, cleared the goods through the customs and arranged for pack animals for caravans into the interior of the country. They were so indispensable that in one instance in 1647, an English voyage from Mocha to Tuticorin had to be cancelled because of the illness of the broker. The English, from time to time, found the brokers convenient for helping circumvent governmental restrictions. In 1619, when the Governor of Baroda put a general ban on the English buying goods there for their Red Sea cargo, they attempted to buy through their brokers. In 1632, they arranged for a caphila or caravan to take their goods to the house of Surji Naik at Variao near Surat, to avoid paying Mughal customs-dues on 20,000 rials intended for Ahmedabad and Agra.

The brokers, on their part, also used the European traders for their own designs. They used the advances in money given to them by the English for their own investments, circulated defective coinage, lent money to Englishmen for private trade, and controlled the weavers.

The broker, indeed, was the local and invaluable expert. His knowledge of the markets was intimate and whenever the costs were to be determined by the quality of goods involved, especially in such commodities as textiles and indigo, his expertise was indispensable. He had contacts with the transportation industry, and virtually controlled the weavers and retailers of victuals. He had his own contacts with the markets in the hinterland.

The brokers became so powerful that in 1650, they hindered Merry's succession to the Surat Presidency, and in 1662, Oxenden feared that he might be poisoned by some of the brokers disciplined by him. The number of brokers employed by the English, Dutch, French and the Portuguese in Surat, Agra, Ahmedabad, Burhanpur, Broach, Baroda, Bulsar, Gandevi, Navsari, Bombay and Rajapur runs to some 150 known names.

The earliest known broker, Jadu, began his association working for Captain William Hawkins in 1608. In July 1609, his brother too was employed by Hawkins on a salary of 8 mahmudis a month. In October 1614, Jadu is reported to be in prison for selling a fake ring for 2,500 rupees. He remained in prison for 20 days. He had his own sarrafs and had his relatives such as Gurudas working for the English. During 1616 and 1617, he worked for Sir Thomas Roe as a broker and linguist. During the subsequent years, until 1632, he travelled to Agra, Burhanpur and Ahmedabad for the English factory. He was particularly useful for work at the imperial court at Agra and seems to have worked for the English for nearly three decades.

Another better-known early broker was Tapidas Parekh. He is first referred to in 1609,and the last available reference to him comes in 1660, thus covering a period of more than half a century He helped the English find accommodation in Baroda and performed a variety of chores for their establishments. In 1634, he was paid an annual allowance of 500 mahmudis, though he continued to deal on his own account in several commodities such as coral and silver, gave his own bills of exchange for Agra, dealt with the Dutch, stood sureties for Englishmen when they were in trouble, lent large amounts of money to them (upto Rs 50,000), hired boats like the Prosperous for 5,000 mahmudis for transporting his goods to Basra and back, and travelled to Goa and other parts on the Company's business. Another Parekh was Tulsidas, probably the brother of Tapidas, who served the English roughly from 1636 to 1667. His sons, Bhimiji Parekh and Kalyan Parekh continued in the Company's service till the end of the century. The Parekh family, thus, was associated with the English factory at Surat throughout the 17th century. Their successes and difficulties are generally characteristic of the mercantile broker community of this time. Tulsidas dealt in coral and textiles and lent large amounts of money. He was paid an annual salary (more correctly, what may be called a retainer fee) of £25, which was about what some of the junior servants of the Company were then paid. He served as a cashier for the Company and was always spoken of as being honest and industrious. In 1652, he wrote a letter in English, but signed in Gujarati, complaining of the delay in settling debts due to him in his claims against the estate of President Bretton. In a communication dated 6 August 1662, the English factory at Surat wrote about Tulsidas, *"a faithful and industrious servant of the Honourable Company... his deplorable condition, that having lived many years in great repute, abounding with riches, much respected for his faithful dealing, he is reduced now (by reason of the great debts owing unto him by some of our nation) to so great poverty he depends on the small profit he makes in the service of the Company which is not sufficient for the subsistence of his family"*. As a gesture, his annuity of 500 mahmudis was then proposed to be revived. In 1664, Tulsidas sought the help of the Surat English factory in recovering his claims against Virji Vora, so that he may discharge his debts to the Company. The problem of Tulsidas' debts was pending until 1668-69.

In 1662, Tulsidas' son Bhimji Parekh began working as a broker for the English. During 1668-71, Bhimji tried to get an English printer to print some ancient Brahmani writings. One was procured in 1674, but the experiment proved less than satisfactory, as the English printer refused to teach the art to Indians. In July 1683, Bhimji was given a medal and a chain of gold worth £150 for his services to the Company. In 1669, a nephew of Tulsidas Parekh was tricked into becoming a Muslim by the local Mughal authorities. This was a great shocking news to all the traders in Surat. In the same year, some charges were made against Bhimji by the Mughal authorities, but the English factory defended his ability and integrity vigorously. Earlier in 1668, Bhimji wanted to move to Bombay with his family because of religious persecution in Surat. In September 1669, such persecution led to a large number of Hindu merchants of Surat, led by Bhimji, to leave Surat. The boycott lasted till 20 December 1669, when the baniyas returned to Surat on being assured by Aurangzeb personally regarding the safety of their religion. This incident forcefully shows the organizational capabilities of the baniyas and the leading role played by Bhimji in their affairs. Bhimji Parekh died in 1686.

Of a different kind were two brokers who worked in tandem. They were Somji Chitta and Chota Thakur. The former seems to have worked for the English for close to half a century. In 1633, he was held responsible for the theft of some calico by the wrappers, but was later released. Somji was a specialist in the trade in baftas and helped Andrews, a President at the Surat factory, in his private deals in 1661. In

December 1662, Somji was dismissed on the allegation that he had tried to set the English warehouses on fire. Somji used to employ a large number of weavers for the manufacture of cloth to be exported on his own account and used to receive advances in money from the Company, which he then gave out to the weavers *"at 12, 14, 15 and 16 mahmudis per cent, rupees exchange"*, by which he made a profit for himself. He paid the weavers 5 mahmudis 3 paisa in kind, whereas he received 6 1/4 per cent of textile from the Company as their payment. He was also alleged to have committed fraud in buying cotton yarn. The English report states: *"It is made or spun in the out villages by the poorest sort of people; from whence it is gleaned up by persons that trade in it with whom two of your brokers' relations are joined that are partners. These drive the same trade of giving out old worm-eaten decayed corn in the several neighbouring villages; which they take out in yarn, and in parcels bring it to your warehouses to sell, where these two forenamed kinsmen of Somji Chittas set as buyers in your behalf, thereby making what prizes pleases them for their own goods..."*

Somji Chitta died in 1668, owing the Company a large debt. But his influence with Virji Vora was such that the latter intervened in a civil matter on behalf of Chitta's and Chota's sons.

The list of English complaints against Chota Thakur is equally long. In October 1623, he was imprisoned by the Mughal authorities, but released on English intercession. In November 1623, he left the English and hid himself and in February 1632, he left Cambay where he was posted, to go to Surat where his brother Gurudas was on his deathbed. His action caused the English factory in Cambay some embarrassment. Gurudas was also a broker for the English, and in 1631, helped Richard Wylde, then President, make a small fortune through a questionable deal in indigo. Chota, like Somji, was an expert in baftas and was also a linguist like him. Time and again, he was suspected of questionable deals, though by 1647, he had become the Company's chief broker at Surat. An English communication of 25 January 1650, complained that *"there is a tribe of family of them now in your service, all brought in by their patron, Chout Tocker (Chota Thakur), our chief house broker and linguist here in Surat, who (since Mr Methwold's leaving India) has so wrought with your former Presidents that his kindred are become your chief brokers not only at Agra (where an arch villain has been long held in by Virji Vora) but in Ahmedabad, Sind etc. and his creatures in almost all other employments of your abroad and at home. Neither is there a possibility on the sudden to dismiss them, without drawing on you some present inconvenience..."* In 1660, Chota Thakur was robbed when he was in the region around Patna, and the English claimed the same privilege for him in seeking redress from the government as was claimed for Englishmen. He was dismissed by 1662. He then tried to enlist Virji Vora's help in forging a boycott of the English factory in reprisal. Until his death, sometime before 1668, Chota Thakur was involved in a dispute about English debts to him for which an interest of Rs 3,28,000 was claimed. He had obviously enriched himself through his numerous transactions. Some of the activities of Somji Chitta and Chota Thakur are indicative of the patterns of operation adopted by many brokers. They had established themselves firmly in the mechanics of European trade, and had especially made themselves indispensable not only for the Company's corporate trade, but more so in the private trade pursued by English factors in spite of the constant complaints from London.

Another leading broker for the English from the 1640s to the 1670s was Benidas. He was sent to several places in the south on errands, which he alone could successfully accomplish. From 1645 to 1660, he often travelled to Raibag, Rajapur, Tuticorin, Goa, Calicut, Cannanore, Bijapur, and through the Malabar. He was also sent to negotiate matters pertaining to trade with the kings of Bijapur, and to Shivaji. In November 1662, for instance, he was asked to send a Brahmin to Shivaji to deal with Shivaji's Brahmins, in order to prevail upon the Maratha leader for the release of the English factors at Raigarh. In 1652, he replaced Tulsidas Parekh when he agreed to work for a lower salary. The Company sent him a piece of scarlet cloth as a present in appreciation of his services. He was a man of considerable means, as in 1652, he agreed to furnish the Surat factory an amount up to Rs 200,000 at 1 per cent per month. He owned a ship called the Diamond, and specially arranged for the Company's lading for Persia. He later seems to have also acquired another ship, the Seaflower, which was used for coastal trade to south-western ports such as Karwar. His fortunes were therefore built not only on his connection with the English, but also on his own mercantile and banking activities.

Another notable merchant of Surat was Mohandas Parekh, usually described as the broker to the Dutch. The Dutch often sold selected goods from the cargoes brought by them from Indonesia – spices and tin. On one occasion, in January 1654, he tried to pass off Dutch goods as those of Muslim merchants in order to circumvent the English blockade. Shivaji, during the course of his raid on Surat, spared his house since Parekh was well known for his charities to Hindus. Though called a broker, Parekh was obviously a man of great wealth and may have carried on his own business outside of his work for the Dutch.

In the wake of the establishment of the English Company factory at Surat, and the increasing demand for textiles and other commodities, the English signed contracts with the merchants of great repute to avoid any risk. They preferred to deal with one or two selected individuals for transacting the business of the Company. As outsiders, it was a problem for them to deal with too many small-scale merchants.

They relied on the few merchants who had substantial means for the supply of commodities, and who enjoyed a good reputation in the market. Small-scale merchants and pedlars thus began working under merchants of greater importance, the brokers or middlemen. With the expansion of trade and commerce, the rich and influential persons among the local merchants emerged as the chief merchants of a region or town, and supplied goods to the Company. They were assisted by a number of smaller merchants and middlemen or brokers.

Due to the increased demand for supplies, the chief merchant employed persons other than his kinsmen as brokers or assistants and sub-brokers to meet the shortage of manpower. After sometime, the office of the chief merchant was institutionalized. He played a major role in the commercial activities, as a link between the middlemen and the Company. The increased importance of trade, and the volume of export, made him assume the responsibility of fulfilling the contracts. If he failed, his property was seized. For this work, he received ten to fifteen per cent of the total transaction as commission – both on the sale and the purchase of commodities.[94]

This indigenous merchant class, apart from the usual broker-associated activities, performed a wide variety of other functions as well, on behalf of the Company. In the first instance, the English Company concluded contract or agreement with the chief merchant or broker to supply the required items. These agreements involved a number of things. The price of a commodity was fixed by the two signatories depending on its quality. The merchant was responsible to maintain the quality and quantity of the goods according to the terms of the contract. In some cases, if a merchant failed to supply the stipulated quality as per the agreement, it resulted in price reduction of the commodities. During natural calamities, the English agents showed sympathy at times, but generally, they were strict in demanding the supply as per the contract. After the conclusion of the agreement, the merchant received an advance in the form of bullion or coined money, as well as European goods. Generally, a merchant received fifty per cent of the agreed amount as an advance from the Company. The merchant was ultimately responsible for this amount until he delivered the manufactured goods.

This chief merchant gave sub-contracts to the lesser merchants on terms favourable to him. This agreement between the chief merchant and the Company was renewed annually. In this contract, the chief merchant was made responsible for the fulfilment of the obligations assumed by ordinary members. Further, the contracts specified the obligations of the merchant, such as the date by which the stipulated goods were to be delivered, and the indemnity if they failed in their supplies. At the time of the delivery of goods, experienced officials were appointed by the Company, and they sorted pieces according to the samples agreed earlier. In case of deviation from the muster, it resulted in either rejection of the piece or the reduction of its price. Only after the fulfilment of contract could the merchant claim the balance agreed amount.

At the time of the Company's financial crisis, English factors borrowed money freely from Indian merchants and bankers to invest, in return cargo for England. As mentioned earlier, throughout the 17th century, big merchants like Virji Vora at Surat, Shantidas at Ahmedabad, Seshadra and Timmanna on the Coromandel coast, etc., were the chief sources of commercial credit to the English Company in India. The Company was heavily indebted in India, and as per their own records, by 1635, it owed £100,000 to several rich Indian bankers. The rate of interest varied from four to sixteen per cent.[95] But sometimes, indigenous bankers would lend money free of interest. There are references to the fact that sometimes they advanced money to the weavers through their subordinates on behalf of the Company for future supplies.[96] This money was borrowed as commercial credit through the use of hundis or bills of exchange. This meant a promissory note stating the repayment of money within a specified period of time. This was the method in vogue during that period. In many ways, this system was helpful for the Company to transact commercial operations without any hindrance. It also provided an opportunity to local merchants for investing their money in productive ways. They thus operated through a group of their own agents posted in market centres all over India. This money market was a source of income for the sarrafs and the rich bankers.

The practice of changing mahmudis into rupees and vice versa, another lucrative source of income for the sarrafs, was called vatav or exchange. It brought good profit to the money-lenders in the form of dasturi or commission for their transaction. The practice of direct moneylending to the European companies was mainly done by the sarrafs or money-lenders who had enormous capital at their disposal. It was one of the means for capital accumulation through interest among the indigenous merchants. In addition to direct borrowings, the indigenous merchants helped the English factors to raise short-term commercial loans through bills of exchange. The professional moneychangers took a certain amount of gold and silver from the English merchants, and in return, supplied hard currency or coined money for easy transactions. For this work, they received commissions. Sometimes, with the help and influence of these local merchants, the English factors got their imported bullion minted into coins at the local mints, because in the early stages, the English were not given minting rights.[97]

Other than commercial activities, the local merchants performed a number of other functions on behalf of the companies. Through their access to the Mughal emperor, the kings in south India, and the nobles or governors in other regions, they were able to defuse any tension that came up in the relations between the English and the local powers, under the pretext of transit duties and customs-duties. The best remedy used to clear any misunderstanding, was to give a peshkash or gift to the person concerned and get his acquaintance. For this, the indigenous merchants used imported European curiosities as gifts. European curiosities like toys, comb-cases, spectacles, pictures, a pair of gloves, rich-looking glasses, burning glasses or anything of rarity, were sent from England to be presented to the king or nobles and merchants as gifts.[98] For example, Benidas, the English broker at Agra, represented their case and obtained the release of the goods whenever English goods were seized or men were detained by Mughal authorities. He, through his influence, met the emperor's mother with presents, usually English curiosities, and the latter asked the ruler to free the goods and men.[99]

In addition to their business activities with the English Company, the indigenous merchants of Surat had their own traditional commercial activities with foreign countries and they also owned ships. They had age-old commercial contacts with the Persian Gulf and South East Asian ports. For example, Virji Vora had commercial operations with regions up to the Persian Gulf in the West, and the Spice Islands in the East. The agents who worked under him travelled far and wide for procuring and disposing off goods. Similarly, Shantidas too maintained his position in the commercial world of Gujarat. The smaller merchants travelled to production centres inland in search of textiles or any other commodity. The bigger merchants were completely dependent on their own brokers to procure supplies to be handed over to the European companies according to the terms of the contract. For their service to the chief merchant, these intermediary brokers received commission of up to two per cent. Below them were a number of subordinate brokers who assisted the head brokers. According to the nature of the supplies, they received commissions ranging from one to one-and-a-half per cent. Sometimes, the brokers also acted as dubash or linguists to the English merchants, and received a salary of four shillings and six pence per month.

Upon the establishment of European factories, there was a major transformation among the smaller merchants. Many indigenous merchants realized that it was more advantageous, profitable, and less risky to work on behalf of the companies, instead of making voyages on their own. So the widely scattered weaving villages in India gave an opportunity to these indigenous merchants to act as links between the producers and the European companies. Further, the Indian merchants' relationship with the political authorities as tax-farmers, helped them generate money for trading purposes and enrich themselves. They grew, and in turn, transformed the small-scale merchants as being merely dependent on them. So capital accumulation remained in the hands of a few, and small-scale merchants began to decline, as an outcome of this situation.

Relationship of Surat Merchants with the Administration

The Mughal administrative apparatus, through which the mercantile policies were run and executed, was headed by the mutasaddi, the chief official at the Surat port, who was directly appointed by the imperial court. One of the qualifications of a person to be appointed as mutasaddi, was that he should have a sound knowledge of judging the qualities of horses and jewels.[100] Lahori says that one Ali Akbar, who was a merchant from Isfahan or Persia, and came to Hindustan, stayed on at Cambay and conducted his business from there, and was later appointed mutasaddi of Surat and Cambay ports.[101] His jurisdiction included the realization of customs from port and overland; and the safety of port from the sea and land. The mutasaddi of major ports usually looked after the administration of adjoining minor ports as well. The mutasaddi of Surat usually enjoyed the additional charge of the ports of Cambay, Broach, Gandhar and Gogha. He was responsible for the purchase of horses and rarities for the emperor.[102] He was also the caretaker of imperial treasury in the town. At times, merchants were also appointed to this post. Mirza Ishaq Beg who was the mutasaddi of Surat in 1616[103] was also an influential merchant. Mirza Ali Akbar Isfahani, who was the mutasaddi of Surat and Cambay in 1646-41, was a substantial merchant whose area of operations included these two places. Another merchant, Muiz-ul-Mulk, was appointed as mutasaddi of Surat from January 1648 to November 1649. He, however, had a dispute with the Dutch and ultimately lost his job.

The official responsible for the realization of customs at the port was shahbandar or harbour master. He acted as the deputy of the mutasaddi.[104] In the European records, he is described as darogha of the custom-house. The shahbandar was generally a family member or relative of the mutasaddi, and if otherwise, then his office was often farmed out to the highest bidder. In one case, it was farmed out to Haji Muhammad Zahid Beg, the shahbandar between 1629 and 1669, who himself was an influential merchant. He was a shipping magnate whose ships plied from Surat and Cambay to both the Red Sea and the Persian Gulf.[105] The main function of this office was the assessment and collection of customs on the import and export of goods and bullion.

The port administration was beset with corruption and mal-administration. The most common practice was of enhanced valuation and assessment of merchant goods passing through the custom-house. The practice of over-valuing the goods in the custom-house was very common at Surat. Reporting this, the English factors wrote, *"Here the Governor's will is a law; so that hee setts what prices hee pleaseth on commodities, that thereby it cometh to pass that, while you think you pay but 3 1/2 per cent, you customs stands you in twice as much, for the goods are often-times rated at double the price they cost, as was that indigo I bought in Agra, which costing 61 rupees, because (he said) it was worth so much in Persia."*[106] Over-valuation was a widespread corrupt practise at all the Mughal ports as well. So to rectify this abuse, the Dutch made a representation at Shah Jahan's court. The emperor issued a firman in 1642, to fix the prices of goods for assessing the custom-dues. As per the firman, goods bought at Akbarabad[xi] were to be determined after raising the cost price by 'the twelfth' (by 20 per cent) and those purchased at Ahmedabad, 'by ten-half' (by 5 per cent). The assessment on merchandise bought at Surat, Baroda and other places in the vicinity of Surat was to be at their cost price stated in the account books (bihckik). Though the firman was issued to the Dutch, it was applicable to all merchants.

Apart from over-valuation, the merchants also complained that the custom official, the mutasaddiyan-i-farza at Surat, while valuing the goods, estimated the value in Ibrahimi and in rials, but took the custom in rupees and did not charge the custom (ushr) as share in kind of each species of coins.[107] The other tactic was to realize unsanctioned money and force the merchants to sell their goods at the depressed prices by delaying the clearance of these goods at the custom-house by the mutasaddi and shahbandar.[108] Fryer wrote, *"till a right understanding be created betwixt the Shawbunder and them (the merchants) which commonly follows when the fist is mollified."*[109] This prevalent corruption was also suffered by the English factors, which

---

xi Agra

they recorded at Surat in 1621, *"It is evident that the goods for England & c. / cannot be cleared from the custom-house without bribes, it is resolved the value of Mahmudis 600 in cloth should be given to the Customer, Mahmudis 300 in like commodities to the Cheeffa Scrivan (writer), and Mahmudis 200 in money amongst writers and other officers"*.[110]

No discussion on the local administration could be complete without describing the kotwal. His main job was to maintain law and order in the town, and provide security to its inhabitants. European travellers have described him as 'city magistrate', and 'criminal judge'. The graphic description of the duties of a kotwal is provided by Fryer, *"The next in the executive power is the catwal, the governor of the night or nearer our constitution, the sheriff of the city: For after the keys are carried to the Governor, it is the catwal business with a guard of near two hundred men, to scower the streets and brothels of idle companions; to take an account all people late out, to discover fires and horse breakers, and to carry all lewd persons to prison which is solely committed to his c(h)arge, so that all night long he is heard by his drums and trumpets, shouting and hallowing of his crew in their perambulation through all parts of the city; with lights and flame beans, with some of his companions in coaches or palankeens. Moreover he seized all debtors and secures them, and has the care of punishing and executing all offenders"*.[111] The kotwal used to realize a 'protection cess' from the residents and shopkeepers, and these cesses were known as rusum-kotwali. He also realized money from criminal and law breakers as fines or jurmana.[112] The other taxes he collected were rahadari (road tolls), tarazu kashi (a tax on stamping weights and measures) and chhati (a cess per cart load).

Attitude of Merchants Towards Other European Factories

Surat was a great place for producing indigo and textile industries in the 17th century. The first recorded attempt to enter the Indian cloth market was made by the Dutch at the end of the year 1601. Their earliest connections with Gujarat started via Achin. In 1618, two factors, Messers Wolff and Lafer, started from Achin[xii] for Akbar's court with articles of trade and a letter of recommendation to the Mughal emperor, given to them by Sultan Alauddin of Achin.[113] After a trip of three months and six days, they arrived at Surat, rented a house and the trade started.

After the establishment of English and Dutch factories at Surat, Asian trade was practised by them from Surat. This Asian trade was a serious threat to the interests of the Surat merchants, and they petitioned Prince Khurram. He issued a firman on 13 December 1619, in response to the request of merchants of Surat, categorically prohibiting the English from trading in the Red Sea. The firman further prohibited them from bringing coral to India from the Red Sea, which was in great demand in the Indian market. The Surat merchants also exerted influence over the Mughal Emperor in 1619, to discourage the English from buying textiles for the Red Sea market, which could jeopardize the interests of the local merchants.

When in 1622, the Dutch confiscated the sea-borne goods of the Gujarati merchants, not only were they duly punished by the Mughal authority, but even the English had to pay for this outrage. The English and the Dutch, in spite of their superiority on the seas, were still junior partners in the Indian trade. The stage was still held by the big Gujarati merchants such as Virji Vora of Surat and Shantidas of Ahmedabad.

In 1618, the Dutch managed to obtain a firman from the Mughal emperor Jahangir when he was visiting Ahmedabad, permitting them to establish factories in Gujarat. Indian textiles were so essential for getting South East Asian spices, that before the establishment of factories in India, the

---

xii Present-day Aceh, Indonesia

English and the Dutch frequently purchased these goods from Gujarat merchants at Bantam and elsewhere, and then exchanged them for pepper.

The Gujaratis were a sizeable community in the Spice Islands. Gujarati merchants had their agencies in all the major commercial centres of South East Asia. According to one estimate, in the 16th century, at Malacca alone, there lived a thousand Gujarati merchants, and about three to four thousand were constantly shuttling between Gujarat and Malacca. The activities of these merchants, in fact, predated the arrival of the Dutch. For when the Dutch arrived in Bantam and the Spice Islands, they found that many Asian merchants including the Gujaratis, were active in commercial traffic.

During the first half of the 17th century, there was stiff competition between the Dutch company and the Indian merchants in the textile trade, each trading to undersell the other. This led to a fall in prices in Bantam. Relations between the Dutch and the Gujarati merchants could not thus be very friendly. Van Leur has rightly pointed out that the Dutch company's economic, military and diplomatic forces were limited, and it could only survive and flourish because of the co-operation of Asian traders and rulers, adjustment with the local circumstances, and immense flexibility on the part of its servants with regards to operating in the Indian Ocean.[114] In principle, the expressed aims of the VOC were limited, viz. trade and commerce. But trade in the prevailing circumstances could not have been peaceful. In the spice-growing areas of South East Asia, the Dutch company gained a monopoly by conquest and expulsion of the local merchants, and by excluding all other traders from engaging in spice trade by use of naval power. Elsewhere in Asia, the company tried to control and restrict indigenous trade and shipping by a system of passes.

Yet the Dutch efforts to control and suppress indigenous trade and to interfere in the activities of Asian merchants were not always very successful. This failure is most clearly reflected in the fact that the settlements of the Gujarat merchants continued to be found in abundance in the South East Asian markets.[115] Haji Zahid Beg's ships called on almost all the South East Asian ports, especially for buying tin at Johore, and the Dutch were unable to stop them.[116] In the face of Dutch hostility, the Gujaratis also started hiring spaces for their cargoes on English ships going to Bantam. Until the middle of the 17th century, the Gujarat merchants were taking tin from Achin to India. In 1688, the Dutch undermined the Sultanate of Achin, and established their monopoly over the tin trade which had so far been in the hands of the Asian merchants. Even then, they could not displace the Gujarat merchants. The evidence of collaboration between the Dutch and the Gujarat merchants is also forthcoming from the Dutch records. When in 1648, the peace treaty between Spain and the Netherlands was signed, the Dutch conceded by an article of the treaty that the Spaniards in Asia would not open their harbours to the Dutch. Nevertheless, the Manila trade was so attractive that it could not be ignored by the Dutch. They, therefore, solicited the services of the Gujarat merchants (as also of the Armenian merchants based in Surat), who in Manila, could pass commodities belonging to the Dutch as their own. The ships of Abdul Ghafur of Surat that sailed from Batavia to Manila in 1682, carried Dutch merchandise. Khwaja Minas, a prominent Armenian merchant of Surat, sent Dutch freight along with the goods of some other merchants on board his ship to Manila in 1669.[117] The ships of Abdul Ghafur sailing between Batavia and Manila carried the VOC flag to placate the Dutch. As these ships came closer to Manila, these flags were removed.[118]

The French factory at Surat was established in the year 1668. They were late entrants. The English and Dutch had already established their factories at Surat in the years 1612 and 1618, respectively. But the French took an interest in India long before the foundation of the Compagnie des Indes Orientale's in 1664. The contact between India and French was established by three classes of people, first by missionaries, second by travellers, and the third by traders who had a field already prepared for them by the first two classes of people. Travellers like Jean de Thévenot, François Bernier and Jean Baptist Tavernier, wrote detailed accounts of the condition of India. The missionaries established contact with the local population and the indigenous authorities, and the travellers gave their countrymen the benefit of their knowledge about India, about the social, political and economic condition of the country, and about the immense possibilities of rising trade and commerce with it. Thus, was heightened the impatient desire felt in France, to share with the Dutch and the English, Europe's trade in the precious goods of India. Beber and La Boullaye started from Surat to the Mughal court at Delhi, to seek trade privileges. They were welcomed at the Mughal court, and presented the personal letter of Louis XIV, to Aurangzeb. The Mughal emperor granted them a firman dated 11 August 1666. Through this firman, the French were allowed to establish a factory at Surat. Francis Caron, who had a vast knowledge of Eastern trade and had served the Dutch East India Company for twenty-two years, joined the services of the French East India Company. He began his travel from France in 1667. Passing through Madagascar and touching at Cochin, he reached Surat in the beginning of 1668. He established the first French factory at Surat.

The political chaos towards the end of 17th century affected the Gujarat merchants very adversely. The local Mughal administration fleeced the Gujarat merchants to augment their dwindling resources. Due to the frequent Maratha raids, the towns and countryside of Gujarat became quite insecure. To maintain security and peace within the four walls of the cities, huge amounts of money were demanded from the merchants in the first quarter of the 18th century. Whenever there was threat of a raid against the city, the officials forced the merchants to pay money. The forced contribution was no innovation, but the sustained pressure which began to develop was certainly new.[119]

Another major problem at Surat which seriously hampered European commerce during the entire 17th century, was that Surat in particular, and Gujarat in general, had its share of climatic and tectonic incidents. On 27 May 1625, wrote Broecke (the Dutch chief in Surat) that there was a strong hurricane at 10 p.m. causing great loss to houses and ships. On 29 March 1626, he received the news of an earthquake at Patan, north of Ahmedabad, which wrecked nearly 250 houses and left behind 180 casualties, though Surat was fortunate to escape it. In August 1636, there was a mild earthquake in Surat, but there was no damage to life and property. Around 1683, a violent pestilence broke out in Surat, and from the details given by the English clergyman Ovington who used the word 'plague' to describe it, it was a severe epidemic of influenza. The death toll is reported to have been 300 a day. Years of scarcity also punctuated periods of plenty, but the city was able to spring back to life and prosperity with remarkable resilience.

References

[1] Shireen Moosvi, *Economy of the Mughal Empire,* c. 1595: A Statistical Study, Delhi, 1987, p 315-16.

[2] Tome Pires, *The Suma Oriental of Tome Pires: An Account of the East from the Red Sea to Japan,* trans. Arnando Cortasao, London, 1944,1, p. 42.

[3] *The Book of Duarte Barbosa,* Vol. 1, ed. M. L. Dames, New Delhi,

1989, p. 108.

[4] Brigg's *Ferishta* Vol IV p. 147

[5] J. Ovington, *A Voyage to Surat in the year 1689*,ed. H. G. Rawlinson, London, 1929, p. 130.

[6] Purchas Samuel, *Hakluytus Posthumus or Purchas his Pilgrimes*, Glasgow, 1905, Vol. iv, P. 27

[7] Abul Fazl, Ain-i Akbari, ed. H. *Biochmann, Bibliothica Indica*, (Calcutta, 1867-77), II, p. 57. For the use of the word baqqal for Baniya, see also. Ali Muhammad Khan, Mirat-i-Ahmedi ed. Nawab Ali, 2 vols. & Supplement, Baroda, 1927-28, 1930; Suppi. p 132, 138.

[8] Ovington, *A voyage to Surat in the year 1689*, ed. H. G. Rawlinson, London, 1929, p. 130.

[9] E. W. Lane, *Arabic-English Lexicon*, Edinburgh, 1867, Book I, part 3, s. v. 'dallal' see also A. Jan Qaiser, 'The Role of Brokers in Medieval India', in *Indian Historical Review*, New Delhi, 1974,vol. I,no. 2,p 220-46.

[10] Varthema, *Travels of Varthema*, ed. Badger, Hakluyt Society, p. 169; Streynsham Master. The Diaries of Streynsham Master, 1675-80 and Other Contemporary Papers Relating There To, ed. Sir R. C. Temple, London, 1911, Vol. II, p M-15.

[11] *Ain-i Akbari*, Vol I, p. 254.

[12] VOC/OB 1383, 31 January 1684, f. 683 Cf. R. J. Barendse, The Arabian Seas, Delhi, 2002, p. 97.

[13] *The English Factories in India*, 1618-69, ed. W. Foster, 13 Vols., Oxford, 1906-27, 1642-56, p. 30 (henceforth EFI).

[14] Jean-Baptiste Tavernier, *Travels in India*, 1640-67, transl, V. Ball, Second edition, revised by William Crooke, 2 vols, London, 1925, vol. II, p 30-31.

[15] "The Voyage and Travel of M Caeser Fredericke, Merchant of Venice, into East India and beyond the Indies", contained in Richard Hakluyt, ed., the Principal Navigations Voyages, Traffiques and Discoveries of the English Nation – Made by Sea or Land to the Remote and Farthest Quarters of the East at any Time within the Compasse of these 1600 years, London, n. d., Vol. III, p. 206.

[16] John Fryer, *A New Account of East India and Persia in Eight Letters Being Nine Years Travels Begun 1672 and Finished 1681*, ed. W. Crooke, Hakluyt Society, 1909-15 (reprint, Delhi, 1985), p. 83.

[17] Caeser Frederike, op. cit., p. 207.

[18] Tavernier, op. cit, I, p 155-56.

[19] Fryer, p. 83.

[20] Ibid., p. 85.

[21] Ibid., p. 82.

[22] EFI, 1637-41, p. 91.

[23] EFI, 1634-36, p. 171-172.

[24] EFI, 1634-36,p. 182.

[25] EFI, 1634-36, pp. 264-265.

[26] Fryer, p. 85.

[27] Tavernier I., p. 156.

[28] VOC/OB 1383, 31 January 1684, f683 vo Cf R. J. Barendse, p. 183.

[29] Streynsham Master, vol. II, p 14-15.

[30] EFI 1661-64, p 166; EFI, 1665-67, p. 263; EFI. 1667-69, p 7-8; see also A. Jan Qaiser 'The Role of Brokers'.

[31] ARA, HRB, Memoir by Schreuder, f 54.

[32] Tavernier, op. cit., I, p. 24.

[33] Irfan Habib, 'The Currency System of The Mughal Empire, in Medieval India' Quarterly, Aligarh, 4, 1961, pp. 3-12; 'Banking in Mughal India', in Contributions to Indian Economic History, 1, ed., Tapan Raychaudhuri, Calcutta, 1960 pp. 1-20. Usury in Medieval India, in Comparative studies in society and History 4, 4 1964,p 393-419 and 'The System of Bills of Exchange (Hundis) in the Mughal Empire', PIHC, 1972, pp. 290-303.

[34] Tavernier, I, p. 24.

[35] Ibid., p. 25.

[36] Ibid., pp. 29-30.

[37] Ibid., p. 24.

[38] Ronald Ferrier in *The Cambridge History of Iran,* vol. 6, ed, P. Jackson and L. Lockhart, Cambridge, 1986, pp. 469-70.

[39] Shireen Moosvi, 'Indian Brokers, The Dutch Company and Monetary Crisis in Iran in the 1680s', in PIHC, Kolkata, 2003, pp. 1121-1122.

[40] Farhad Daftary, *The Ismailis: Their History and Doctrines,* Cambridge, 1992, p 298-99; see also AAA Fyzee in Encyclopaedia of Islam, vol. I, Leiden, pp. 299-301.

[41] B. G. Gokhale, *Swat in the Seventeenth Century*, pp. 113, 129.

[42] Ashin Das Gupta, *Indian Merchants*, p. 83.

[43] James Douglas (1883). *A book of Bombay*. Bombay Gazette Steam Press. p. 133.

[44] EFI 1618-21, p. 86. ; EFI 1618-21, p. 114.

[45] EFI, 1630-33, p 301-02; EFI 1642-45, p. 18; Ibid. p. 99; Ibid., p. 210; EFI 1646-50, p 281; EFI 1646-50, p. 257.

[46] S. Arasaratnam, Maritime India in the 17th Century, Delhi, 1994, p. 104.

[47] EFI, 1646-50, p. 206.

[48] EFl 1661-64, p. 93.

[49] EFI 1642-45,p. 108.

[50] EFI, 1661-64, p. 207; EFI. 1630-33, pp. 137-151, 249.

[51] EFI 1634-36, p. 218.

[52] EFI, 1642-45, p. 145; EFI 1655-1660, pp. 16-17.

[53] EFI, 1642-45, p. 7-8.

[54] EFI, 1634-1636,p. 24.

[55] EFI. 1642-1636, p. 108.

[56] EFI, 1634-1636, p. 114.

[57] Van Santen, De VOC in Gujarat, p. 45-47.

[58] Van Santen, De VOC in Gujarat, pp. 73-74.

[59] Van Santen, De VOC in Gujarat, p. 124.

[60] Om Prakash, *The Dutch East India Company and the Economy of Bengal*, 1650-1717, Ph. D. dissertation, University of Delhi, 1967, p. 19.

[61] Van Santen, De VOC in Gujarat, p. 119.

[62] Van Santen, De VOC in Gujarat, p. 126.

[63] EFI 1655-60, pp. 215, 211.

[64] EFI. 1642-45,p. 108.

[65] EFI 1630-33, p. 154.

[66] EFI, 1630-33, p. 262-63.

[67] EFI, 1630-33, p. 193-94.

[68] EFI 1668-69, p. 195.

[69] EFI, 1655-60, p. 369.

[70] EFI, 1665-1667, p. 3.

[71] EFI 1668-1669, p. 193.

[72] EFI. 1661-64, p. 308; S. N. Sen (ed.), Indian Travels of Thevenot and Careri, New Delhi, 1949, p. 22.

[73] EFI, 1624-29, p. 189.

[74] Mirat-i-Ahmadi, P. 207; Commissariat, Studies in History of Gujarat, p. 54.

[75] This firman was issued in 1635-36 A.D. 2nd Shahriwar, 8th R.

Y.) see Mughal firmans, K. P. Srivastava, p. 31.

[76] The firman was issued on Sept, 26, 1642, see Mughal firmans, p. 33.

[77] See Mughal firmans, p. 34.

[78] EFI 1634-36, p. 314.

[79] EFI 1637-41, p. 225.

[80] EFI, 1624-29,p. 215.

[81] Makrand Mehta (1991). "Special Base of Jain Entrepreneurs in the 17th Century: Shantidas Zaveri of Ahmedabad". Indian merchants and entrepreneurs in historical perspective,pp. 91-113.

[82] EFI 1634-36, pp. 196, 259, 314.

[83] Commissariat, *Studies in History of Gujarat*, p. 56, Now the locality in known as Saraspur.

[84] Thevenot, p. 13; *Commisariat*, Mandelso, p. 23-25.

[85] Mirat, I, p. 220, This has also been attested by the French traveller Thevenot who visited Ahmedabad in 1686; See Thevenot, p. 113.

[86] M. S. Commissariat, *Mandelso's Travels in Western India* pp. 101–102.

[87] Ibid. ; *Gazetteer of the Bombay Presidency:* Ahmedabad. Government Central Press, 1879, p. 285.

[88] Mughal firmans, p. 39.

[89] Sen, S. N., *Indian Travels of Thevenot and Careri*, The National Archives of India, New Delhi, 1949, pp. 13-14.

[90] Mughal firmans, pp. 50-51.

[91] Mughal firmans, pp. 51-52.

[92] EFI, Vol. VII (1642-1645), p. 204.

[93] Gokhale, op. cit., p. 119; Letters., Vol. 1 (1602-1613), p. 26, 227, 284, 304; Vol. VI (1617), p. 237; EFI, Vol. 1 (1618-1621), p. 21, 42, 194: Vol. II(1622-1623). p 280, 281, Moreland, Akbar to Aurangzeb, p. 157.

[94] Indrani Roy, "Of Trade and Traders in the Seventeenth Century India, An unpublished French Memoir by Georges Request", in *Indian History Review*, Vol. IX, No. 1-2, 1982-1983; pp. 88-90.

[95] Court Minutes, Vol. 1 (1635-16391, p. 24., EFI, Vol. IV (1630-1633), p. 160; Chicherov, op. cit., pp. 146-147.

[96] EFI, Vol. VIII (1646-1650), p. 223.

[97] S. Najaf Haider, "English Merchants and the credit market

of India in the 17th century", in the *Proceedings of the Indian History Congress*, (Goa University), Bambolim, 1987, p. 296.

[98] Letters., Vol. II (1613-1615), pp. 117, 193.

[99] EFI, Vol. VIII (1646-1650), p. 252.

[100] Mirat, I, p. 222.

[101] Badshahnama, I, pt. I, p. 607.

[102] Akhbarat, document no. 2533, dated 19th Safar, 28th regnal year of Aurangzeb; Badshahnama, II, p. 607; Mirat, I, p. 222.

[103] Letter Received, IV, p202,347-49, Pieter Van Deu Broceke, p. 213, EFI 1618-21, pp. 147, 150, 281, 320.

[104] Mirat (Suppl.), p 194, 222; Hawkins in Early Travels, p 71-72; Letters Received, I, p. 150; Letters Received, V, p 193, 210-1, 220, 253; EFI 1646-50, p. 120; EFI 1656-60, p. 81.

[105] EFI 1633-36, p 251-255; EFI 1642-45; p 161, 247; EFI 1661-64, p. 297; also see Farhat Hasan, *State and Locality in Mughal India*, Cambridge, 2004, p. 38.

[106] EFI 1634-36, p. 224.

[107] Surat Documents, AMU, No. 2.

[108] Letters Received, IV, p. 79; EFI 1618-21, p. 319; EFI 1655-60, pp. 312-13.

[109] Fryer, I, pp. 247-48.

[110] EFI 1618-21, p 317-18; also see EFI 1630-33, p. 326.

[111] John Fryer, *A New Account of East India*, Persia: Being Nine Years' Travel, 1672-1681, ed. W. Crooke, reprint, Delhi, 1985, p. 98.

[112] State and Locality in Mughal India, p. 39.

[113] Shireen Moosvi, 'Indian Brokers, The Dutch Company and Monetary Crisis in Iran', pp. 11,21-22.

[114] Indonesia Trade and Society, pp. 240-45.

[115] F. S., Gaastra, "Merchants, Middlemen and Money: Aspects of the trade between the Indonesian Archipelago and Manila in the 17th century", in the papers of the Dutch-Indonesian Historical Conference, 1980, pp. 301-02.

[116] EFI. 1646-1650, p. 169.

[117] EFI 1668-69, p. 195.

[118] EFI, 1670-7, p. 226.

[119] Ashin Das Gupta, Indian Merchants, the chaotic and confusing political situation around 1720s has been graphically depicted by Das Gupta. The account is primarily based on Dutch sources.

Chapter 5
Mughal Perception and European Piracy

Beyond generalized impressions, very little has been written on how the Mughals viewed Europe and the Europeans, and more importantly, how their perception of Europe shaped the course of their interaction with the European merchants and traders before the intrusion of colonialism. Since the English first came to India mainly as merchants and Company servants, and established their factories and settlements at different places in the Mughal domain, it is important to unravel the connection between perceptions and policies – the extent to which the Mughal perception of Europeans shaped their commercial policy responses toward them. The expansion of European trade in India that ultimately led to India's subjugation by the English East India Company, was crucially facilitated by a concessional (practically Free Trade) policy of the Mughal rulers. The Mughal perception of the European merchants not only explains their largely favourable policy towards the European merchants and traders, but also provides important clues to the Mughal commercial policies towards them.

When two civilizations interact, they create a dialogic process of immense potential. However, what one civilization can learn from the other depends on their mutual perceptions. Often, unequal relations of power convert the dialogue into a monologue, thereby disrupting the creative potentialities that such an encounter provides. Equally importantly, appreciation of mutual differences can thwart the dialogic process, and cause to construct the 'other' in hostile and irreconcilable terms.

According to historian Irfan Habib, the polity of the Mughal ruling class was based on an internally stable system of extraction of agrarian surplus, its transfer to towns through sale of foodstuffs and raw materials, and the existence in the towns of a large urban population offering craft-goods and services of all kinds. So long as an internal agrarian crisis did not break out, the Mughal ruling class did not feel a scarcity of resources, and were unwilling to accept European technology. Only in war weaponry was this need felt; and this could be met by importing European guns as well as gunners. Habib also explores the possibility that the fairly sizeable amount of merchant capital which existed could have been a source for investing in new technology, and left to itself, capitalist development would have taken place organically. If this did not happen, it was because, says Habib, "the agrarian exploitation pursued successfully by the Mughal Empire made its economy immune, by and large, to the temptations of imitating European technology until it was too late".[1] A.J. Qaiser has, however, enumerated several important sectors in which interaction with the Europeans crucially led to the development of technology in Mughal India, such as artillery, ship-building, and in subsequent periods, glass technology, artillery, clockmaking, etc.[2] It still remains an intriguing problem of Indian history as to why the Mughals showed an unusual lack of interest in European science and technology. The accounts of the time are replete with references to the technological ingenuity of 'the Firangis', it being mentioned with pride when craftsmen at any place could manufacture articles that might compare with those of European manufacturers.

By the end of 17th century, European physicians and surgeons had made far-reaching developments in medical science. This was probably not lost on the Mughals as well, for European physicians were employed not only by the Mughal emperors, but also by the members of the nobility.

In fact, it was the medical expertise of the English doctors that got them the permission to trade in India. Jahangir's younger daughter Bahar Bano Begum got sick, and none of the vaidyas and hakims could cure her. Jahangir was very upset and went to several holy places to pray for her to get well. No miracles happened. Captain Hawkins asked Jahangir to give permission to a British doctor to check her and Jahangir agreed reluctantly. The doctor checked on the princess and gave her some English medicines. Bahar began recovering within a week, and very soon got well. Jahangir, who had given up hope, was very grateful to Captain Hawkins and gave him many gifts and gold for saving his daughter's life. Captain Hawkins asked nothing for himself. Instead, he asked Jahangir to give trading rights to the East India Company. Jahangir, though under pressure from the Portuguese, allowed the East India Company to trade.[3]

By the time the Mughals established their rule in India, the Portuguese had already established a monopoly on the Asian trade. The main method of enforcement of this so-called monopoly was first, by issuing cartaz or passes, by which they imposed restrictions on the personnel and armaments allowed on the ship; and second, through piracy. The control of the Portuguese on the Red Sea trade was particularly irksome to both the Ottomans and the Mughals, since the Portuguese posed a potential danger not only to indigenous traders, but also to hajj pilgrims. Akbar, in a letter in 1586 to Abdullah Khan Uzbeg, expressed displeasure regarding the unrest that the Portuguese created by harassing traders and pilgrims to holy places.[4]

Akbar, however, maintained cordial relations with the Portuguese by accepting to take cartaz from them to send off his pilgrim ships,[5] a practice which continued under Jahangir. Akbar signed a firman on 18 March 1573, instructing the Captains, Governors, administrators and other officials working especially in Surat, Broach, Naussari and Velodra

(Baroda) in the province of Gujarat, not to disturb the Portuguese in their possessions like Diu. It further enjoined to them not to favour Malabar pirates, but extend help to the Portuguese. As for the general Portuguese merchants, like all other traders, they had to pay customs-duties. The final decisions regarding the fiscal administration rested with the Mughal emperor. As Akbar went on to occupy the port cities of Surat, Broach and Cambay, some Portuguese merchants at Cambay sought from him the special favour of exempting them from the obligation of paying customs-duties for the commodities imported into Cambay. Akbar granted the request and reportedly agreed to take the lumpsum payment of 300,000 cruzados[i] every year instead as duties, payable to the captain of Cambay.[6]

The overwhelming and intimidating presence of the Portuguese and their dominance of the maritime trade was one of the factors that shaped the Mughal perception and policies towards the English. The presence of the Portuguese also prevented the Mughal officials from developing better trade relations with the English. In 1618, Sir Thomas Roe wrote to the Company, *"the Portugal houlds all the coast to slaverie, and there is no way to remedie it, unless either the Kyng would build or give us a port or hyre our shipping"*.[7] The experience of the Mughal ruling elite with the Portuguese, who had introduced an element of 'force' in the maritime commerce of the high seas, was probably responsible for their wary attitude towards the English merchants. And this fear was not unfounded. The English also resorted to piratical activities against Mughal shipping on the western coast. They began to issue passes to unprotected Indian vessels as early as 1613. As a consequence, Mukarrab Khan, the Governor of

i Cruzado was a Portuguese gold (later silver) coin, valued at 400 reis (plural for real), later raised to 480 reis by king Pedro II (1683-1706). The Portuguese word 'cruzado' means cross, referring to the cross of the patron saint of Portugal, St George, on the reverse of these coins.

Surat, did not allow the English to establish a factory at Surat, and also rebuked them for the robbing of the ships coming from the Red Sea, by one of their factors, Henry Middleton.

For the same reason, in 1608, when William Hawkins arrived at Surat, Mukarrab Khan (who was the mutasaddi of both Surat and Cambay) allowed them to unload their cargo. But the local Mughal officials did not permit them to engage in any commercial transaction in Surat.[8] In 1612, Middleton was also refused trade at Dabul[ii] not because of Portuguese instigation, but ostensibly because as Hawkins himself states, Surat merchants had made a declaration at court that encouragement to the English would mean the ruin of trade of Gujarat.[9]

In the initial phase, the English traders tried to make an impression upon the Gujarat merchants that they were powerful enough to succeed against the Portuguese. In 1612, Captain Best, and in 1614, Nicholas Downton, inflicted crushing defeats on the Portuguese. But these only served to make the ruling elite more watchful of their activities. The emperor allowed the English to trade in Mughal dominions, but he also took care to not let them settle and build a factory or even buy a house.[10].

Mughal perception and policies towards the English in the 17th century were not uniform and can be demarcated into two distinct phases. In the first phase that lasted till about 1630s, the Mughal administration perceived the English as petty merchants, foreign and inferior. During this phase, the Mughals rejected outright the English claim to a superior status based on their political connections with the ruler of England. Hawkins' embassy failed miserably in getting privileges for English merchants at Surat. Jahangir was fully aware that Surat had become a place of contention between the English and the Portuguese merchants. In 1615, Sir Thomas Roe, the ambassador of King James I,

ii Dabhol

came to the court of Jahangir and made a deliberate effort to present himself at the court as an ambassador of the English monarch, besides working upon getting trading privileges. For the Mughals, however, he was a representative of the English merchant body, and they were foreign merchants not to be placed on parity with Indian merchants. Obviously, this embassy was also unsuccessful. Nevertheless, Roe devised a plan of escorting Mughal vessels to the Red Sea in order to gain acceptance in the Indian trade alongside the Portuguese. They had realised that they needed to generate profit from Asiatic trade to finance their purchases of Asian goods for European market.[11] Linked with their desire to gain acceptance in the Red Sea trade was the desire to get permission for settlement in Surat, which was a principal port on the western coast from where the Red Sea and Persian Gulf trade was carried out.

In 1618, Roe drafted proposals for a firman which was submitted to Prince Khurram. It included a demand to allow him to land with arms, to defend themselves against the Portuguese, which was rejected by the prince. Further, Roe's demand for complete freedom of trade throughout the empire was completely ignored by Khurram. With the mediation and assistance of Asaf Khan, a revised firman was issued and Roe had to agree not to build any house in or about Surat without obtaining permission from Jahangir. They could only rent houses for merchants' residences and for storage of merchandise. In fact, in 1617, when the news regarding a ship containing building material, reportedly for a factory at Swally reached Prince Khurram, an embargo was placed on English trade and they were not allowed to unload the ship. Also, their goods were not to be passed unchecked. Roe had to sign an undertaking that the English would live at Surat according to the laws and regulations of the empire.[12]

The English claimed that by 1613, they had the permission (by a firman supposedly given to Thomas Best) to trade at Surat, but this firman had little value. The permission to settle at Surat (build a 'factory') was not yet given,[13] and the idea of making a fortress on the coast of Gujarat had been rejected by Prince Khurram. The English could not get the Mughal Emperor to sign the treaty or have an exclusive alliance with them against either the Portuguese or the Dutch. This was because the emperor considered it below his dignity to sign a treaty with the representatives of a foreign merchant body. Roe's proposal to Prince Khurram to allow them to settle at Surat, against which they would assume the responsibility of the naval defence of Surat against the Portuguese, was scornfully rejected by Khurram. Apparently any such 'help' which would put the emperor under obligation to a foreign trading company, was unacceptable to him. In 1616, Roe tried to convince Jahangir that the Dutch in Southern India and Eastern India were building forts, as in the case of Masulipatam, and would become masters of the port. But this news only served to 'somewhat trouble' Jahangir.[14]

By the end of the first phase, ie 1630, the Portuguese were virtually wiped out by the English, and the latter had established complete supremacy in the high seas. The English were able to impose successive defeats on the Portuguese, one after the other. In 1622, they captured Ormuz in the Persian Gulf from the Portuguese In 1633, they defeated the Portuguese at the port of Hugh, thoroughly routing them. Their successive victories enabled them to establish a maritime supremacy in the Indian Ocean, which came to be gradually recognized by the Mughals.

An important instance of Mughal perception of the English merchants comes from the Red Sea trade dispute, in which Thomas Roe played an important role. In 1618, the English East India Company, under the initiative of Roe, decided to participate in the trade to Red Sea, in order to enhance its profits from the Indian Ocean.[15] In 1618, the English despatched a ship, Anne, to Mocha. Encouraged by the profits, in 1619, another ship, Lion, was despatched to the Red Sea. This trade, Roe told the Company, *"in tyme may be enlarged by the English, and will be the life of Surat and Persia trade"*.[16] The English decision to participate in the Red Sea trade created quite an uproar among the Surat merchants, who, in alliance with the local authorities, seized the English factories and prevented them from buying merchandise from the merchants of Gujarat. When the factors started their investments for the fleet expected in the autumn, a general boycott was organized. They were plainly told that unless they undertook to abandon the Red Sea traffic, they could not buy a yard of calico for that purpose. When the English took the matter to Ishaq Beg, Governor of Surat, he flatly refused to help them.[17] They were specially prevented from buying linen or making big investments in buying for the lading of the Lion. When the English were suspected of buying linen from adjacent places, a meeting of all the brokers in Surat and nearby places was called and it was decided not to buy and sell any commodity to the English. Not only Surat and Navsari, but the governors of Broach and Baroda were also informed that the English were to be boycotted as per the orders of the prince. The English had to agree to not making any investments in the Red Sea until further orders came from the prince.[18] Sir Thomas Roe was forced to take the matter to the Mughal court. In response to his petition concerning the blockade of the Red Sea trade, Prince Khurram issued a firman, which forbade them from trading between Gujarat and the Red Sea on the ground that this was the only avenue of overseas trade left to the Indian merchants in the wake of the advent of the European Companies.[19]

Another issue of dispute was the coral trade. It was a major item of import from the Red Sea, although most of the coral that they sold at Surat was brought by land to Bijapur.[20] The governor and merchants of Surat wrote a joint petition to the prince for a firman to forbid the sale of coral to the English merchants, and that any further trade by the English in that commodity was against their interests, and it was accepted. Khurram's firman forbade the English from importing coral. The firman is significant in highlighting the Mughal perception of the English. It would seem from the firman, that the Mughal court did make a distinction between the Indian and the foreign merchants, and believed that the Indian merchants being their subjects, deserved a more favourable treatment than the foreign English merchants. William Biddulph, one of the factors of the English Company at the Mughal court, found *"the prince and all generallye tenderinge their own peoples goods and complaints before our shutes and benefits"*.[21]

The monopoly system was an important part of the imperial economic policies which directly affected the European merchants and their trade. Monopolies in certain articles were imposed for various reasons, such as according to the military exigencies of state as in the case of saltpetre in 1636, or for revving the revenue for the state, as in the case of indigo, which was monopolized in 1633, and the gold and silver monopolies. Mostly, these temporary monopolies had to be terminated before their stipulated time. One of the reasons for this was the opposition put up against them, as in the case of indigo, where the combined opposition of the Anglo-Dutch made the monopoly difficult to sustain. The Governor of Surat, apprehensive of the falling revenues of his port, petitioned to the emperor to restore the freedom of trade in indigo. Through his mediation, some relaxation was given to both the English and the Dutch through three firmans – one to the Governor of Surat, one to the English and one to the Dutch, to make arrangements to buy indigo at Agra. The proposal was rejected by both the English and the Dutch. This shows that a foreign merchant body could expect a revision of the emperor's firman if its interests were adversely affected. It also reflects the collusion between the Mughal officials and the European merchants, who through the mediation of important nobles at the imperial court could get imperial orders revised. These nobles, either for financial reasons (e. g. Muiz-ul-Mulk, the Governor of Surat,) or for political reasons (e. g. Asaf Khan, the vakil and Afzal Khan, the Diwan-i-kul) supported them. The English decided to take advantage of the enmity between Mir Jumla and Asaf Khan, who belonged to different factions at court, and looked on to Asaf Khan for help. Consequently, on 14 April 1635,[22] the English received the imperial firman dissolving the indigo monopoly and its sale once again became open to all. In 1636, when the emperor received complaints from the Dutch about the attempts of Saif Khan to monopolize the stock of indigo in his district,[23] a firman was issued by the Emperor on 22 February 1636, reiterating that the indigo monopoly had been taken off, and that no one could monopolize indigo in an unauthorized manner.[24] Thus, while making it clear that the European merchants like all other merchants of his domain, were protected from any arbitrary act of Mughal officials, another firman which was simultaneously issued, showing that he would neither let the foreign merchants disrupt the trade of Surat, nor let the Mughal ports be harmed by them. He wanted the heads or principals of both the English and Dutch factories to be accountable for the activities of their merchants. The firman said that the Dutch and the English must always keep a deposit of Rs 12 lakhs at Surat, and that the principals of both nations must always remain in Surat and must not go aboard their ships at any time. The firman further sought to regulate their movement and activities by ordering that the

English and Dutch must not resort to any other ports in the Mughal Empire. They were also not allowed to bring ships to any other place except Swally Hole (Swally Marine), where it shall not be lawful for them to build any frigates.[25] Likewise, a document dated 10 September 1645, a hash-ul-hukum[iii] issued by Saadullah Khan stated that the English were not expected to a) fortify their factories, b) employ armed guards in their factories, c) refuse to pay regular taxes, and d) construct fortresses for residences.[26]

A similar example can be taken in the case of the saltpetre monopoly when the co-operation of a governor helped in making the monopoly ineffective. George Tash took the assistance of Governor Mir Musa through gifts and succeeded in clearing all obstructions to the saltpetre business, which was very important for them, as in Bengal, they had "less trade except in saltpetre". They had large factories in Patna, Kasimbazar and Hughli. When President Methwold said that the English would not submit to conditions of such 'slavery', the governor pretended that the firman was merely a formality. When the Dutch also complained through Shahbandar Mirza Mahmud, they got the reply that the firman was not meant for them, and that it was meant to restrain the English who had taken to frequenting Portuguese settlements with their small vessels, and were planning to use them in fetching goods by water from Broach and Cambay, which would injure the customs-revenue of Surat.[27]

After the 1630s, however, a new phase in Mughal perception and policies towards the English began to take shape. By this time, the Portuguese had been virtually wiped out by the English. During this phase, two developments seem to have shaped the Mughal policy towards the English. The first was the English maritime supremacy – Mughal

---

iii An order issued by a lower officer, but in the name of the emperor.

aggressions on land were responded to by the English in equal measure on the high seas. Thus, there existed between the English and the Mughals, a reciprocal 'balance of terror'.[28] The second important development was the growth in the overseas trade carried on by the Mughal officials since the time of the Portuguese. Mukarrab Khan's commercial links with both the Portuguese and English merchants are time and again alluded to in the English factory records. Middleton tells us of the commercial transactions which he conducted along with Mukarrab Khan and Khwaja Nizam. This Khwaja Nizam, who appears to have been a business partner of Mukarrab Khan, was reportedly such an influential merchant that no other merchant dared to trade with the English "without his prevention and leave".[29]

During the second half of the 17th century, a large number of Mughal officials were participating in overseas trade. Mughal officials such as Shaista Khan and Mir Jumla had important trading interests in West Asia and South East Asia. Referring to Mir Jumla, Walter Littleton and Venkata Brahman reported to the Company in 1651, that *"concerning forran negotiation, hee (Mir Jumla) hath trade to Pegue, Tennassaree, Acheen, Rackan (Arakan, Persia, Bengalla, Moka, Peruck, Maldeevaes and Macassar. Hee hath ten vessels of his owne, and intends to augment them, makeing much preparatyon for building of more"*.[30] Imperial ships were regularly despatched to the ports of Aden and Mocha by members of the imperial court. Nur Jahan, Jahan Ara and other imperial princesses had ships of their own, participating in overseas trade.[31] The result of this was that the interest of the Mughal officials came to be tied up with the interests of the Company. This led to a nebulous and undefined alliance between the two. Though conflicts between the Mughals and English officials were common and frequent, these conflicts did not undermine the larger co-operation between them. This ultimately led to the development of an alliance based on a framework of a mutually-accepted code of conduct and practices. It was this alliance that considerably facilitated the trading activities of the English in India, and contributed in a large measure to their ultimate success, leading to the gradual undermining of the interests of the Indian merchants.

The Interlopers, 1633-39

On 7 November 1633, Hopkinson was succeeded by William Methwold as the President of the Surat factory. Methwold was in many respects a remarkable man. He was a scholar of distinction and had contributed a chapter to Purchas' famous work. He spoke Dutch fluently. Methwold's first task on his arrival was to do his utmost to repair the damage done by the famine, which had come very close to ruining the Surat factory. Another important thing to be done was to put an end to the lingering hostility with the Portuguese, which had long ceased to profit either party. He, therefore, set to work at once to negotiate a treaty with Goa, overtures for which had been put forward by his predecessors, Thomas Kerridge and Thomas Rastell, and which had been scornfully rejected by the Portuguese. Now, however, neither side was in a condition to continue the struggle. The poverty of Goa was only equalled by her pride, and the English were utterly crippled by the famine. Besides, both parties viewed with apprehension the growing power of the Dutch who helped the English when it suited them, but were dangerous allies. Preliminaries were arranged with the help of Father Tavares and other influential priests, who were as eager now to help the English as their predecessors had been to oppose them. Methwold and his council went to Goa, which they reached on 6 January 1635, amid much firing of guns and other courtesies.[32] They had a long interview with the Viceroy, at the end of which they concluded *"not only a cessation, but union of arms, against the common enemies"*. They were *"to observe the like peace here in East India, as hath been so happily begun and continued between our illustrious Princes and their subjects respectively in the parts of Europe"*.[33] The terms were then drawn up in detail and despatched to Europe. Methwold was at first inclined to suspect that *"not love towards us but hate to the Hollanders hath in policy humbled them, that, our opposition being taken off by a neutrality, they may the better vanquish them first; whilst we shall have the favour which was promised unto Ulysses from Polyphemus, in being last devoured"*. However, the suspicion was an unworthy one, and when Portugal became free from Spain in 1640, the peace was made permanent. It proved advantageous to both sides. From this time onwards, English ships plied up and down the coast and anchored in Portuguese harbours without hindrance.

Another scheme of Methwold's was to abandon the Surat factory altogether, and to move the English headquarters to Ahmedabad. But before these ideas could be discussed, a fresh calamity fell upon the Company. Without a word to them, Charles I, in direct violation of the Charter, had licensed one Samuel Bonnell, an employee of Sir William Courten, to fit out an expedition *"to range the seas all the world over"*, and *"to make prize of all such the treasures, merchandizes, goods and commodities, which to his best abilities he shall be able to take of infidels, or any other prince, potentate or state not in league with us beyond the line equinoctial"*. It was difficult to imagine anything more scandalous than a licence to commit piracy upon unoffending vessels, couched in such terms. The holders promptly took advantage of it. They fitted out two ships, the Samaritan and the Roebuck, under one William Cobbe, flying the colours of the Royal Navy, and despatched them for Aden in April 1635. The Samaritan was wrecked, but the Roebuck held up two ships, the Mahmudi of Diu and the Taufiqui of Surat, and cruelly tortured the crew. They took the nakhuda or master as prisoner, bound both his hands, tied a match to his fingers, which burnt first the flesh and then the bones. Once he confessed to where the money was, they burnt the nakhuda, the boatswain, the merchants and the carpenters, until they were near dead and confessed all they knew.[34]

To make matters worse, the Taufiqui belonged to Mirza Mahmud, a prominent Surat merchant and a loyal supporter of the English factory. When Methwold heard this report that English pirates had been plundering Indian vessels, he rushed to the Governor's house to contradict what he thought was a ridiculous bazaar rumour. But he found a sad assembly of dejected merchants, some looking through him with eyes sparkling with indignation, others half dead in the sense of their loss, already present there. Amid a profound silence, the Governor questioned him as to the whereabouts of the English vessels, to which Methwold truthfully replied that he only knew of the Crispiana, apparently delayed by a breakdown. The Governor then read out a letter received from the Taufiqui, and *"whereupon the whole Company mouthed at once a general invective against me and the whole English nation; which continued some time with such a confusion as I knew not to whom to address myself unto to give a reply until they had run themselves out of breath"*.[35] Methwold argued in vain that it might be French or Dutch pirates, but realized that further denials were useless, as the Taufiqui, ravaged, had returned to port. A guard was set at the English factory, and Methwold was locked up at night in a filthy, airless chamber swarming with vermin. Finally, Methwold settled the claims as far as he could with the cash and goods which he had in hand, and a formal reconciliation was reached. In the meantime, the pirates were run to earth by captain John Proud of the Royal Navy off the Comoros. Proud arrested Cobbe, but the crew took up an impregnable position on a neighbouring hill, where they had mounted four big guns commanding the ship. Proud did not dare to attack them, so he came to a compromise. Cobbe handed over the money and jewels amounting to £9,700, taken from the Surat boat.[36] Soon, the Blessing, sent by Methwold, arrived on the scene and Cobbe fled. He landed in England in 1637 with nearly £40,000 worth of booty, and the Company prosecuted him in vain. It was known that Courten had nothing to do with the business, his name only being used, and what was done was his Majesty's act.[37]

Worse, however, was to follow. Courten, encouraged by the ease with which the first body of interlopers had obtained sanction for their nefarious work, now started an expedition to the Indies on a large scale. He assembled a fleet of six vessels, for which he paid £120,000, and placed it under Captain Weddell, an old servant of the Company. The expedition, from one point of view, may be looked upon as a rival concern, organized by discontented or discharged Company's servants, who used the knowledge gained in its service to spite their former masters. The king's excuse for his action was that he was "*credibly informed that the East India Company had neglected to settle trade in those parts, and had made no fortifications to encourage any in future times to adventure thither, contrary to the practice of the Dutch and Portuguese*", and he went on to state that "*this neglect has resulted in loss of trade to His Majesty's subjects, as evidenced not only by the complaints of some of the adventurers, but especially by the decrease of the royal customs, which is due to the said Company's supine, neglected discovery of trade in divers places in those parts*".[38] The new Association was authorized to trade on the African and Arabian coasts, in the Persian Gulf, along the Malabar, Coromandel and Bengal coasts, and was specially enjoined to put into Goa and make an arrangement with the Portuguese government. After that, the fleet was to proceed to the Far East, and open trade with Siam, China, and Japan, and finally, if possible, to return home by the Northwest passage.

The expedition reached the Comoro Islands in August 1636, and Goa (where they were courteously, but coldly received) in October. Weddell sent a polite note to Methwold at Surat, saying that he could not forget to wish well his old masters, enclosing the king's commission ordering the President and Council of the East India Company to render them assistance. Methwold wrote a furious reply, accusing Weddell's promoters of being responsible for "Cobbe's pranks", and containing other "flashes and peremptory jeering menaces", which Weddell answered in a similar strain. He was particularly nettled at the imputation of piracy, which he considered a slur upon a respectable Association trading under Royal Warrant. Weddell went on to the small port of Bhatkal on the Malabar coast, where he obtained permission from the local Raja to establish a factory for trading in pepper. It was an unhealthy spot, and the graves of members of the little band still exist in a tiny cemetery on the edge of the sea.

A small English vessel, the Comfort, on its way from Bantam to Surat, was attacked by the notorious pirates of Malabar. A desperate struggle followed. The pirates boarded the ship and the captain, Walter Clark, decided to blow it up rather than surrender. Comfort's survivors were picked up and imprisoned. However, with the help of a renegade, Henry Weygive, a fugitive from the Company who had embraced Islam, they got in touch with Weddell, who generously ransomed them for 2,200 reals (£550).

The End of the Interlopers and The Dutch War, 1639-54

President Fremlin's term of office was not marked by any event of great importance. The benefits of Methwold's treaty with Goa soon began to be felt. The English began to build a large number of coasting vessels in local shipyards, which proved much cheaper than ships built in England. They drove a lucrative trade from the Portuguese ports along the shores of Western India. They were still troubled by the depredations of the Malabar pirates, but here again, the 'frigates', a type of vessel in which the Goanese authorities apparently specialized in, proved a very useful protection. In 1640, the Hope was waylaid by eight 'prowes'[iv]. But a Portuguese patrol arrived in time to rescue the ship, though the marauders got away with prisoners and booty. The former was, as in the case of the Comfort, generously ransomed by Courten's factory at Karwar.[39] The Swan, from Bantam to Surat with a valuable cargo, was beset by a fleet of sixteen of these interlopers, but its captain courageously navigated his ship away.[40]

In 1640, the Company decided to extend their trade in the Persian Gulf to Basra. William Thurston and Edward Pearce were despatched to that port, where they were courteously received by Ali Basha, the rebel Badshah of the Turks, and made an agreement to open a factory there. The chief exports were pearls, spices, dates and Arab ponies, while the imports most in demand were lead, tin, quicksilver, indigo, sugar, coffee, pepper and cloth. Merchants came from Diarbekir, Mosul and Aleppo, and a few Janissaries from Baghdad, to trade at Basra.[41] The factory at Surat was in an unsatisfactory condition, in spite of the efforts of Methwold and his successor, Fremlin. The Civil War was now practically inevitable, and trade in England was dislocated. The Fourth Joint Stock, started in 1642, with a capital of £105,000, proved a failure. The Company had to endure several losses in ships and money. The Discovery was lost with all men aboard in 1644, taking with her a cargo worth £30,000. The John was shortly afterwards carried off by its captain.

Added to all this, King Charles I, not content with the harm which he had already done, robbed the Company of £63,000 in 1640. The Company had on hand a stock of

iv The 'prow' was a Malay galley propelled by oars, but the word was often used to denote any small craft.

£600,000 of pepper, unsold. Lord Cottington, on behalf of the king, offered to buy it at the current rate of two shillings and a penny per pound. The Company was reluctant to sell. Their sympathies were with the Parliament and they themselves had a long list of grievances against the Court, which remained un-redressed. But while they hated the king, they also feared him, and he could do them infinite harm by refusing to negotiate on their behalf with the Dutch or Portuguese. So, the pepper was handed over, on the word of a king that the bill, amounting to £63,283, would be settled as soon as possible. Meanwhile, Charles sold the stock for £50,626 cash. Needless to say, the Company never saw a penny of their money again, and a rich cargo, representing the major part of a season's trade, had to be written off the books of the Third Joint Stock, adding to its other heavy losses.

The Company's rivals, Courten's Association, were faring no better. Their factory at Bhatkal, after all the money spent on adding manpower by rescuing men captured by Malabar pirates, had to be moved to Karwar. In 1639, a mission was sent to Muhammad Adil Shah at Bijapur, with presents consisting of a set of knives, spoons, and cups mounted in agate, a pearl richly set, a 'gurgalet', and a 'spitting pot', of the total value of 2,500 pagodas. In return, they demanded a firman for trade. But it was a bad year for pepper and little came out of it. Between 1639 and 1644, they lost the William, the Talbot, and the pinnace Thomasine, and to crown everything, in that year, Weddell himself, the life and soul of the venture, was drowned. His two vessels, the Dragon and the Katherine, went down with all men aboard. The Association sank into bankruptcy. In a desperate attempt to stave off the inevitable, they started coining debased reals and pagodas, some of which they palmed off on the Surat factors. In 1646, they issued a piteous appeal to the Company to take over the Karwar factory, which the

Company, not unnaturally, refused to do. Shortly after, the local governor seized it to recover the rent which had been owing for four years, marking the end of an ill-fated venture. Courten, a ruined man, fled to Europe and died there.[42]

Fremlin returned home in 1644, and was succeeded by Francis Breton. But Fremlin had a disastrous return voyage, being caught in the storm which proved fatal to the Discovery and to Weddell's fleet. His own ship, the Dolphin, had to return to Surat. He managed to reach England safely the next year, but died soon after his arrival. In 1649, Breton died, and was buried in a stately tomb, the first English President to lie in the graveyard at Surat. The factory now had branches at Ahmedabad, Agra, Lucknow, Tatta, Baroda, Broach, Basra and Gombroon. In 1652, Thomas Merry (1649-52) was succeeded by Captain Jeremy Blackman, in whose favour the Company made several important concessions. His pay as President was to be £500 per annum, to commence from his departure from England, with £40 allowance for servants. He was permitted, as a special favour, to take his wife with him. This was an unusual thing. Mrs Blackman must have felt strange in the bachelor establishment in which she found herself, though she had, of course, the companionship of the ladies of the Dutch factory. This, however, was destined not to last for very long. In 1652, the long commercial rivalry between the two nations led to the outbreak of war. The factors at Surat made the usual mistake of underrating the enemy. They were confident, they write, that *"our people would show themselves Englishmen here in India as well as our friends at home, where one Englishman thinks himself as good as two Dutchmen, and by God's blessing have proved themselves so"*.[43]

They were to find, however, that the well-equipped Hollanders were very different opponents from the ill-equipped Portuguese. Most of the fighting was in the Persian Gulf, a new field of trade, which both sides were endeavouring to exploit. The Dutch captured the English ships. The loss of prestige, so carefully built up since the time of Roe by able diplomacy and successive victories over the Portuguese, was under threat. President Blackman warned the Court of Directors that the impression of English inferiority must be dispelled, or "you must bid adieu to your East India Trade". He pointed out that what was chiefly needed was a permanent port of their own, to serve as a depot and naval base for the English, where they would not be at the mercy of a native potentate, thus confirming an idea which was steadily gaining ground among the younger members of the Company. He suggested that Portugal might be willing to give up Bombay, Bassein or Mozambique.[44] The idea was put before Cromwell, but nothing came of it. Blackman also complained of the insubordination caused by the presence of a number of unattached Englishmen not under the control of the Company – interlopers and independent traders, and members of Courten's Association and of the Assada plantation in Madagascar.

Finally, by the Peace of Westminster, after a prolonged discussion of claims and counter-claims, the Company received a net sum of £85,000 in compensation for various injuries and damages.[45] Unfortunately, the government borrowed £50,000 of this and there is no record of its repayment. In all probability, the matter drifted on until the Restoration, when it was hopeless to expect further redress. The balance of £35,000 was mostly expended in settling various outstanding claims, and very little seems to have actually reached the pockets of the shareholders.[46]

European Piracy

Piracy was not unknown either in Europe and in the Islamic world[v] or in the Indian Ocean. Long before the Portuguese

---

v The Ottoman Sultan Suleiman II's (1520-66) pirate-ships operated in the Mediterranean Sea.

arrived on the scene, the Indian Ocean had been infested with Malabar pirates who operated in the gulf of Persia and Red Sea. Merchants had to make their own arrangements to protect themselves from them. According to the Indo-Persian historian Khafi Khan, who lived in Aurangzeb's time, the one difference between the Indians and the Europeans, particularly the English pirates, was that while the former never attacked the hajj pilgrim traffic, the latter thrived on it.[47]

By 1556, the Portuguese were firmly established on the west coast with a large number of factories and forts. By the first half of the 16th century, the cities of Diu and Bassein with lands attached to them in the kingdom of Gujarat, were also in the possession of Portugal. Similarly, the Portuguese had fortresses in Chaul, Bhatkal and other areas. Bombay was under Portugal since 1550. The Portuguese were able to regulate and restrict the traffic of Indian merchants in the Indian Ocean to a large extent by the introduction of a system of cartaz, which was introduced by them in 1502, after a war with the Zamorin of Calicut. Cartaz was used to implement monopoly and supremacy over maritime trade in the Indian Ocean regions.[48] Portuguese officials were soon detailed to guard coastal regions to prevent other ships from conducting trade with any part of India, and were asked to capture all ships not equipped with cartazes. They compelled Bahadur Shah of Gujarat, to accept the system of cartaz under the terms and conditions of the treaty signed on 23 December 1534. Under its terms, vessels going to the straits of Mocha via Bassein, had to buy cartaz. This treaty was repeated between the two parties on 25 October 1535. Their claim to maritime supremacy had piracy as an essential element, to reinforce it. They prevented journeys to Mocha, and deterred Malabar ships by burning them. They guarded the ships to Cambay coming from Goa and other places, and gave cartaz for southwards trade as well as for Red Sea trade.[49]

Akbar broadly maintained cordial relations with the Portuguese by accepting to take cartaz from them to send off his pilgrim ships, a practice which continued under Jahangir. In the cartaz issued to Bhimji Parekh under the orders of Jahangir for the ship called Mubarakshahi on 18 May 1620, special reference is made to the tradition of issuing a free cartaz every year.[50] Akbar was of the opinion that the 'Feringis' who turned out to be a great threat to the pilgrimage to Mecca as well as to the trade, should be driven away from the Indian Ocean. It was considered quite humiliating for so powerful an emperor as Akbar to ask for passes from the Portuguese. Though Akbar had instructed his officials in Malwa and Gujarat to take necessary steps to drive away the Portuguese with the assistance of the Deccan rulers, there is no record of any effective expedition for this. Private traders like Abdur Rahim Khan paid tax to obtain passes and ensure the safety and security of the passengers aboard their ships. Malik Ayaz, Chief Governor of the Sultanate of Gujarat in 1573, was able to keep the Gujarat ports secure from the feringis,[vi] but later, their influence increased and no ship could dare depart without their pass or cartaz.[51] Several attempts were made by Akbar to control piracy, but these measures were unsuccessful.

For as long as Portuguese naval power was held in esteem, Mukarrab Khan, the Governor of Surat, did not allow the English to establish a factory at Surat. He also rebuked them for robbing the ships coming from the Red Sea by Henry Middleton, and refused to give them any explanation as to why he did not let them establish a factory at Surat. The English started issuing passes to unprotected Indian vessels as early as 1613. They even began holding Gujarat ships for ransom and claimed that ships could

---

vi The Portuguese

not dare go out of the river of Surat without their passes. However, they also admitted that the transportation of their own goods to Surat was dangerous due to Portuguese frigates.[52] The English asserted their maritime supremacy on the conventional methods used earlier by the Portuguese, namely, (1) the system of licences, as inherited from the Portuguese practice of issuing cartaz, according to which any ship sailing in western Indian waters without the cartaz would be sacked, looted or sunk; and (2) organizing convoys for Indian ships. Just as the Mughals accepted the Portuguese passes, they were willing to tolerate the English passes, as well. In 1613, the Portuguese organized a raid on the port of Surat and sacked four ships. In retaliation, Mukarrab Khan got St. Xavier and other Jesuits arrested at Surat in 1614, and closed their churches. Meanwhile, the Portuguese were defeated in a naval fight by the English, wherefore they had to approach Mukarrab Khan, suing for peace. This victory gave the English a temporary edge over the Portuguese. The next year, when the Portuguese seized another ship of a local merchant at Surat, Jahangir debarred Portuguese trade and laid a siege at Daman. The English were asked to help against Portuguese. The refusal of the English displeased the Mughals but their trade was not stopped. Finally in 1615, the Portuguese had to yield to the Mughals, and in a truce, they had to pay three lakh rupees for the ships taken, and for licence to go to Red Sea.

In 1621, despite a warning by Prince Khurram to the President and Council at Surat that they "should live quietly or else leave", Prince Khurram's ship arriving from Red Sea was taken by the English pirates.[53] In October 1621, some English pirates sunk an Indian ship which carried valuable treasures. In March 1622, English factors appeared before Mohammad Taqi, Diwan of the Subah, to make compensation for the alleged loss. Although they tried to lay the blame on the Dutch, they were imprisoned and had to make compensation. Despite these occasional friction and conflict, Anglo-Mughal relations were, in the long term, that of considerable co-operation. Once the dispute subsided, they were permitted to rent a house for the establishment of the factory. They were also allowed to buy or construct four frigates each year, and were freed from land tolls. An arrangement was made by which a sum of 40,000 mahmudis was to be paid yearly by the English, in lieu of all custom-dues in Surat, both inwards and outwards. The agreement was sent to the emperor for confirmation, and accordingly, a firman was received on 7 September 1624. By this agreement, the English were allowed to have access to the Red Sea. They also secured the right to convoy the Mughal ships from Surat to Mocha and back. By 1630, the English fleet at Surat was providing convoys to Indian vessels trading with the Red Sea.

In 1616, Asaf Khan, who was virtually protecting the English factors at Agra, told Roe that he should endeavour to prevent the Dutch from robbing the prince's ship, for that would be hazardous not only for the Dutch, but for the English as well.[54] Later, in 1622, when a few Indian merchants claimed that their ships had been taken off Chaul and demanded compensation, the English tried to blame the Dutch. But the Mughal officials held them also responsible, arguing that they 'shared the booty'.[55]

The capture of the Taufiqui, Mirza Mahmud's ship at Surat in 1635, by an English pirate named Roebuck, and the Mahmudi, a Diu ship by other English pirates, led to the imprisonment of some factors of the East India Company, as these vessels belonged to a prominent merchant of Surat who also was a broker of the Governor of Broach, Yaqub Khan.

In the 17th century, the overseas trade and commercial activities of the members of the royal family and nobles such as Nur Jahan, Khurram, Mukarrab Khan, Zulfiqar Khan, Saif Khan, Muiz-ul-Mulk, etc. increased. Nevertheless, the growth of trade in the Indian Ocean in the latter half of the 17th century, also saw a corresponding increase in the incidents of piracy. Most of the pirates were chiefly English, most notorious among them being Teach, Henry Every, Kidd, Roberts, England and Tew, who had extended their operations to the Indian Ocean. They were helped by friends among English factors on shore with supplies and information of rich prizes to look for, or armed ships to be avoided, which put a strain on this arrangement. The commercial interests of Prince Khurram had already started to clash with that of the East India Company.

The origins of the European pirates were in the culture of privateering in the Atlantic, where different European monarchs granted commissions to private parties to carry out acts of piracy against rival states. The English, for instance, would use privateers to great effect against the Spanish in the Caribbean. However, once this culture of piracy had been established, it was not long before well-armed European pirates began to expand their operations into the Indian Ocean, often out of bases in Madagascar. Perhaps the most successful of these was Captain John Avery[vii] who would become a legend and an inspiration for the likes of Captain Kidd and Blackbeard.

Born in Plymouth, England, Avery had served as a junior officer in the Royal Navy. In 1693, he signed up for a privateering expedition aimed at French shipping in the Caribbean, and was assigned to a forty-six-gun flagship. The owners of the ship, however, did not pay the crew on time and Avery led a mutiny, taking over the ship and renaming it the Fancy. Using the ship's firepower, they now looted and pillaged their way down the Atlantic, before heading for the secluded harbours of Madagascar. The original mutineers had been British. But along the way, they had picked up Danish and French sailors, who had volunteered

vii Also known as Henry Every

to join the pirates. They now set their sights on the shipping that passed between India and the Yemeni port of Mocha, which was famous for its coffee exports.

In1694, Avery headed for Bab-el-Mandeb. But when he arrived there, he found small sloops[viii] also flying English colours, waiting for the Mocha fleet. They were privateers from Rhode Island and Delaware, with licences to raid enemy shipping in the Atlantic, but had decided to try piracy in the Indian Ocean. Seeing Fancy's firepower, they agreed to work for Avery. The collaborating fleet hunted like a pack of wolves over the next few months. One of the ships they captured was the Fateh Mahmudi, bigger than the Fancy, but armed with only six guns. The ship belonged to the Surat merchant Abdul Ghafur, and yielded £100,000 worth in gold and silver, enough to purchase the Fancy many times over!

Just two days later, the pirates came across the enormous Ganj-i-Sawai, owned by Mughal emperor Aurangzeb himself. The ship was heavily armed and confidently prepared to put up a fight. However, as the battle began, one of the Mughal cannons exploded and killed several of the ship's own gunners. Just then, the Fancy fired a full broadside that knocked over the main mast of the Ganj-i-Sawai and turned the main deck into a disarray of rigging and sail. Amidst the confusion, the pirates boarded the crippled ship and took it over. The Mughal captain would later be accused of cowardice.

According to stories that would later circulate in the taverns in England, the ship was carrying the stunningly beautiful granddaughter of the Mughal emperor. Avery immediately proposed, and on receiving her consent, married her on board the captured ship. Her gaggle of beautiful hand-maidens was similarly married off to various members of the pirate crew. This is the origin of several

---

viii One-masted sailing boats

Hollywood scripts. The reality was that Avery presided over an orgy of violence, and several women preferred to kill themselves by jumping into the sea. The treasure they found on the Ganj-i-Sawai is said to have been worth £150,000 in gold, silver, ivory and jewels. The pirate ships headed for the island of Reunion in the Indian Ocean, where they shared out the loot before heading their separate ways. Avery and his crew headed for Nassau in the Bahamas, where they too split up. Some of the pirates were later apprehended, but the captain himself simply vanished. Avery became a legend. For the next couple of decades, rumours would circulate among the world's sailors that Avery made his way back to Madagascar, where he lived with the Mughal princess in a heavily-fortified pirate hideout. This legend inspired a new generation of pirates.

The victims ascribed the attack to Englishmen closely connected with the Bombay factory. Some of them said that at the time of plunder, they recognized some Englishmen. Tremendous pressure prevailed upon the Governor Itimad Khan to punish the English. On 14 September, he sent a party of regular troops under his Lieutenant Ashur Beg to occupy the Surat factory, and confine the merchants there. Forty-nine Englishmen, including President Annesley and other members of the Surat Council, even interlopers like John Vaux and Uphill who had been expelled from East India Company's service, were imprisoned. At Swally, sailors of the ship Benjamin were jailed too. At Broach also, their arms were confiscated and the factors imprisoned. Their trade was totally stopped. Annesley, the President, protested to the governor and the emperor, upon which the emperor demanded that the English, the Dutch and French should scour the seas in pursuit of the pirates and provide a regular escort for the pilgrim ships making the trip to Mocha, till this demand was satisfied. "European trade would be stopped and the prisoners detained till piracy stops." This order dated 12 January 1699 asked all Europeans to either undertake to pay compensation in future, or leave the Mughal Empire. Annesley offered to provide an escort for the convoying of pilgrim ships between Surat and Jeddah, and finally, the port was reopened and the prisoners released. For some time, all went well. Itimad Khan introduced the system of a convoy to the Red Sea. Both the Dutch and the English were to detach one or more ships every season, to escort Indian vessels to and from Mocha. These European warships would for the time, be in Mughal service, and they would be paid according to a fixed rate. For a large ship, the payment for a round trip would be Rs 20,000; for a smaller ship, it would be Rs 5,000. Half the payment was to be borne by the imperial treasury and the other half of the payment was to be borne by the merchant whose ship was to make a trip.[56] European Factors had to sign the undertaking. The Indian Ocean was divided into zones among the three companies – the French were given the Persian Gulf, the Dutch were given the Arab coast from Muscat to Jeddah, and the English, the South, which took in the West coast of the Indian and Indonesia areas. The idea was that they would be responsible for the piracies committed in their areas, and if piracy was committed in their area, either they would capture the pirates or pay money. On 2 February 1698, William Kidd captured Quedah Merchant, 400 tonnes, bound from Bengal to Surat, with a rich cargo worth 4 lakhs of rupees belonging to Mukhlis Khan, one of the nobles of the Mughal Empire. Its captain was an Englishman, the gunner was French, and there were two Dutchmen as well. Therefore, all three nations were held responsible for this piracy. In August, the emperor ordered that all three nations pay damages amounting to 14 lakhs. A guard was placed on the English factory and they had to pay 2 lakh rupees as compensation.

Piracy was a sensitive issue for the Mughals as it undermined trade and commerce and affected the revenues accruing from trading activities indirectly. When an imperial ship was attacked, however, it amounted to an open infringement upon sovereign authority. Perhaps no one suffered more from all this piracy than Abdul Ghafur of Surat, the owner of the largest trading fleet in the Indian Ocean. He repeatedly complained to the Mughal authorities, who in turn, accused the European companies of aiding the pirates. The Ganj-i-Sawai incident was the last straw. The Europeans were also forced to pay compensation to Indian merchants who lost their ships to European pirates.[57]

The Dutch, however, asked for a monopoly of trade in the Mughal Empire in lieu of convoying the Red Sea fleet. The Dutch threatened to abandon trade rather than pay damages. But they signed bonds to suppress piracy and jointly engage with the Mughals to make good all future losses.

English fortunes at Surat had reached its lowest ebb. Their trade had been almost extinguished, and at this critical moment, Annesley was replaced, on 13 May 1698, by Stephen Colt, his junior in the council. President Colt emphatically denied any responsibility for these piracies, as it was not possible for him to meet the demand without consulting the authorities in London. The result was the arrest and imprisonment of all English merchants at Surat.

The prospect of a settlement seemed remote on account of a strong representation made to the emperor, that in spite of repeated orders, the Company had not yet discharged its debts. It was further complicated at this juncture, by the fact that an English ship had again captured one of Abdul Ghafur's ships sailing from Mocha, along with three other ships carrying considerable sums of money. In December 1701, acting upon instructions, the governor seized some of the Company's factors at Surat, forbade the entry of all provisions, and confiscated goods amounting to over Rs 140,000. These were given to Abdul Ghafur as part of the compensation for losses incurred through the pirates.

Piracy vs Privateering

In international law, privateers are defined as "vessels belonging to private owners, and sailing under a commission of war empowering the person to whom it is granted to carry on all forms of hostility which are permissible at sea by the usages of war." Privateers are usually required to post a bond to ensure their compliance with the government's instructions, and their commissions are subject to inspection by public warships.[58] In contrast, "piracy may be said to consist in acts of violence done upon the ocean or un-appropriated lands, or within the territory of a state through descent from the sea, by a body of men acting independently of any politically organized society."[59] But, to put things very simply, privateers were pirates having the support of a state and who shared the plunder with the sovereign.

English privateering apparently began in the 1200s, when the king ordered vessels of the Cinque Ports (Hastings, Hythe, Dover, Sandwich, and Romney)[60] to attack France. In 1243, Henry III issued the first privateer commissions, which provided that the king would receive half the proceeds. The English monarchy was also the first to issue a letter of marque,[61] which was directed against Portugal in 1295. Letters of marque, which were issued in peacetime, allowed individuals to seek redress for depredations they suffered at the hands of foreigners on the high seas. By the 13th century, in an attempt to gain control over this incessant private warfare, many governments provided that a private person could only take up arms with the sovereign's permission in the form of a letter of marque or reprisal. For example, if an Englishman's vessel were attacked by a Frenchman, a letter of marque would authorize the Englishman to seize something of equal value from any French vessel he encountered.

Privateering was a strictly wartime practice in which states authorized individuals to attack enemy commerce and to keep some portion of what they captured as their pay. Early on, however, the two practices became confused, apparently because whenever a war broke out, each party always claimed to be the party aggrieved, and when it justified its acts of hostility at all, it did so by connecting them in some way with the notion of reprisals. Already, boundaries between the legitimate and illegitimate were under practical challenge.

England had gained naval superiority over Spain largely through the action of the Elizabethan Sea Dogs.[62] These private adventurers, in collusion with the English Crown, engaged in all kinds of violent activities directed against Spain in the New World. Besides plundering Spanish ships and settlements, Sea Dogs such as Drake, Cavendish, Clifford[ix] and Raleigh engaged in what might be termed as state-sponsored terrorism. For example, Drake extorted large ransoms from two Spanish colonial cities by threatening to burn them to the ground. He actually destroyed three other cities. His sack of Peru netted him and his backers £2. 5 million, and repaid his backers, including Elizabeth, "47 for 1". Cumberland, leading a purely private expedition, captured Puerto Rico in 1598.[63] Other Sea Dogs behaved similarly, plundering, destroying and extorting their way to fame and fortune in England, and sharing their loot with the English Crown. Drake and Raleigh, of course, were knighted for their achievements.[64]

Mercantile companies were, as a rule, granted full sovereign powers. In addition to their economic privileges of a monopoly on trade with a given region or in a particular

ix The third earl of Cumberland.

commodity, and the right to export bullion,[65] they could raise an army or a navy, build forts, make treaties, make war, govern their fellow nationals, and coin their own money.[66] The companies' outposts were headed by governors who "remained the appointees of the companies, as did the military officers, even when they were officially invested with their offices by their governments."[67] The English East India Company,[x] was in 1661, granted a new charter that "gave the Company criminal and civil jurisdiction 'over all persons belonging to the said Governor and Company or that shall live under them'; it empowered the Company to make war or peace with non-Christian princes or people; and it authorized the Company to erect fortifications and to export munitions from England." The reason the companies needed the military element of the infrastructure – armies, navies, forts, and so on – was, according to their defenders, to protect the trade against attacks by 'rampaging natives", other Europeans, and pirates.

In the late 1670s, the English president at Surat was appointed Captain-General, Admiral and Commander-in-Chief of the Company's forces in all its possessions, and Director-General of all its mercantile affairs. He established the English company's first regular military force made up of infantry, cavalry and artillery. Eurasians and Indians made up these regular forces, with Indian mercenaries recruited as needed to supplement the regulars.[68] Once the English company's conflict with the Dutch company subsided and its principal foe became the French, it began to rely more on Europeans, especially Swiss and German mercenaries.[69]

Towards the end of the 17th century, piracy went out of hand and became a menace the world over – from the Americas to the Indian coast to China. The conversion of privateering from "patriotic piracy" into "a kind of piracy

---

x The Governor and Company of Merchants of London Trading to the East Indies.

which disgraces our Civilization"[70] was revealed. There simply is no doubt that piracy was a legitimate practice in the early European state system. Pirates brought revenue to the sovereign, public officials, and private investors. They weakened enemies by attacking their shipping and settlements. They supplied European markets with scarce goods at affordable prices. They broke competing states' trade monopolies. The most successful of the British pirates were knighted and/or given important posts in the Royal Navy or the British Admiralty.[71] By the early 18th century, however, pirates were being hanged *en masse* in public executions. Privateers were implicated in piracy for a number of complex reasons. Some privateers faced prosecution for piracy. The question was, if no state exerts authority over the high seas, who is responsible for individual acts of violence launched from the sea? If individual states do not assert jurisdiction over the seas, then "unless complete lawlessness is to be permitted to exist, jurisdiction must be exercised either exclusively by each state over persons and property belonging to it, or concurrently with other members of the body of states over all persons and property, to whatever country they may belong."[72] Clearly, the former became the normal practice towards the end of the 17th century.

The first state to define piracy as a problem and one within its own empire, was England. Formerly a great beneficiary of piracy, the English, towards the end of the 17th century, faced a situation in which the East India Company was demanding the Royal Navy's protection against English pirates, who were operating in collusion with English colonists (in Americas), to plunder English commerce in the East. Rather than providing protection for this trade, the Mughals in India demanded that the company assume responsibility for the safety of Indian ships. In Mughal view, the pirates were English-speaking, and therefore, were probably operating in concert with their countrymen in the Company. The problem was that once the Company began convoying the Mughal ships, the pirates no longer saw any reason to refrain from attacking the company's ships along with the others. In essence, it was the Mughals who defined English piracy as a problem for the English company to deal with, and the English company in turn, defined it as a problem for the State's attention.

But sending the Royal Navy to patrol the Eastern waters merely motivated the pirates to move to the Bahamas. In order to permanently resolve the piracy problem, England had to put its own house in order. American colonial markets for pirate booty had to be suppressed. Plunder of pirate attack used to be openly sold in markets in American English colonies. Colonial legal systems were strengthened, corrupt officials replaced and a new government for the Bahamas established. Pirate attacks on the Americans' own shipping contributed to the decline in colonial support for piracy.

But having suppressed piracy in the Americas, it was found that this had merely succeeded in driving the pirates back to Madagascar. This time, Company complaints about them led to the quick despatch of Royal Navy vessels to the region. So, in the case of major, organized piracy, it was the Mughals of India who alone among those who defined piracy as a problem, were able, through pressure on the East India Company, to define piracy as a problem for England.

References

[1] Irfan Habib, "Changes in Technology in Medieval India", paper presented at the Symposium on Technology and Society, Indian History Congress, 1979.

[2] A. J. Qaiser, *Indian Response to European Technology and Culture (I498-I707A.D.),* DeM, 1982, pp. 35-77, 139.

[3] Jauhar Aftabchi, *Tazkira-ul-Waqiat,* tr. Charles Stewart, Calcutta, 1904, p168; Also see Niccolao Manucci, Storia Do

Mogor, 1656-1712, translated with Introduction and Notes by William Irvine, 4 vols., Calcutta, 1966, vol. iii, Pt. iii, p. 214.

[4] Abul Fazl, *Akbarnama*, vol. III, p. 275;Badauni also testifies to the fact that Akbar detested Portuguese control of the high seas. Abdul Qadir Badauni, Muntakhab-ul-Tawarikh, vol II, p. 150.

[5] M. N. Pearson, *The Portuguese in India*, Hyderabad, 1987, p. 27.

[6] Diego de Carto, Da Asia, Decada IX Lisboa,1786,Part1, p64-87. Cf. K. S. Matthew, Akbar and Portuguese Maritime Dominance, Akbar and His India, Irfan Habib (ed.), Delhi, 1997, p. 257.

[7] EFI, 1618-21, pp. 12-13.

[8] Orme, Robert *Historical Fragments of Mughal Empire* 1659-1689, pp. 323-4.

[9] Foster, W. (ed.) Early Travels in India 1583-1619, p. 66.

[10] EFI, 1624-29, pp. 20-21,310.

[11] Foster, W. (ed.) Thomas Roe, The Embassy of Sir Thomas Roe, 1615-19, p. 308.

[12] Foster, W. (ed.) Thomas Roe, The Embassy of Sir Thomas Roe, 1615-19, p. 485.

[13] EFI, 1624-29, pp. 20-21,310.

[14] Foster, W. (ed.) Thomas Roe, The Embassy of Sir Thomas Roe, 1615-19,p. 27, 303.

[15] Foster, W. (ed.) Thomas Roe, The Embassy of Sir Thomas Roe, 1615-19, pp. 307-08.

[16] Foster, W. (ed.) Thomas Roe, The Embassy of Sir Thomas Roe, 1615-19, p. 52.

[17] Foster, W. (ed.) Thomas Roe, The Embassy of Sir Thomas Roe, 1615-19, p. 52.

[18] EFI, vol. I, pp. 134-35.

[19] Farhat Hasan, Two Official Documents of Jahangir's Reign relating to the English East India Company, p. 333, Indian History Congress, Amritsar Session, 1985, (cyclostyled).

[20] EFI,1624-29, p. 258.

[21] The English Factories in India, 1618-21, ed. W. Foster, vol. i, p. 174.

[22] EFI,1634-36,pp. 70-71.

[23] EFI,1634-36,p. 157.

[24] President Methwold's Diary, 22 January-6 April 1636.

[25] EFI,1634-36, p157, xvi.

[26] Tavernier, Jean-Baptiste Travels in India, 1640-67, vol. i, pp. 6-7.

[27] EFI, 1634-36, p. 57.

[28] EFI, 1618-21, p138, 237. Also see The Diaries of Streysham Master, 1675-80, ed. R. C. Temple, London, 1911, vol. II, p. 35.

[29] Purchas His Pilgrims vol. iii, p. 176; vol. iv, p 224-5; EFI, 1618-21, p. 19.

[30] EFI, 1651-54, p. 12.

[31] Shireen Moosvi, *Mughal shipping at Surat in the first half of Seventeenth Century*, p. 312, Indian History Congress, Calcutta Session, 1990.

[32] English Factories in India, 1634-6, p. 88.

[33] Ibid., pp. 21-22.

[34] Letter to Mirza Mahmud (English Factories, 1634-6, p. 199).

[35] Methwold's narrative, ibid, p. 232.

[36] Report, ibid., p. 265.

[37] Records, Court Book 17, p. 385.

[38] Court Minutes, 1635-9, p. 127.

[39] English Factories, 1637-41, p 243, 289.

[40] English Factories, 1637-41, p. 310.

[41] English Factories, 1637-41, p 249-51, and 1642-5, p. 58.

[42] Court Minutes, 1644-9, introduction.

[43] English Factories, 1651-54, p. 146.

[44] English Factories, 1651-54, p. 170.

[45] Court Minutes, 1650-4, p. xxi, introd.

[46] Ibid., 1655-59, p i-viii, introd.

[47] Khafi Khan, *Muntakhab-ul-Lubab,* Calcutta, 1870,vol. II,p. 428.

[48] M. N. Pearson, *The Portuguese in India,* p. 78.

[49] Jourdain, The Journal of John Jourdain, 1608-17, p. 173.

[50] MSS. Historical Archives of Goa, Codex no. 1043 f. 150, cf. K. S. Mathew, Akbar and Portuguese Maritime Dominance, Akbar and His India, Delhi, 1997, p. 264.

[51] Ashin Das Gupta and M. N. Pearson(ed.), *India and the Indian Ocean,* 1500-1800, p. 85.

[52] Letters Received, vol. I, p. 279.

[53] EFI, 1622-3, p. xv.

[54] Foster, W. (ed.) Thomas Roe, The Embassy of Sir Thomas Roe, 1615-19, p. 204.

[55] EFI, 1622-23, p. xvi.

[56] Das, Harihar: *The Norris Embassy to Aurangzeb*, 1699-1702, p. 113.

[57] Das, Harihar: *The Morris Embassy to Aurangzeb*, 1699-1702, p. 34.

[58] William Edward Hall, *A Treatise on International Law*, 8th ed., ed. A. Pearce Higgins (Oxford: Clarendon Press, 1924), 620–21.

[59] Ibid., 314.

[60] Sherry, Raiders and Rebels, p. 57.

[61] See Francis R. Stark, "The Abolition of Privateering and the Declaration of Paris", in *Studies in History, Economics and Public Law*, ed. the Faculty of Political Science of Columbia University, vol. 8, no. 3 (New York, 1897), pp. 52–53.

[62] Kenneth R. Andrews, Elizabethan Privateering: *English Privateering during the Spanish War, 1585–1603* (Cambridge: Cambridge University Press, 1964), 198–99. Elizabeth's privateers' prizes amounted to "some ten to fifteen per cent of England's total imports." Ibid., p. 128.

[63] Andrews, Elizabethan. *Privateering*, pp. 77-78 and 177.

[64] Stark, "Abolition", 61–64. See also James G. Lydon, Pirates, Privateers and Profits (Upper Saddle River, N. J. : Gregg, 1970), 27–28; and Hugh F. Rankin, The Golden Age of Piracy (New York: Holt, Rinehart and Winston, 1969), pp. 3–5.

[65] K. N. Chaudhuri, "The East India Company and the Export of Treasure in the Early Seventeenth Century", Economic History Review, 2d ser. 16 (1963): pp. 23–38; idem, *The English East India Company: A Study of an Early Joint-Stock Company, 1600–1640* (New York: Augustus M. Kelley, 1965), p. 13.

[66] Furber, *Rival Empires*, 91.

[67] Coornaert, "European Economic Institutions", 249.

[68] Furber, *Rival Empires*, pp. 93-94.

[69] Ibid., p. 150.

[70] Stark, "Abolition", p. 66,70.

[71] Julian S. Corbett, *England in the Seven Years' War* (London: Longmans, Green, 1907), p. 26.

[72] Piggott, Declaration of Paris, p. 121.

Chapter 6
Life at the Surat Factory

In 1612, English merchants received permission to settle for trade at Surat. In time, they built a factory and in 1618, established the hierarchy and precedence of their community, the chief of the factory taking the title of President, in imitation of the Dutch. Surat lies twelve miles up the river Tapti, on the fertile plains of Gujarat. Few boats came up the river to Surat, and these few were always flat-bottomed coasting vessels. The ocean-going European merchants anchored at the port of Swally. There, one could always count the masts of several hundred ships, only a minority of them European. Arab dhows with red sails, Chinese ships, and Mughal vessels carrying pilgrims to Jeddah, the port of Mecca, were more numerous. The first experience of life at Surat for the Europeans was at the customs office at the Surat port. European travellers found the customs examination a tedious ordeal. Every trunk, box and parcel had to be opened and sometimes shoes and hats were removed and peered into.[1] Fryer says: *"The Custom-house has a good front, where the chief customer appears certain hours to chop (chaap = stamp), that is, to mark goods outward-bound, and clear those received in."* The place was usually filled with officials and their servants, merchants and their brokers. The customs officials wandered about the port with a retinue of black slaves, mostly from Abyssinia, carrying whips to dissuade intending smugglers. They were little kings in their own domain and levied duty on articles at their own valuation. They insisted on levying duty even on the buttons worn by Europeans in their coats, not only on their first arrival at the port, but each time they left their ships. This was particularly annoying for the pursers of

English ships who often had to make several visits ashore to arrange for the re-provisioning of their ships. As one of them complained, *"in a short time, the very intrinsick value of the buttonnes would be spent in customs"*. If the customs officials found anything especially attractive in the foreigner's luggage, they would put it on one side, pretending that they were not sure of the rate at which customs-dues should be levied on this article, and the owner never saw it again.

Emerging from the customs, a newly-arrived would hire a conveyance to take him to Surat. There was a wide choice in carriages. One could travel in a chariot drawn by two buffaloes attended by local footboys, or one could engage a coach, as most English merchants used to, drawn by two white oxen *"with circling horns as black as coal, each point tipped with brass, from whence came brass chains across to the headstall which is all of scarlet, their flapping ears snipped with art"*. Jangling and jolting, the carriage carried the traveller through the alleys of the port. Beggars stared at the foreigner and clamoured for bakshish. But, as Fryer noticed with relief, you were not troubled. Their main fault was their curiosity. They followed every foreigner with inquisitive comments. Otherwise *"they are very respectful unless they get drunk, when are they Monarchs and it is madness to oppose them"*.[2] It was a relief to come out of the port into open country and enjoy the prospect of wide green fields, richly cultivated. The roads were shady with over-arching banyan-trees and the traveller would remark on the green parrots chortling and screaming as they flew from tree to tree.

From 1609 onwards, there are references to a number of gates through which the city could be entered. In 1609, William Finch saw three gates. One was at the northern end, leading to Broach via Variao, a suburb of the city. The second was the western gate leading to Burhanpur, and the third, the southern, leading to Navsari. In 1630, Peter Mundy mentions some seven gates, though he names only three, those already listed by Finch. De Laet also mentions three gates, while Ovington refers to six or seven gates *"where are sentinels fixed continually requiring account, upon the least suspicion, of all that enter in, or pass out of the city"*. The inner walls were called Saharpanah (succour of the city) while the outer walls were named, rather pretentiously, Alampanah (succour of the world).

Then, at a distance one could see the Surat fort, surrounded by strong walls and a wide ditch, the circumference of wall being punctuated by canons for safety as well as grandeur. It was built in 1540 to protect the city against the Portuguese, by one Khudawand Khan, a minister of the Sultan of Gujarat, Mahmud II. The length of the wall was thirty-five yards and the breadth, fifteen yards, and their height as well as the depth of the moat was twenty yards. The centres of every two stones were joined with iron clamps and the interstices and joints were made firm with molten lead. The battlements and embrasures were lofty and elegant. On the bastions which overlooked the sea, a gallery was made, which in the opinion of the Europeans, was a Portuguese invention. During Akbar's siege in 1572-1573, some breaches were caused to the walls which the emperor later ordered to be repaired. When he inspected the fort after its surrender to him, he came across large cannons and immense pieces of ordnance. They had been brought by sea by Sultan Sulaiman, the Emperor of Turkey, when he came with a large army intending to take possession of the ports of Gujarat. However, due to adverse circumstances, his army retired and the cannons from that time were left behind on the river bank. At the time of building of Surat, Khudawand Khan brought most of them into the fort, and the remainder, the Governor of Junagarh dragged to his own fortress. The emperor commanded that they be removed from there and be carried to the fortress of Agra.

"There were many fountains and rivulets of fresh water and Grottoes descending underground by huge Arches and Stone Steps shaded by Trees on each hand. And so, passing through the clamour of the streets thronged with as cosmopolitan a crowd as you could find anywhere in Asia, the traveller reached at last the English factory and must have felt a sober satisfaction to note that it was built of stone and excellent timber with good carvings, without representations, very strong for that each floor is half a yard thick at least, of the best cement, very weighty... with upper and lower galleries, or terras walks. The President had spacious lodgings with noble rooms for counsel and entertainment".[3]

In the vicinity of the fort, facing the custom-house, was the Mint, a large set of offices within itself where all the sarrafs or bankers worked. Between the Mint and the custom-house, there was an open stretch of ground called the maidan. About this, Ovington says: *"In the midst of the city is a spacious vacant place, called Castle-green, because of its nearness to the castle, on which are laid all sorts of goods in the open air, both day and night, excepting the Mussoun time. And here the English, French, and Dutch, with the natives, place their bales, and prepare them as loadings for their ships."* This was the open-air bazaar where a large number of buyers and sellers met everyday.

Fryer says that the city smell was very nasty because of the *"want of privies, and their making every door a dunghill; yet never had they any plague, the heats evaporating, and the rains washing this filth away"*. The walls of the fort enclosed only some parts of the city and there was the eagerness for many families, during the second half of 17th century, to move into the protected part because of the fear of Maratha raids. Also, from time to time, the more tyrannical elements among the Muslims were threats to Hindu women, especially after dark. Broecke mentions an incident when a daughter of a prominent broker was abducted from a 'narrow' street by a servant of a Muslim noble and kept in confinement for a few days. She was later released on payment of ransom. Such apprehensions added to the unsanitary state of the city.

Surat had three sarais for lodging for visitors, especially merchants. They were used by the Persian, Armenian, Turkish and Central Asian merchants who frequented Surat during the trading season. One special institution noticed by European travellers was the hospital for animals. Ovington says: *"For within a mile distance from Surat, is a large hospital supported by the Banians in its maintenance of cows, horses, goats, dogs, and other animals diseased, or lame, infirm or decayed by age; for when an ox, by many years of toil grows feeble, and unfit for any further service; lest this should tempt a merciless owner to take away his life, because he finds him an unprofitable burden, and his flesh might be serviceable to him when he was dead; therefore the Banian reprieves his destiny and the animal is placed in the shelter to spend the rest of its life."*

The first English factory was established near the house of Mulla Badkani. This place was used for trade from 1612 A.D. to 1800 A.D. The English rented another house with a terrace, upper rooms and warehouses from Khwaja Arab Turbati in 1616, on lease for three years.[4] After the expiry of the term of lease, the Mughal officials, presumably for security reasons, strictly forbade the heirs of Arab Turbati[i] from renewing the lease and ordered them to evict the English out of their house.[5] In March 1619, on expiry of the lease, the English had to accommodate themselves in three separate dwellings at some distance from one another, besides having to hire three other houses for warehouses and a set of stables, however, none convenient for lodging or with sufficient warehousing space. It was not until 1623 that they were able to occupy the building owned by Khwaja Hasan Ali with a garden, stables and other conveniences. It was to this house that William Methwold, who was the President of the English factory from 1633 to 1639, came on

i Arab Turbati had died in the meantime.

his arrival. A description of the English house in Surat in 1629-1630 just before Methwold's arrival is given by Peter Mundy: *"Surat house is of the best sort in town, very fair and strongly built, the roofs in general flat and terraced aloft to walk on, very substantially done with lime etc. so that no rain can pierce it, and below a fair hall, chambers and rooms for the President and Council etc. merchants, with complete warehouses, walks (etc.) below. We have also a garden which for its bigness is the neatest and costliest in all the country hereabouts; being near 4 square, having 4 very fair long walks round about, all covered over with vines supported with timber; very curiously contrived. It hath 4 other allies which go from the middle of the long walks into the middle of the garden, where stands a chowtree (chabutra), or pretty room, covered overhead to sit and pass the time. Before it stands a little tank to wash in time of heats and rain, in the midst of which is a spout, which at pleasure is let to run, upon which they add others (as occasion serveth) among the rest, this first six spouts running outwards from the top of the main spout, and one right up, over which is a round plate fastened so that the water, striking with violence against it, causeth it to diffuse and disperse itself so equally, every way, and every part of tire water so conjoining with the other that it perfectly resembles the half of a great glass globe or a crystal cupola, the edge whereof is again by the under spoutes cut into so many divisions like the valens of a canopy"*. The water for this fountain came from a well and was drawn by oxen. It was in this garden that the German traveller Mandelso was invited to a grand party given on the occasion of the transfer of charge from Methwold to his successor William Fremlin in 1639. All the English employees had then assembled to listen to an oration followed by a great dinner, at which various delicacies were served.

Another description of the English house, as it was toward the end of the 17th century, is provided by Ovington: *"The house provided for the English at Surat belongs to the Mughal, and is fitted with the best accommodations in the city. It is situated in the north-west part of it, and is able to give convenient lodgings to forty persons, besides several decent apartments to the President."* The English buildings formed a rectangle, with a courtyard separating the two wings. The main gateway was on the south of a bend in the river and led to the administrative offices on the ground floor in the western wing. The private quarters of the President and other members were situated on the upper storeys. The eastern block consisted of storerooms, and besides these, were the rooms for the servants. The whole complex was fortified with a strong wall. An inventory of articles at the Surat house dated 6 December 1629 makes interesting reading. It had 'silver plate'[ii] worth 2,639 mahmudis, copper utensils, brassware, chairs, stools, tables, cots, carpets, table linen, seven horses, oxen, one great coach and five small ones, tents with their furniture, china (porcelain wares were referred as china or fine china in those days) and earthenware, and a garden valued at Rs 1,000 or 2,250 mahmudis. The clerks used sercatores or desks, paper secured either from Ahmedabad or England, and some 1,000 quills a year. By the 1660s, the house had its own modest library with six volumes of books containing the Old and New Testaments in Hebrew and other languages.

An essential part of the factory was the warehouse where the goods brought in from England or other countries as well as commodities meant for export were to be stored, awaiting transportation to their destinations. In places where built-up warehouses were not available, goods were stored under a thatched roof or chappar. The Company also had a warehouse at Swally, which was surrounded by a thick hedge of thorns to prevent thefts. The Surat warehouses were well-guarded and the establishment always had a good supply of firearms and ammunition.

---

ii Spoons, wine cups, an ewer and basin, beer bowls, saltcellars, a rosewater bottle, a betel box, a spittoon, etc.

Fryer, in 1673, described the daily life as: *"The House the English live in at Surat, is partly the King's gift, partly hired; built of stone and excellent timber, with good carving, without representations; very strong, for that each floor is half a yard thick at least, of the best plastered cement, which is very weighty. It is contrived after the Moor's buildings, with upper and lower galleries, or Terras-walks; a neat oratory, a convenient open place for meals. The President has spacious lodgings, noble rooms for counsel and entertainment, pleasant tanks, yards, and an hummum to wash in; but no gardens in the city, or very few, though without they have many, like wildernesses, overspread with trees. The English had a neat one, but Seva Gi's coming, destroyed it: It is known, as the other factories are, by their several flags flying."*

The English continuously maintained a full battery of personnel – President, chaplain, factors, writers and apprentices from 1613. These men were responsible for ordering and gathering the company's investment or yearly stock of Indian goods destined for England. From the roof of their establishment rose a number of flag-poles, with English flags moving in the wind. This dignified exterior was, however, somewhat spoiled by the confusion and uproar in the courtyard where the packers and warehouse-keepers, together with merchants bringing and receiving goods for business, for *"if you make not a noise, they hardly think you intent on what you are doing"*.[6]

The head of the factory was called the President and he lived in almost as great a style as the Mughal governor. Outside the door of his bedchamber, servants stood with silver staves and when he came out, they followed him from room to room. If he went downstairs, guards came to attention in the hall, and if he left the factory, they marched with him. He was provided with "well-filled stables for pleasure or services" and he had his own chaplain, physician, surgeon, linguist and mint-master. At his entry into the dining-room, trumpets blew and while he sat at table, violins played softly. All the English merchants dined together in the hall of the factory, the President sitting at the head of the table and the others seated around him in order of seniority. On church festival days, they dined in the gardens outside the city. They went in solemn procession, the President and his lady in a palanquin with banners ahead, or in ox-drawn coaches of special splendour, each having "a four-Square Seat, inlaid with Ivory", and the factors on Arabian horses whose saddles were of embroidered velvet and whose headstalls, reins and cruppers were of solid silver. All the dishes and drinking-vessels were of solid silver. Each diner was attended by a servant with a silver basin and ewer, so that he might wash both before and after the meal. A peculiarly English grace prescribed by the elders of the council, was intoned by the chaplain. "We, Thy unworthy creatures do most humbly; implore Thy goodness for a plentiful effusion of Thy grace upon our employers, that we may live virtuously in due obedience to our superiors".

Rising at dawn, the factor would 'comfort' his stomach with 'burnt wine'. At six, he would hurry to the chapel, unless he wished to incur the fine of half a crown for non-attendance. After prayers, the factory gates would be thrown open, and the baniyas and traders would stream in. Till noon, pandemonium reigned in the courtyard, when business was closed down at four, and the factors, all except the President, adjourned to the dining hall. They dined early, and the lunch (curiously, the records mention mid-day meal as dinner) was a portentous affair. All the dishes were of pure silver and substantial, and so were the 'tosses' or cups. Silver was cheaper than china or glass, hence the abundance of silver plate in all well-to-do establishments of the 17th century. Before the meal, a large silver ewer and basin for washing the hands was taken around by a peon.

Indian, Portuguese and English cooks were employed, so as to please the curiosity of every palate.

Generally, there were several courses in the meal. 'Cabob' was a favourite dish, followed by 'dumpoked fowl',[iii] that is, chicken boiled in butter and stuffed with raisins and almonds and mango pickle. This was washed down with plenty of Shiraz wine and arrack punch, served around the table. On Sundays, for dinner, there would be "deer and antelopes, peacocks, hares and partridges and all kinds of Persian fruits, Pistachios, Plums, Apricots, Cherries". European wines and bottled beer were added. The meal sometimes ran to sixteen courses. This explains the complaint that excessive indulgence in meat and alcohol was responsible for many deaths and much more sickness. But meat was sometimes scarce and though the senior merchants never went without meat, the common sailors had to do without it twice a week, contenting themselves with saffron rice. Beef was unprocurable. Captain Downton had attempted to start an abattoir, that is a slaughter house, but local Hindu merchants bribed the Mughal governor to prohibit this. Pork was, of course, unheard of in Muslim territory, and so the English had to satisfy their 17th century appetites with mutton and chicken. At first, some of the young factors tried to supplement their meagre diet by shooting doves and pigeons, but the local Hindus would implore them not to do this, and would, as a last resort, offer them money to spare the poor birds. This method of persuasion was so successful that it became a regular practice for impecunious young sportsmen (the contrast between their splendid style of living and their small salaries was responsible for general indebtedness among all the junior factors) to take out a gun near some rich Hindu's house and talk loudly and ferociously about the number of pigeons they would

iii Persian dampukhta = stewed

massacre that afternoon, till the man ran out of his house with tears in his eyes and money in his hands.

Only on Sundays were European wines served at the table. On weekdays, they drank Persian wines and more commonly, arak. Arak was evidently an acquired taste and the French traveller Bernier was surprised at the English liking for it. He described it as "*a drink very hot and penetrating like the brandy made of corn. It so falls upon the nerves that it often causeth shaking hands to those who drink a little too much of it*". On the other hand, Captain Symson attributed to arak various medicinal properties. It was "good for the gripes... in the morning laxative and in the evening, astringent". But he added that immoderate indulgence in arak made drinkers "*so restless that no place is cool enough; and therefore, they lie down on the ground all night which occasions their being snatched away in a very short time*". Occasionally, the factors dined with their Muslim friends and found the pulavs and biryanis delicious. These meals were, however, of enormous length and coffee was served between courses. Regarding the drinking habits of Muslim friends, Fryer writes, "they were not content with such little glasses as we drink out of, nor Claret nor Rhenish (which they call Vinegar) but Sack and Brandy out of the Bottle". But Western science could still score a minor success, and Indians who first witnessed the opening of a bottle of beer expressed a George II-like surprise at the bubbles and froth. "It is not," they cried, "the sight of the drink flying out of the bottle, but how such liquor could ever be put in".[7] On occasion, however, the effect of beer and brandy on the temper of a Muhammadan not used to alcohol was unfortunate. A party at the Mughal governor's house was interrupted by the host going into a sudden rage with some dancing-girls and ordering their instant decapitation in the dining-room itself, before the eyes of his startled English guests. Whatever their opinions, however, the guests couldnot have ventured on too open an expression of disapproval, even when they left the palace, for there were spies everywhere. The chief of these spies in Surat was called 'Harcarrah', and he sent his reports directly to the Mughal emperor. He listened to all kinds of news, whether true or false, listened to everything that happened and reported to the Mughal emperor whatever was done or spoken of, but with so soft a pen that nothing may offend him, considering the profound veneration due to such a powerful monarch whose frowns were mortal.[8] On holidays, the factors amused themselves with archery and musket-shooting, or they would just stroll in the bazaar, the temples and the old palaces.

In the initial days, the English factors at the Surat factory were not normal men. Most of them were prisoners from Newgate prison or inmates from the lunatic asylum at Bedlam. India was too distant and the voyage too risky for normal young men to venture into. Their life at the factory resembled those of students in a well-conducted college. All had to sleep in the factory whose gates were open only from dawn till dusk. At night, the Company's servants retired into a virtuous seclusion, congratulating themselves on their self-imposed remoteness from the tumult beyond their gates, where like any other city, Surat awoke to new liveliness in the cool of twilight. And in addition to the strains of music and songs, there came faintly through barred windows, to the ears of the factors, the noise of police activity. Any factor returning to the factory after sunset was fined five weeks' salary, to be distributed among the poor. Absence from prayers, which were held twice daily, incurred a fine of half a crown on weekdays and five shillings on Sundays. There was a variety of punishments for being drunk. Even the maximum amount to be drunk was regulated and though the allowance would appear to be liberal – "not more than half a pint of brandy together with one quart of wine at any meal" – yet, no doubt, many grumbled at the restriction.

But wine was not the only refreshment, for as Mandelso noted, "at our ordinary meetings, we took only tea which is commonly used all over the Indies as a drug that cleanses the stomach and digests the superfluous humours". It was not drunk with milk, though sometimes candy sugar was dissolved in it. But the factors with more delicate palates brewed it with a variety of spices and the more curious ones, with conserved lemons. A few packets were sent home to friends in England where there was an outcry against this 'hay water'. But the doctors, as usual scenting profit in this new drug, were loud in their advocacy of its qualities. For long, however, tea was considered an oddity and, in an order, despatched in 1664, it was included in a cargo of oil of cinnamon, marked as "rarities of birds, beasts or other curiosities".

An effort was made, not very successfully, to reduce the use of alcohol by the use of tea, thereby reducing the mortality caused by excessive drinking. Among the Dutch, the teapot was seldom off the fire, but apparently the English factors, as in Mandelso's days, preferred 'burnt wine', punch and arrack. Ovington wrote very highly of the medicinal properties of tea.

Sundays were tedious, for in addition to the church services, there were two sermons read out by the President. But there were compensations on *"the great Feasts of Christmas and Easter, for then, we have the Solemn Service, publike Feasts and noe great busynes permitted to be done in the factory house and all the country people know why we are soe solemn and feast and are Merry"*. Interest in the arts was viewed with some suspicion, and when one Mr Lenton ventured on an ode (he tried to write a poem and recite in one of the gatherings), he was told "the Court did not well relish his conceits and desired him neither to print them nor proceed any further in making verses". Nor was the local council the only tribunal of taste as the Leadenhall Street[iv] kept a close eye on the morals and behaviour of its employees, and had on every possible occasion commented on it.

To judge by the rules of conduct prescribed for the English merchants in 17th century Surat, it would be difficult to find another community of such sobriety and discipline. Unfortunately, the rules represented an ideal state of conduct and often had little relation to reality. Sir Thomas Roe found most of the factors liable to frequent bouts of drunkenness and to "other exorbitances proceeding from it". Sir Thomas, of course, felt deeply on the subject of Surat liquor since his own servant's drunkenness had caused him some embarrassment. His servant, probably sick to death of ship-board rum, discovered a taste for the Armenian wine which was served to him on the very first day he arrived at Surat. After slaking his thirst, he staggered out into the streets at precisely the same moment when the Mughal governor's brother was passing by with his great train of attendants. Swaying into the middle of the road, he addressed the governor's brother with a "How do you do, you heathen dog?" Fortunately, the governor was in a good humour and when Sir Thomas Roe hurried to apologise, he dismissed the incident with a smile and a suave gesture. This was not poor Sir Thomas's only trouble with a servant in India. One of his fellow countrymen at Agra nearly took him to the gallows, when, in a state of inebriation, he decided to climb up the minaret of a mosque and give call for prayer in the name of Jesus.

The Italian traveller Della Vallee reported that not only the junior factors drank to excess, but that the President himself, as soon as he awoke in the morning, shouted for 'burnt wine' which he "drank frequently to comfort the stomach, sipping it little by little for fear of scalding".

---

iv Headquarters of the Company

The East India Company maintained a policy of not employing gentlemen as factors, or as servants of the Company during the formation years. Initially, the reason for prejudice against employing aristocratic employees or gentlemen as servants of the Company, was the fear that they would not be amenable to the discipline imposed on all the servants of the Company. This prejudice rapidly declined after the fall of Charles I. The Company had to appease the voracious appetites of the Parliamentarian oligarchs by enrolling as many of them as possible among their shareholders and finding jobs for their stupid nephews. With the return of Charles II, courtiers succeeded to the privileged positions of the East India Company's Court of Directors, and a new, almost aristocratic, tone becomes evident in the communications of the Company's servants. *"We thought it necessary,"* they wrote when recounting Streynsham Master's resistance to the Marathas, *"to maintaine your honour and that of the Nation (which wee had hitherto reputably preserved) from any scandall that might be cast upon us of deserting the Towne in Time of danger."* The tone of letters had changed from merchant-like to aristocratic within a span of 50 years.

The changes in manners that marked the Restoration in England had their effect on the life of the Surat factors. The almost convent-like life of the first half of the century was disturbed by a new spirit of atheism and indifference, and in spite of President George Oxenden's order from England for *"a large Table in a frame gilded and handsomely adorned with Moses and Aaron and in ye midst and at ye Topp God's name writt"*, the prevailing sentiment of many of the sceptical or lazy juniors was expressed by Shem Bridges who exclaimed *"that we have divine service once on the Sunday is as much as can be expected in these hot countries"*. Instead of attending the President's sermon, the young factors preferred to spend their time with their fighting cocks, especially imported from Siam, or with their other pets with which the factory was crowded – fantail pigeons, Basra turtle-doves, tame cockatoos and even a performing cassowary. They were less interested in pomp and ceremony than in comfort, and while the officials stationed at Swally, the port of Surat, had been formerly satisfied with tents, they now demanded bungalows. Private rooms began to be furnished with an elegance that disturbed the Directors.

The court of Directors became increasingly anxious at the "riot, prodigality, carelessness and folly and expensive and vicious habits" and soundly denounced its employees as "incorrigible lumber", most of whom ought to be dismissed "in a summary way, without formality of tedious, impertinent examinations or other trumpery". But as threats were more often uttered than put into effect, the factors attended office when they chose to and, in the evenings, strutted around the gardens of Surat in their big hats of velvet and taffeta, with bunches of feathers, followed by troops of servants in elaborate liveries. The uniform of one's servants was an important matter. Even visitors to the factory had to decide how they would dress their retainers. Sir Thomas Roe, after some thought, chose for his servants an elaborate outfit, including "red taffeta cloaks guarded with green taffeta" as the proper dress for an English ambassador to the Mughal court. The extravagance of European costume, the ruffs "of twelve, or sixteen lengths, set three or four times double", the slashed silks and heavy folds of lace, always impressed Indians and brought on awe. Most wore clothes that seem to have differed in no respect, not even in materials, from those worn in London. It was in vain that the Company issued sumptuary decrees directing with a shrewd combination of Puritan sobriety and protectionist zeal. "*...that for the encouraging good husbandry, by preventing the vaine and immoderate excess of apparell... no apparell or outward garments, to wit, Tunicks, vest.*

Doublet, Breeches be used or worn, of what quality, nation and condition soever but such as are made of English manufactures, of silke, wooll or cotton." The Company's employees were less interested in the climate or material of their clothes than in their approximation to the latest fashions at home. They begged their friends in London for advice on dress. No present was more gratefully received than some sample of the recent fads and fancies of the English world. In return, they would send Indian curiosities, and these would often take a strange form in that superstitious age when people expected material benefits from Eastern magic. Sir Streynsham Master sent to his daughter, Lady Coventry, along with the most elaborate directions for use in an Indian silk bag and paper, an Eagle Stone to prevent miscarriages of women with child, to be worn around the neck. Snake Stones, believed to be an infallible protection against the cobra bite was another popular gift sent to England by the factors.

It must have seemed a waste of all this male finery that there were so few women to admire the feathered hats, watered silks and lace cuffs. English women were rare and though on festive occasions, the local Armenian and Portuguese ladies might sit at the table with the English merchants, such reunions were not encouraged, for there was "*no knowing when some Englishman might wish to marry a Portuguese and then the children through their father's neglect, be brought up in the Roman Catholic principles, to the great dishonour and weakening of the Protestant religion*". The Dutch merchants of Surat had no such foresight and often married Catholics. Many of these Portuguese women had started for India as the intended wives of officials in Goa, as the Portuguese government in its concern for the morals of its employees in the East, used to send out annual batches of women who had failed to find husbands at home. It was assumed that the obedient officials might not cavil at such trifles as lack of physical attraction, and thus, sent with them substantial dowries. These women, however, as often as not, were provided by fate with non-Portuguese husbands in other parts of India, their ships being captured by pirates and they themselves despatched to the slave-market at Surat. A famous beauty of 17th century Surat was one Donna Lucia, who having arrived at Surat in this manner, attracted the attention of a rich Dutchman. They were married by the rites of the Dutch Reformed Church and all the foreign merchants in Surat attended the wedding dinner. It was a successful marriage and the English merchants found, as a proof of the Dutchman's unreasoning devotion, that he allowed his wife to practise her religion, though in private. Some of these Portuguese captives brought to Surat reached even more exalted stations. In the 16th century, one had become an empress and another, the wife of a Mughal Chamberlain, the renegade Bourbon, the founder of the house of the Bhopal Bourbons.[v]

Most, however, were bundled into the harems of local officials and were never heard of again. Senior members of the English Company discussed the dangers of these Catholic women and warned susceptible juniors against their seductive charms. But no one seems to have thought of the emotions of these mild convent-bred girls looking forward to a quiet and dutiful existence as wives of minor civil servants, caught away suddenly from their curtain-shaded cabins and their stout duennas, and paraded through the cosmopolitan bazaars of Surat with less ceremony than a herd of cattle.

The medical facilities available to European merchants at Surat left much to be desired. Many of the deaths which the factors ascribed to Surat heat were really due to the

v She married Jean-Philip, the French noble who was granted a small principality around present day Bhopal and a Portuguese wife by Akbar.

ordinary diseases, aided by the antics of contemporary surgeons. Cholera, for example, was considered to be due to eating fish and meat together. The favourite method of treating cholera was to apply a red-hot iron to the patient's foot. If he winced, that was proof he would recover; if he gave no sign of pain then all hope was to be abandoned. How many cures resulted from these methods of treatment are not recorded. The doctor, having delivered this diagnosis, pocketed his fee and drove to the next patient's house. With the advance of science, new methods came into favour and for a time, the following treatment was recommended as invaluable in all fevers.

"Take an iron ring about an inch and a half in diameter and thick in proportion. Then heating it red hot in the fire, make the patient lie on his back, and apply the ring to his navel, in such a manner that the navel may be as a centre to the ring. As soon as the patient feels the heat takes away the ring as quick as possible when a sudden revolution will be wrought in his intestines." And the Company was, as always, less interested in the physical, than in the spiritual health of its employees.

With almost limitless credit (local banias were always ready to give credit), life was easy even for most junior clerks. No work was done after one o'clock[9] when everyone went home for lunch, which was eaten in wigs and flowered coats, to the accompaniment of violins. The gentlemen toasted each other with Madeira or Shiraz wine served in cups of rhinoceros horn, which was thought to be an antidote against poison. After food, there would be a long siesta, and in the evening, hairdressers came to attend to gentlemen's wigs before they left their rooms for an evening ride or a formal visit. Servants were mostly slaves from the Malabar.[vi] They were so cheap that they were exported in great numbers, though never with the reckless indifference

vi Except for the butlers who were mostly Parsis.

to morality that characterised some other slave-dealing companies – the directions being always careful to insist that "you should send near as many female slaves as male, because the male will not live so contented, except they have wives". And sometimes, orders for special slaves were received from highly-placed persons in England – once even from King Charles II, who desired one male and two female blacks, but they must be "dwarfs of the least size that you can procure, the males to be seventeen years of age and the females fourteen, giving the commander great charge to take all care of their accommodation and in particular of the females, that they be in no way abused in the voyage by the seamen".[10]

The Company had not forgotten the lesson which they had learnt from Roe, that if they wished to be respected, they must be mindful of their dignity. For this reason, even after death, senior officials of the factory were interred with respect. Ovington speaks with admiration of the magnificent structures and stately monuments in the European cemetery at Surat, "whose large extent, beautiful architecture and aspiring heads make them visible at a remote distance". These were obviously imitated from the tombs of the Mughal noblemen. The English tombs in the European cemetery at Surat were unique in many ways. Nothing quite like them was found in Calcutta or Madras later. These structures, with their mixture of Oriental and European architecture, seem quaint rather than imposing, but they were greatly admired in their day, and Ovington, Fryer, and other travellers in the 17th century refer to them with pride. They were evidently a show for sightseers, and were pointed out as standing monuments to the respectability and dignity of the Company's servants. The earliest and most graceful of the English tombs was the pretty domed mausoleum of Francis Breton, President from 1644-49. Next in order came the grand tomb of the Oxenden, President in the year 1662.

Visitors from Europe

Surat saw many visitors from the West, all of whom found a ready welcome at the hospitable English factory. None, however, was stranger than Tom Coryat – witty, linguist, buffoon and crazy, who arrived at Agra in 1616, after wandering through Egypt, Turkey, Palestine and Persia. He was born in Somerset and before his excursion to India, he had tramped over half of Europe. He had a marvellous gift of tongues, and on his arrival at Agra, delivered an oration before Jahangir, in which he compared himself to the Queen of Sheba and Jahangir to Solomon. Jahangir contemptuously tossed him a purse of one hundred rupees. Roe, who was there at the time, was furious at this buffoonery, which lowered the prestige of the English in the eyes of the court. On another occasion, Coryat talked down a loquacious washerwoman to the terror of Roe's entourage, completely silencing her by eight in the morning. But his most remarkable feat was to mount a minaret at the time when the call to prayer was sounding from a neighbouring minaret, and, parodying the muezzin, to proclaim "La alah, ala alah, Hazrat Isa Banala (there is no God but God, and Jesus the Son of God!)". On this occasion, he only escaped with his life because he was looked upon as a lunatic, and religious maniacs were regarded with superstitious reverence. Vanity was not the least of his failings, and he was elated to hear that the King James I had asked about him. But when he was told that the king's actual words were "Is that fool yet living?", it seemed to trouble him very much, because he spoke no more except saying that kings would speak of poor men as they pleased. Coryat's end was pathetic, though. He travelled to Surat from Agra, though he was suffering from a severe attack of dysentery. His co-passenger was a kind-hearted English merchant who gave him a sack which he had brought from England. Coryat called for it as soon as he heard of it, crying, "Sack, sack, is there any such thing as Sack? I pray you give me some sack." He drank all the way to Surat, and travelled no more. He was buried at Surat, on a small hill on the left hand of the road, outside the Broach Gate.[11]

Among other queer visitors to Surat were a young English nobleman and two Spanish renegades from Goa. The Englishman, who had been taken on out of pity by Sir Thomas Roe, distinguished himself by beating a servant and afterwards firing a pistol at him, for which he was sent home. The Spaniards seemed to have stepped straight out of the pages of Don Quixote. One of them, who dubbed himself the Knight of the Golden Rapier, had been forced to flee from Goa on account of his prowess in duelling. He further added that he was now resolved not to live any longer among Christians, but that he desired to live among the English. So, when he got to know that the English were Christians too, he cried, "Jesu Maria", as wondering at it, and further said that he had never heard such a thing before. He was entertained at the factory and proved himself a valiant trencherman. But he was made to sit among the servants, a position unbecoming to a hidalgo of Spain. Terry found him, six months later, alive and well, at the Mughal Court.

And then there were the two musicians, Lancelot Canning, a virginals-player, and Robert Trully, a cornet-player, who hoped to make their fortune by introducing the Mughal court to Western music. After a brief stay at Surat, they reached Agra and were allowed to perform before the assembled court. Canning played first, but the faint watery music of the virginals had no attraction for Jahangir's flamboyant court, and the audience became restive. It was left for Trully to uphold the reputation of European music. The first notes of his cornet caused a sensation. The emperor asked if he might try this gorgeous instrument and finding it hard to manipulate, ordered all his musicians to learn the cornet. The Imperial Chief Bandmaster was annoyed at the favour shown to a foreign musician and insisted on trying the cornet. He blew it so hard that he injured himself internally and later, died. In spite of this dramatic scene, Jahangir's interest in cornets soon waned, and Trully only received fifty rupees for his entertainment. Not disheartened, Trully wandered south, hoping to repeat his success at the court of Golconda. Finding that his offers of a cornet-recital awoke no enthusiasm there, he decided to become a Muslim, *"which was kyndlye accepted by the Kinge. So Tryllye was circumcised and had a newe name given him and greate allowance from the Kinge"*.[12]

Factory Administration

The administration of the Surat Factory was vested in a President and a council of four members. Writing on 10 April 1621, Thomas Kerridge advised the Company to "give the president full powers", as well as control over the agents of the Company operating in other parts of India and Persia, to give him a "council at Surat of four sufficient men and a Register, constantly resident". There was also the need for experienced factors and other personnel. In 1618, the Surat factory had six Englishmen employed, of whom two were young men and one, a steward or book-keeper. In 1628, the number of writers was increased to six. The number of English employees increased to 28 by 1674. In 1624, the salaries of professional employees ranged from £30 to £100 a year, and the salary of the President was £500 a year, half paid here, the other half reserved to be received at home, besides a bond of £5,000 sterling of good securities. The accountant was paid £72 per annum, £50 paid at Surat, the other at home. All the rest were half paid here, half at home, except the writers, who were paid at Surat. The staff included accountants, secretaries, registers, writers, surgeons, ministers, tailors, carpenters, bakers, cooks, trumpeters, warehouse-keepers, besides Indian employees such as brokers, stewards, peons or messengers and guards.

The office of the President was one of importance. The President at Surat controlled all the English factories in western India and Persia, and also Bantam, for a considerable time. The President was usually appointed from England, and could look forward to an honourable employment at the Company's headquarters after his return, if he carried himself well. Three to five years was the usual term of office. The President lived in style; he dined in his own apartments, except on festive occasions, and went about in a palanquin, preceded by guards, flagmen, and mace-bearers, with an ostrich-feather fan, like the noblemen of the Mughal court. Next in importance came the councillors, senior factors, four or five in number, who received from £300 to £100 per annum, according to seniority of service. Of these, the senior member was the accountant. He ranked next to the President, and was a person of high rank in the eyes of the Company, as through his hands passed the receipts for the whole of India. He was, in fact, the Company's treasurer in the East. Next to him came the warehouse-keeper, who registered all Europe goods brought by ships from Europe, and received all Asian commodities bought for sending back to Europe. The purser kept account of all goods exported and imported, paid the seamen their wages, provided wagons and porters, looked after the tackling for ships and ships stores. Lastly, came the secretary, who recorded all consultations, wrote all letters, and carried them to the President and council, to be perused and signed. It was he who kept the Company's seal, which was affixed to all passes and commissions, and recorded all transactions and sent copies of them to the Company.

Two other leading personalities in the factory were the surgeon and the chaplain. The surgeon received £50 per annum, the Company supplying him with drugs and medicines, and with an Indian assistant.[13] The chaplain was a well-known figure. The first regular chaplain was appointed in February 1657-58, the former incumbents having come out spasmodically as ship's chaplains or in attendance on people like Sir Thomas Roe. Some of these Chaplains did not lead very edifying lives. Hence, the Company applied to Oxford and Cambridge for suitable candidates. They were promised an allowance of £100 per annum, with accommodation. Besides this, the chaplain had a carriage to ride in and a peon to wait on him. Unfortunately, even these measures did not always have the desired effect. There are black sheep in every flock, and in a letter dated 16 November 1700, we find a complaint that a chaplain chosen directly by the Bishop of London, fell for a Dutch woman and deserted them for the Dutch camp!

One of the reasons for having chaplains at the factory was to counteract the influence of the Portuguese Catholic priests.[14] Some mission work "for the advancement and spreading of the gospel in India"[15] was contemplated at one time, but besides the conversion in 1617 of a 'Muslim Atheist', nothing appears to have been done. The chaplain was a very busy man. Prayers were held every morning before the doors of the factory were opened, and every night between eight and nine o'clock after the doors were shut. On Sundays, solemn service and sermons were read and preached twice in the day, followed by prayers at night. The chaplain would perform his duty as in churches in England, catechizing the youth on Sundays after evening service, and administering the Sacrament – the three festivals of the year, and of course, burying the dead. In these duties, he kept strictly to the rules of the church. The chaplain also had the duty of visiting the subordinate factories in regular circuit, a toilsome and even perilous task in these days.[16]

Apart from these dignitaries, the rest of the Company's servants may be comprehended in three classes, viz.

merchants, factors and writers. Some blew-coat[vii] boys were also entertained for seven years, which upon expiry, if they could get security, they were capable of employment. The writers were obliged to serve five years for £10 per annum, giving in bond £500 for good behaviour, during which time they served under some of the above-mentioned offices. After this, they became factors, had a £1,000 bond exacted from them, and had their salary augmented to £20 per annum for three years. Then entering into new indentures, they became senior factors, and lastly, merchants after three more years when they were allowed £40 per annum during their stay in the Company's service, besides lodgings at the Company's charges.[17] What strikes one most forcibly is the lowness of the salaries. Even granted that a servant in India used to cost two or three rupees a month, and that everything else in India in the 17th century was on a similar scale, it is difficult to see what inducement even a blew-coat boy could find to set off against the perils and discomforts of life in a far-off country on a salary of £10 per annum, rising to £20 in five years.

The local merchants, the baniyas, during their grand festival of Diwali, had a custom of presenting the President and council, the minister, surgeon, and all the factors and writers with something valuable, either in jewels or silks, according to the respect which they owed to every man at the factory. By this, the young factors, besides their salaries, diet and lodgings, were supplied with clothes sufficient for a great part of the year.[18] And, of course, there was the private trade. It was the most advantageous liberty of trade to all parts, from China to Surat, where they commonly made a fortune. They would borrow from the baniyas, money for China at 25 per cent, only to be paid upon the safe arrival of the ship, which if it met with any accident in the voyage, they were exempt from all damage.[19] Even the

vii Apprentices

chaplain made a good deal of money over and above his somewhat slender salary. Besides many private gifts from merchants and masters of ships who always brought gifts and rarities for the President and the senior merchants, the chaplain constantly received large gratuities for officiating at marriages, baptisms and burials. The surgeon also got fees for officiating at the Dutch factory, as well as for outside practice, from rich locals.

In addition to their normal commercial functions, the President and his council were also given certain judicial powers. These became necessary because of the presence, temporary or prolonged, of a large number of Englishmen in and around Surat. There were two categories of Englishmen that frequented Surat. One was that of crews of the visiting ships who, after their disembarkation from their ships at Swally, roamed around Swally and Surat. Very often, some of these sailors imbibed toddy and arrack much more than what was good for them, and in their inebriation, fought with the locals – common men as well as authorities. Such incidents occurred from time to time as reported in communications from Surat in 1619, 1623, 1633 and 1651. In some cases, such drunken behaviour was punished with instant dismissal or the errant being put in confinement for 24 hours, and then to have 20 'drubs' administered to him with a rattan. It was better for the Surat President to handle such cases through his council than to permit the Mughal authorities to deal with them, not knowing precisely what the outcome could be.

The standing rules of the Company frowned upon English factors taking wives to India or in India. But this did not prevent liaisons as was in the case of one preacher William Leske, who in 1616-17, admitted having relations with a Halalkhor (sweeper) woman, and one John Leachland in 1626, who had for some years privately kept an Indian woman and refused to part with her. The other offences were gambling, desertion, incurring of debts, and apostacy in conversion to Catholicism or Islam. In all such cases, strict action was taken and the offenders punished with fines or even expulsion.

The English establishment at Surat was a curious amalgam of 'monasticism' and commerce. Except the President, all others were forbidden from having their wives with them. They lived together, ate together, prayed together, amused each other and traded on their own personal account privately, and contrary to the Company's regulations with each other's tacit knowledge, including the President. The hours for meals were fixed and the food was sumptuous, cooked in the English, Portuguese, Mughal or Indian manner, by a number of cooks maintained on the establishment's roster. The major meal of the day, dinner, contained a number of courses washed down with liberal quantities of wine. There was a sustained demand for beer. A hot mixture of 'burnt wine' flavoured with cinnamon, cloves and other spices, was also popular. Punch was a particular discovery of the English in India, derived from the Hindi word for five. The five ingredients which gave the drink its name were brandy, sugar, lime, spices and water. Wines from Persia and France were much sought after, and toddy and arrack were often used. Chinese chai[viii] was also popular and the use of this new drink in the factory was noticed in the 1630s and thereafter. On special days such as Christmas, there was much fraternizing with the Dutch at parties given in the English garden in the city. Drinks were liberally served at such parties, and games like archery were played with great enthusiasm.

Famine and Other Disasters

Rastell returned to England in March 1625, and was succeeded by Kerridge for a second term. Kerridge's second

---

viii Tea

term of office was distinguished by the fierce fighting in the Persian Gulf between the Anglo-Dutch fleet and the Portuguese under Botelho. Kerridge returned to England in 1628, and was succeeded by Richard Wylde. Sir Thomas Herbert visited the factory during his period of office. He landed at Swally, where he found that *"the banias had pitched their booths, and tents and huts of straw in great numbers, resembling a country fair or market. Here calico, China satin, escritoires of mother-of-pearl, jewels, rice, sugar, plantains, and arrack were for sale. Peons, olive-coloured Indian foot-boys who can very prettily prattle English, could be hired for four pice a day (2 pence of our money) either to interpret, run, go arrands or the like*".[20] Surat was in his opinion an ugly town.

Mr Wylde, says Herbert, was a bad President. Discipline was poor, prayers were neglected, and Sundays were spent in feasting, drinking, gambling, and the beastly sin of whoredom. Bribes were freely taken by the authorities to ship private goods free of charge on the Company's vessels. Business was left to sarrafs and banias, and all, from the President downwards, indulged in private trade.[21] Under the circumstances, the Company decided to recall him, but Wylde preferred voluntary resignation, and Rastell returned as President in 1630. Rastell came out with special orders to make a clean sweep of private trade and of all concerned in it. He set about his task with the vigour which had characterized his last term of office, but shortly afterwards, he died in a tragic manner. In 1630, the monsoon had failed and in the next year, the rain fell in torrents, sweeping away fields and crops. The consequence was an awful famine. *"When we came to the city of Surat,"* wrote a Dutch factor, *"we hardly could see any living persons, where heretofore were thousands; and there is so great a stench of dead persons that the sound people that came into the town were with the smell infected, and at the corners of the street the dead lay twenty together, one upon another, nobody burying them. The mortality in this town is and hath been so great that there have died above 30,000 people."*[22]

Even in December 1631, the effects were still there, for an English communication of 9 December1631 says that *"places here that have yielded 15 bales cloth made there in a day, hardly yield now three in a month"*. By June 1631, some rain had fallen and a report of 24 January 1632 speaks of the area being slowly "re-peopled" by craftsmen beginning to return. But the famine was followed by torrential rains which "drowned and carried away all the corn and other grains" and there was pestilence which added to the people's misery. In spite of all this, the Mughal government continued its wars with the Deccan powers, and Shah Jahan's efforts consisted of opening a few relief kitchens.

Some four years later, in early 1636, the English records report of a rise in cost of food grains, though the situation seemed to have eased by the middle of the year. The year 1644 was again a year of anxiety, as were the years 1647, 1648, 1659, 1660, 1663, 1664,1685-1686 and 1694-1695, when the prices of essential commodities soared by 50 per cent and 100 per cent because of insufficient rain. Such extraordinary calamities apart, the environment of Surat was prone to the rise of a number of sicknesses. Towards the end of a hot and dry season, foreigners suffered from *"hot fevers, headaches, fluxes of both kinds, boils and botches, most usual in such dry years when the waters are drawn low and savour most of the soil, which is a blackish and sulphurous nature"*.

The famine of 1630 was disastrous for the factory. It was terribly crippled by the loss of their factors and by the paralysis of their trade. It was only able to survive at all by the profits reaped on their Persian trade, especially in silk.

Law and Order

There were frequent challenges to law and order which the local administration was not able to face appropriately.

In 1648, a band of 150 armed robbers attacked the Dutch factory. That such a large group could enter the city without the governor and his officers knowing anything at all is hard to believe. Increasingly, through the second half of the 17th century, the insecurity of life and property began to rise. Following Aurangzeb's order of April 1669 to destroy Hindu temples and suppress Hindu religious practices, Hindu-Muslim clashes began in Surat. In November, the Surat factory wrote to the Company, *"You have been formerly advised what insufferable tyranny the banias endured in Surat by the force exercised by these lordly Moors on account of their religion"*.[23] During the height of the persecution, a nephew of the Company's aged broker, Tulsidas Parekh, was inveigled and converted to Islam. The act was treated as a severe blow by the Hindu employees of the factory. The Hindu merchants decided to leave the city in protest against the violation of their religion, and the commercial life of Surat practically came to a standstill. All the shops remained closed, the mint and the Customs House stopped business, and no money could be borrowed. When the merchants began to leave the town, the qazi who had initiated the persecution, went to the governor and asked him to stop them by force. But the latter replied that they were also the emperor's subjects and were free to travel wherever they pleased.[24] So great was the tension between the two communities that even after the merchants returned to Surat on being promised fair treatment by the Mughal governor, no Muslim trader could borrow money or buy bills of exchange from Hindu bankers.[25]

The Surat disturbance of 1669 was far from being an isolated incident. What is remarkable, however, was that in spite of a long history of mutual suspicion and distrust, the city's communal groups managed to co-exist for centuries. The resilience and the capacity of the Hindu traders to withstand Islamic pressure did not go unnoticed.

In a lengthy private letter written home in 1672 on the social aspects of life in Surat, a servant of the Company commented that the reputation for cunning and subtlety which the Hindu traders of Gujarat enjoyed, was the result of being continually exposed to danger, and the necessity for preserving their wealth and family integrity through sheer political skills. For they are altogether a suffering people, and against all the violent assaults that are made upon them, have no other defence other than their wits and that interest which their money makes.[26]

The biggest challenge to Surat's safety came from the Maratha war of independence, relentlessly carried on by Shivaji. Shivaji sacked Surat twice, the first time in January 1664 and a second time in October 1670. There had been persistent rumours of an impending Maratha attack a considerable time before 6 January 1664. The governor, Inayat Khan, was not only inept, but a coward too. He took no measures to prepare his forces for the defence of the city. At the first sign of attack, he, along with some rich merchants sought safety in the fort, leaving the city open for the Marathas. The town's fortifications were so weak that Shivaji could easily assault it. In October 1670, the English Council reported in a letter from Surat that Shivaji's army approached the walls and after a slight assault, the defendants fled under the shelter of the castle guns. Shivaji's men took control of the whole town including the English house, the Dutch, and French, and the two sarais, one of which was maintained by Persian and Turkish merchants, the other by Central Asian ones. At the time of leaving the city with all the booty he could collect, Shivaji sent a letter to the city government, warning that if they failed to pay him an annual tribute of 1,200,000 rupees, he would return.[27]

Shivaji's two raids in six years demonstrated the deepening crisis of the Mughal empire. In 1664, while Inayat Khan proved himself to be both unprepared and incapable, and deserted his post to flee to the safety of the fort, the Europeans stood firm. Aurangzeb dismissed Inayat Khan and rewarded the English with concessions in the rate of customs-duties as a mark of his appreciation for their valour. The Mughal government also began to construct a fortified wall around the town. But the second raid in 1670 proved this effort feeble. The fact of the matter was that the Maratha war of independence was beyond the capabilities of the Mughal political system to contain, much less defeat.

Equally futile were the Mughal efforts to deal with the problem of European piracy on the high seas. From time to time, the Mughals made efforts to strengthen their naval capabilities. In 1654, a Dutch report said that the Mughals had bought 29 pieces of artillery to mount on their ships. Manucci recounts an incident when Aurangzeb was much enraged at the capture of his royal ships sailing to Mecca and wished to create a navy. He discussed a plan to entrust the Europeans in his pay with the task of building war ships, but his minister Zafar Khan demurred saying that it was risky to trust foreigners on such delicate matters. Undeterred, Aurangzeb ordered an Italian, Ortencio Bronzoni, to build a small ship, which when ready, was floated on a great tank. The European craftsmen demonstrated their skill in managing the sails and piloting the vessel and firing off the guns mounted on it. Manucci says: "*On seeing all this, after reflecting on the construction of the boat and the dexterity required in handling it, Aurangzeb concluded that to sail over and fight on the ocean were not things for the people of Hindustan, but only suited to European alertness and boldness. Thus, at last, he abandoned the project*". Aurangzeb's decision reflected both the political and technological bankruptcy of the Mughal system.[28]

Pay Bills of the Surat Factory in 1628-29

Richard Wylde	President	**£100.**
John Skibbowe		**£200.**
Richard Boothbye		**£100.**
George Page		**£100.**
Arthur Surnld	purser	**£50.**
John Willoughby		**£50.**
Nicholas Wooley	purser's mate	**£30.**
Henry Glascocke		**£50.**
Ralph Rande	writer	**£35.**
Peter Mondaie	writer	**£30.**
Crispen Blagden,	writer	**£40.**
Thomas Smith	writer	**£25.**
Clement Dunscombe	writer	**£20.**
Thomas Joice		**£33.**
Robert Davison	steward	**£20.**
John Calf	writer	**£20.**
Thomas Wilborne	(Mr Wylde's man)	**£20.**
George Turner	(an unprofitable chirurgeon)	**£40.**
John Blewe	cook	**£18.**
Two bakers		**£36.**[29]

Pay Bills of the Surat Factory in 1649

Francis Breton	President	**£350**
Thos. Merry	Member of Council.	**£300**
Edward Pearce		**£100.**
George Oxenden		**£40.**
Andrew Baines	Minister	**£50.**

Anthony Clitherow	warehouseman	**£60.**
John Anthony	chirurgeon	**£33.**
Henry Young		**£18.**
John Adler		**£18.**
Nicholas Buckeridge		**£25.**
Walter Gollofer		**£25.**
John Broadbent		**£20.**
Edward Locke	chirurgeon's mate	**£22 4s.**
John Chambers	'boarder'.	
William Noke	President's servant	**£4 16s.**
George Pepys	Mr Merry's servant	**£9.**
Herman Hill	trumpeter	**£24.**
John Wilson	cook	**£14 185.**[30]

References

[1] Thevenot, Voyage.

[2] Fryer, New Account of the East Indies.

[3] Finch's narrative of Purchas.

[4] Letters Received, vol. V, p. 74.

[5] EFI, 1618-21, p. 150.

[6] Fryer.

[7] Price's Memorials, quoted in Douglas's Bombay and Western India.

[8] Surat Factory Records, 1698.

[9] Forbes's Oriental Memoirs.

[10] Letter to Surat, quoted in Anderson's *English in Western India*.

[11] Travels, 1665 ed., p. 43.

[12] Purchas, His Pilgrimes.

[13] Ovington, p. 402.

[14] Anderson, English in Western India, p. 25.

[15] Yule, Hedges' Diary, vol. II, p. CCCLI.

[16] Ovington, p. 404.

[17] Fryer, I. 216.

[18] Ovington, p. 401-2.

[19] Ovington, p. 391.

[20] Travels (1665 ed.), p. 43-5.

[21] English Factories in India, 1630-3, p. 16.

[22] Ibid., p. 181. A vivid account of the famine, called by the natives the Satasio Kal, or famine of '87 (Samvat 1687), is to be found in Peter Mundy's Travels, ed. Temple, vol. ii (Hakluyt Society, 1914). Mundy went to Patna in November 1630 and returned in May 1633. In the meantime, fourteen out of the twenty-one English factors had perished.

[23] Original Correspondence, 26 November 1669, vol. 30, No. 3373.

[24] The English Factories in India, 1668-1669, p. 192.

[25] Factory Records Surat, 24 December 1669, vol. 3, p. 13.

[26] 'A letter from Suratt in India giving an account of the manners of the English factors etc', 18 January 1672, in Barlow, R., and Yule, H., ed., The diary of William Hedges 1681-1687 (3 vols., London, 1887-9).

[27] William Hedges, II, P ccxxvii ff; EFI, XI, P 307 ff. After 1664 an English report had it that "Surat has become a garrison more than a town of trade". Patel, Suratni Tawarikh, p. 39; EFI, XII, p. 173.

[28] For Maratha incursions in the area see Storia, IV. p. 232; for religious and political policies see IV, p. 57; Generale Missiven. III, p. 271; also see Forrest, Selections, 1, pp. 248-251.

[29] *English Factories in India*, 1624-9, p. 314.

[30] *English Factories*, 1646-50, p. 271.

Chapter 7
A Modern Corporation

A majority of the historical literature about the East India Company has dealt with it as a semi-political entity that negotiated terms with kings, entered into treaties with foreign rulers and waged wars when that suited it. Its character of being a company has often been ignored. But a company it was, and perhaps the greatest in all history – a precursor to many of the modern-day multinational corporations. A model for the present-day multinational enterprise – the English East India Company was 'the greatest corporation in the world', according to Victorian historian, poet and Indian administrator, Thomas Babington Macaulay.[1] Throughout its long life as a trading concern, it confronted and overcame many of the timeless questions facing business enterprise: how to keep employees motivated, customers satisfied, shareholders happy and society content.

Established on a cold New Year's Eve in 1600, the English East India Company, in its more than two-and-a-half centuries of existence, bridged the mercantilist world of chartered monopolies and the industrial age of corporations, being accountable solely to its shareholders. The Company's establishment by Royal Charter, its monopoly of all trade between England and Asia and its semi-sovereign privileges to rule territories and raise armies, certainly mark it out as a corporate institution from another time. Yet, in its financing, structures of governance and business dynamics, the Company was undeniably modern. It may have referred to its staff as servants rather than executives, and communicated by quill pen rather than email, but the key features of the shareholder-owned corporation were there for all to see.

From Roman times, Europe had always been Asia's commercial supplicant, shipping out gold and silver in return for spices, textiles and other luxury goods. European traders were attracted to the East for its wealth and sophistication at a time when the Western economy was a fraction the size of Asia's. And for its first 150 years, the Company had to repeat this practice, as there was almost nothing that England could export that the East wanted to buy. Then, first in Bengal in the decades that followed Plassey, and then in China through the opium trade, the Company broke this long-standing pattern of trade and wealth. By the time of its demise in1858, Europe's economy was double the size of that of China and India, a complete reversal of the situation in 1600. There were many elements in this turnaround, but the East India Company was certainly one of the chief agents that engineered the great switch in global development that marked the birth of the modern age.

What makes the English East India Company special is the way it bridged the medieval concept of the corporation as an essentially public body, with the industrial model of an enterprise acting primarily in the interests of its shareholders. In the rising commercial world of the 16th century England, the chartered company brought together a number of institutional ingredients. The Crown had a long tradition of setting up corporations as independent bodies to manage public services such as municipalities and universities, like Oxford and Cambridge. Indeed, the local government of London's financial district is managed by the Corporation of London even today. From Italy came the concept of 'compagnia', a name deriving from the Latin phrase for the act of sharing bread, 'cum panis'. This was essentially a family firm, where fathers, brothers, sons and other relatives would pool their labour and capital.[2]

In England, the first generation of chartered companies brought together a band of merchants who would buy and sell goods under a common umbrella. These regulated companies operated more like a guild, setting standards for a chosen field of endeavour and collecting fees for shared services such as docks and warehouses. Where the East India Company differed was in its fusion of the institutional structure of the public corporation with the financial mechanism of joint stock ownership. Unlike earlier regulated companies, the East India Company was established as 'one body corporate and politick'. This brought a whole series of financial and organisational benefits, which were especially valuable for the long-distance trade to the East Indies. Capital costs were high in terms of both shipping and the bullion required to buy home-bound goods. In addition, risks were extreme, both natural and political, with a high likelihood of the loss of some or all of the investment. The joint stock mechanism provided a solution to this challenge. First, it enabled a separation of investors and managers, thus broadening the pool of capital that could be tapped to include both city merchants as well as passive investors from elsewhere in the moneyed elite. Second, the risks were shared widely: if profits were made, then dividends could be disbursed, but if losses were incurred, investors would only be liable up to the nominal value of their paid-in capital. This limited liability endowed the Company with a special dynamism, substantially reducing the risks for investors, as compared to the usual partnership model of ownership. Third, trading was conducted by the joint stock company on its own account, rather than by the members themselves. This gave the Company a separate identity and its own legal personality – one that could conduct business using strategies that went beyond the interests of individual merchants. It also gave it a unique institutional structure when confronting merchant partnerships, and the states of Asia.

Leadenhall Street was not the Company's first headquarters. When it was newly established by Elizabeth I as 'The Governor and Company of Merchants of London Trading to the East Indies', its business was done at the city mansion of its first governor (or Chairman), Sir Thomas Smythe. His house was situated on the narrow lane of Philpot Lane, where today stands an appropriately named 'Spice Trader' curry restaurant. The Company then shifted a few hundred yards to the north and occupied Crosby Hall, owned by John Spencer, Lord Mayor of London. Later, in 1648, the Company moved to an Elizabethan mansion named Craven House and renamed it to East India House. This East India House went through numerous incarnations during its 200-year life and remained the London headquarters of the Company till 1858. In the 1690s, it was known as 'the house belonging to the East India Company which are a corporation of men with long heads and deep purposes.[3] By the end of 17th century, it had become one of the landmarks of the city of London, and along with the South Sea Company and the Bank of England, formed the corporate trinity of that era in England.

Initially, the Company constructed separate joint stocks for each voyage, whereby investors would decide to allocate capital on a case-by-case basis. Only in 1657 did the Company become a permanent joint stock corporation, a 'continuous unlimited investment taking place without reference to individual voyages'.[4] This provided the basis for shares in the Company to be valued and exchanged at its headquarters in Leadenhall Street. Later, trading in stock moved to the courtyard of London's Royal Exchange. When this proved too cramped, dealing shifted across Cornhill to the coffee houses of the Exchange or 'Change Alley', until the formal establishment of the London Stock Exchange in 1773. Like a modern corporation, the Company's share price was its heart-beat, communicating to the world the market's estimates of its future prospects. For the jobbers clustered around Exchange Alley, the Company's stock – along with its bonds and annuities – became the trendsetter for the market as a whole. From the 1690s, its share price graph for the next 180 years would be dominated by a series of peaks and troughs, reflecting both the state of its commerce and the health of its relations with governments at home and abroad. For the Company, its share price peaked in 1693, and then fell for the next five years, as successive parliamentary inquiries exposed corruption and proposed potentially disastrous remedies. The low point was in 1698, when a rival company was established, sending the Company's shares which had a nominal value of £100 down to a mere £39. By the turn of the century, the threat had been seen off and prices had returned to well over £100 once more, rising to over £200 in 1717.

As part of its charter, the Company gained a whole series of special rights, the most valuable of which was the monopoly of all trade between England and the lands beyond the Cape of Good Hope. This gave the Company's investors extra confidence by creating a captive home market for its products. In the real-world conditions of global competition, the Company was for many years just one player among many, striving against the Portuguese, the Dutch and the French. It also faced home-grown challenges from so-called interlopers who sought to break its exclusivity, along with the more informal bands of smugglers and pirates. Nevertheless, its monopoly powers were real, keeping prices high and ensuring substantial profits for shareholders.

For the Company, achieving a favourable relationship with the English monarch, was therefore essential. At home, the English Crown and then Parliament, possessed the power of corporate life and death. The state not only set the boundaries of its commercial operations, but laid down the fiscal bargain that would govern the distribution of the

Company's surplus. The Company's great strength lay in its ability to generate extra revenues for the low-income states of the pre-industrial world. Sizeable loans to the British Crown and large-scale bullion imports into Mughal India made the Company indispensable. For the merchants who managed the Company, the arrangement of Royal Charters at home and imperial decrees (firmans) abroad, was all part of the wider business of buying and selling. These were financial transactions that established contractual rights that could not be infringed. What the Company sought was a zone of commercial sovereignty that ensured it had free rein to operate as it wished. Giving presents to princes and paying bribes to Parliamentarians were simply part of the fundamental costs of business.

Business Administration

The English Company shared, or rather borrowed, many structural features from its Dutch rival, the VOC. Both had strictly hierarchical systems of administration, supported by a small army of clerks – known as writers in England, a term borrowed from the Dutch 'shcruyvers'. Both companies were publicly held and publicly traded, with the VOC usually offering the more attractive investment opportunity throughout the 17th century. But in their governance, the two companies differed markedly. The VOC's directors were chosen by its six provinces – Amsterdam, Middelburg, Hoorn, Enkhuizen, Delft and Rotterdam. In Amsterdam's case, their representatives on the board were nominated by the burgomasters and appointed for life. The directors had to hold a substantial portion of VOC stock. The VOC's shareholders provided the capital, but had no say either in the choice of those who would manage their investment or in the direction of policy. The public origins of the English company's corporate form gave its shareholders not only a financial stake, but the franchise as well, and the Company' operated as a limited, property-based democracy, one that was run by and for its shareholders. Just as the right to vote in Georgian England was restricted to those with property, so too the Company's shareholders had to have £500 of nominal stock before they could vote either in the quarterly meetings of the Court of Proprietors held in March, June, September and December, or at the annual meeting in April. This was the most important event on the Company's calendar, when over a thousand shareholders would gather to elect 24 directors. No matter how big a shareholding, each individual with more than £500 in stock only had one vote. In turn, only shareholders with over £2,000 in stock could put themselves forward as candidates to be directors. Once elected, these directors would then choose from among themselves, a chairman and a deputy chairman. Until 1709, the chairman went by the name of governor, and directors were assigned to committees. Power was controlled within a relatively narrow group of affluent merchants on the Court of Directors. But shareholders had the right to override executive decisions taken by the directors till as late as 1784.

The Court of Directors oversaw the operations of a hierarchical system. At the helm was the chairman, who presided the weekly board meetings of the 24 directors every Wednesday. Each director was assigned to one of the ten committees that looked after different dimensions of the Company's operations. Among these, three committees were regarded as most important:

(1) Correspondence, which handled all the communications with the distant factories
(2) Treasury, which handled the finances, buying bullion and paying dividends
(3) Accounts

In addition, there were committees for buying commodities, warehousing, shipping, managing East

India House, regulating and preventing private trade and lawsuits. Then there was the all-powerful Secret Committee which defined the Company's political and military strategy in times of war. From East India House, the directors would send precise orders to their overseas factories dictating the quantity, quality and price of goods to be purchased. In the case of textiles, this could cover details such as the type of thread, weave, colour, pattern, stiffness and packing. These orders were implemented by a system of autonomous presidencies headed by a president, who controlled the operations of his particular port or factory, as well as smaller outposts in his zone of operations. Although the East India House laid down clear parameters on the contents of its commerce, it gave considerable freedom to local managements to determine how these goals were to be achieved, including their relationships with the host governments. As the fortunes of trade fluctuated, different presidencies took the lead.

Below the president lay another hierarchy, with promotion strictly by seniority. New recruits would enter the Company's service as 'writers', where they would stay for five years, before progressing to the rank of 'factor' for a further three years. This would be followed by a promotion to junior and then senior merchant, and thereafter, a possible selection for their president's council, and even governor. The expectations of employment were clearly set out for all employees in a covenant, backed by a bond, while giving employees a strong incentive to stay and make their fortune in India. For its executives, the purpose of a career with the Company was to make enough money to be able to retire. This could not be achieved by saving from the salaries received from the Company, which barely covered living expenses. As a result, the ambitious Company man had to use his position as a platform for patronage and private trade. The privilege of private trade also exacerbated the inherent tension between the corporation and its employee, making the staff both executives and entrepreneurs in their own right.

Compared with the Dutch VOC, the English Company proved more adept at moving into new markets, shifting from pepper to textiles, and then to tea. This was a strategy that the East India Company applied for minimising the amount of bullion to be sent to the East, keeping the costs of supply as low as possible, and then maximising the price of goods sold on auction back in England. One of the fundamental things that the Company sought from the English monarch, was a monopoly over trade with the East. Like most present-day multinationals, the Company was eager to avoid the mere interplay of supply and demand. The Company jealously guarded its exclusive rights over imports from Asia, lobbying and bribing the authorities to retain its charter. It also wanted to eliminate competition in Asia so that it could force down the costs of supply. By controlling both ends of the chain, the Company could guarantee high profits for its shareholders. Negotiation was the preferred method of achieving market dominion. But if required, it would use both force and fraud.

The Rivals

For the first hundred years, the VOC was the arbiter of European trade relations with Asia, overshadowing the efforts of its English rival in both the scale and scope of its operations. The Dutch were the first of the North European nations to break the Portuguese maritime monopoly of the Asian spice trade, with the Compagnie van Verre (Company of Distant Lands) sending its fleet to the East in 1595. Over the next six years, eight rival companies sent 15 fleets to tap the Spice Islands of Indonesia. Competition proved good, both for the spice producers, who saw increased purchase prices, as well as Dutch consumers, who enjoyed falling sale prices. But it was a disaster for investors. So, on 20 March 1602, the various companies put their differences aside and merged into a single body. The united company received a monopoly over all trade with Asia – just like the English Company – and worked diligently to channel trade for its own benefit. Although England had launched its own East India Company two years earlier, the VOC had ten times the capital base, and quickly achieved a dominant position. It became the First Joint Stock to trade its shares on an open market, and in its lifetime, the VOC would pay out 3,600 per cent in dividends based on the initial investment in 1602.[5]

The English East India Company's voyages between 1601 and 1612 generated returns of 155 per cent on an invested capital of £517,784. Cloves sold from the Company's Third Voyage alone made profits of over 200 per cent. The first 'joint stock' then raised £420,436 to finance fleets for each of the four years between 1613 and 1616. But returns were much lower, though still substantial, at 87 per cent. As time went by, a series of factors – including recession at home, mounting competition overseas and a growing glut of spices – meant that profits continued on a downward course. The Second Joint Stock raised £1.6 million to finance annual voyages between 1617 and 1622, but could only offer 12 per cent back to investors, a rate of less than 1 per cent a year.[6] Driven from the Moluccas following the massacre of English traders at Amboyna in 1623, the English Company was finally expelled from Bantam by the Dutch in 1682. Step by step, combining financial acumen with colonial brutality, the VOC achieved mastery of the Asia trade. Jan Pieterszoon Coen, who had established Batavia (modern Jakarta) as the VOC's capital in Asia, symbolised the single-minded commercial aggression that brought it such success. Writing back to the Heren XVII in 1619, he famously claimed"*we cannot carry on trade without war, nor war without trade*".[7] Violence in the East was matched by corruption at home. Just 20 years after its foundation, angry investors forced the directors to publish the accounts and introduce a modicum of responsiveness to shareholder concerns. In the 18th century, it failed to diversify its product range, and was weakened from within by administrative sclerosis and fraud. By the end of the century, its three initials were being used by critics to spell out its doom 'Vergann Onder Corruptie'– 'perished by corruption'. Expelled from India by the English, the rest of the VOC's Asian operations became untenable following the last Anglo-Dutch war in the 1780s. In 1799, the Compagnie ceased to exist.

Permanent peace was signed with Portugal at Goa in 1635, giving the Company access to the Estado's ring of ports stretching all the way to Macao. It also paved the way for the establishment of the new base at Fort St George at Madras on the Coromandel coast, in 1639. Bombay would follow in 1668, a wedding gift to Charles II from his Portuguese wife, Catherine of Braganza. The cash-strapped king promptly leased Bombay to the Company in return for a sizeable loan and an annual rent.

Monopoly Under Attack

Before the benefits of Bombay's transfer could be realized, the Company almost ceased to exist, undermined by interlopers and civil war. For many in the 17th century, monopolies were regarded as the economic expression of royal despotism, powers to be opposed by the rising Parliamentary forces. As early as 1604, a bill was introduced in Parliament to abolish all exclusive privileges over foreign trade. Supporting the bill, Sir Edwyn Sandys spoke out for the importance of commercial freedom: "*...it is against the natural right and liberty of the subjects of England to restrain[merchandise] into the hands of some few*". This was a spirit that would be echoed throughout the Company's career, with varying degrees of success. In 1604, the free trade bill failed. But the kings of

England were always seeking additional sources of finance. As a result, the Crown was happy to back rival ventures, such as the short-lived Scottish East India Company of 1618 and the Courten Association of 1636. Courten's venture lasted for 15 years, disrupting the Company's monopoly presence. Yet, it would come together with the original Company in 1650 under the banner of the 'United Joint Stock' to found a permanent English factory in Bengal, at Hugli.

By then, however, the Company had been hard hit by the aftershocks of the British civil wars that raged from 1640 to 1647. The Anglo-Dutch struggles during Oliver Cromwell's protectorate in the 1650s also profoundly damaged Company interests. In addition, Cromwell refused to renew the Company's charter in 1653, allowing its monopoly to lapse. This produced a brief window of open commerce, boosting trade and reducing prices, thereby crippling profits – a result almost exactly the same as the Dutch experience before 1602. On 14 January 1657, the situation had grown so bleak that the Company's directors voted to liquidate its affairs. This proved to be an effective ploy to force Cromwell's hand. By October, a new charter had been granted, and a permanent joint stock was established with capital to the tune of £740,000 – although only 50 per cent of this was actually subscribed at the time. It would take another half-century before the Company could match the invested capital of the second joint stock of 1617, and the Company could finally be called a modern corporation. For the next three decades, it experienced an economic boom. Between 1658 and 1688, the Company managed to complete 404 voyages between London and the East Indies, an average of 13 each season.[8]

The return of King Charles II in 1660 secured the Company's position. From established bases at Surat and Madras, the new port of Bombay and the emerging trade with Bengal, Company imports surged. In 1664, it imported a quarter of a million pieces of cloth, almost half from the Coromandel coast, a third from Gujarat and less than a fifth from Bengal. By the end of the decade, cotton and silk textiles made up 56 per cent of Company imports, pushing pepper to the second place, followed by raw silk, indigo, saltpetre, coffee and tea. Indian textiles hit an all-time peak of 1.76 million pieces in 1684, representing 83 per cent of the Company's total trade. This influx of cheap, easily-washable clothing, created a health and lifestyle revolution. By the end of the century, the value of the English Company's trade was fast catching up with that of the Dutch, with Bengal taking an ever-greater share. If the VOC was the commercial hare among the north European trading companies, the East India Company was proving to be the tortoise. The 1680s were the peak of the boom, when 200,000 pieces were exported from Bengal alone each year. This produced generous dividends and capital growth for the Company's investors. The Company's share price more than quadrupled in the two decades following the Restoration, growing from £60–£70 in 1664 to £245 in 1677 and £300 in 1680. Dividends were also substantial. For most of the 1670s, the Company paid out a 20 per cent dividend. But in 1680, fortunes improved and a 50 per cent pay-out was made, to be repeated in 1682, 1689 and 1691. And in 1682, so strong were the Company's finances that each proprietor received matching shares as a bonus, taking the Company's capital stock to £740,000. In all, from 1657 to 1691, proprietors received 840 per cent in dividends on their original investment. And for India, there was a steady influx of bullion, stimulating growth in income, output and employment. Between 1681 and 1685 alone, the Company exported 240 tonnes of silver and 7 tonnes of gold to India. Financially, these were perhaps the best days of the Company's life.

A Bid for Dominion

It was at this point that the Company's directors in London made a fundamental shift in corporate strategy, a turnaround engineered by one of the most influential executives in its history, Sir Josiah Child. In 1671, Child became a shareholder in the Company for the first time, and only two years later, he held 2 per cent of the entire stock, becoming the largest shareholder in 1679. Shares brought power in the Company, and for the next 15 years, from April 1674 until his death in 1699, Child was on the Company's board. Throughout the 1680s, he was either governor (chairman) or deputy-governor. Child's influence stretched to London's embryonic financial markets, where he had the reputation as 'the original of stock-jobbing'.[i]

The rising markets of the 1680s and 1690s made it clear that "every man's eye, when he came to Market, was upon the Brokers who acted for Sir Josiah, enquiring 'does Sir Josiah sell or buy?'" But it was not just Child's wealth that moved markets, but his skill for manipulating the news from India. Known today for his story of Robinson Crusoe, writer Daniel Defoe was also a leading economic analyst of his age. Defoe cast Josiah Child as a pivotal figure of his *Anatomy of Exchange Alley*. Published in 1719 as an investigation into the causes for the South Sea Bubble, he wrote "*there are those who tell us, letters had been order'd by private management to be written from the East Indies with an account of the loss of ships which have been arrived there, and the arrival of ships lost; of war with the Great Mogul, when they have been in perfect tranquillity, and of peace with the Great Mogul when he has come down against the factory of Bengal with*

i Stock jobbing is a term that means making quick profits on small moves of a stock. The term is mostly out of date now and comes from a British slang term for certain financial market participants. The more common terms for a similar kind of activity in the markets nowadays might be scalping, or more generally, day-trading or even high-frequency trading.

100,000 men, just as it was thought proper to call those rumours for raising and falling of the stock and when it was for this purpose to buy cheap or sell dear."[9]

As he rose to prominence in the Company, Child put in place a radical plan to implement his vision. The first step was to make a new alliance with the Crown to guarantee the Company's privileges at home. Elected as the governor in 1681, Child quickly gifted King Charles II £10,000, to help smoothen the renewal of the Company's charter, a payment that became annual for the next seven years. Next, he broke with his former partner Thomas Papillon, who was proposing to open up the East India trade to a much wider pool of investors and merchants. Driven from his position on the Company's board and hounded by the court, Papillon was forced into exile in 1685. Child rapidly became a favourite at court, marrying his daughter to the eldest son of the Tory aristocrat, the Duke of Beaufort, and transferring £10,000 of Company stock into James' name. With his position at court secured, Child clamped down mercilessly on the growing band of interlopers who sought to break the Company's monopoly. Child wanted the Company to become a sovereign power in India, forcing the Mughal Empire to trade with it on terms of equality. The prize was Bengal, where the Company had increasingly important trading operations, but lacked a fortified stronghold like Goa or Batavia. This left it exposed to the fiscal exactions of the provincial Mughal governor of Bengal, who, for example, in 1680, introduced a 5 per cent duty on imported bullion and a 3.5 per cent duty on exports – in spite of the Company's technical duty-free export status. In January 1686, Child arranged for an expeditionary force of ten ships and six companies of infantry to force concessions from the Mughals in Bengal. Writing to the President of Fort St George in Madras on 9 June 1686, Child underlined the imperative for the Company to transform itself from 'a parcel of mere trading merchants' into a 'formidable martial government in India'.[10] The same tone filled his visionary call on 12 December 1687, for the new President and Council in Madras, to 'establish such a politie' of Civil and Military power, and create and secure such a large revenue to maintain both at that place as may be the foundation of a large, well-grounded sure English dominion in India for all time to come'.[11]

Child had begun what has become known as the Anglo-Mughal war – although it would perhaps be better described as the first Company-Mughal conflict. The Mughal Emperor Aurangzeb was a military zealot intent on asserting his power throughout the subcontinent. In 1686, for example, he took Bijapur, and the following year, Hyderabad. In Bengal, the local forces of the Mughal governor were equally overwhelming. Three years of skirmishing through the swamps of the Bengal delta followed. In Gujarat, the Company raided Mughal shipping, provoking the capture of the Surat factory and a full-blown siege of Bombay in 1689. Aurangzeb eventually restored the Company's trading rights, but at the cost of diplomatic humiliation and a fine of Rs 1,50,000 plus damages. Only one piece of consolation could be drawn from the whole affair. A new 'factory' was established among the villages of Kolikata, Govindapore and Sutanuti on the river Hugli in 1690, for which fortifications were begun in 1696, and zamindari rights purchased two years later. Calcutta had been born.

The Role of the Armed Force

Writing home to the Company in 1616, Sir Thomas Roe had expressed his view that trade and war were incompatible. The policy of armed trading, according to him, was responsible for impoverishing the Portuguese. The Portuguese did not profit from trade with India, as they decided to defend their possessions by force, and the same mistake was made by the

Dutch who also took plantations in the east by the sword. As war was a risky business, Roe's advice to the Company was to seek profits by quiet trading at sea.[12]

A high-ranking Mughal official, Khafi Khan, visited Bombay in 1696. He has left a unique Indian view of the English East India Company's activities in these years. The author of the report strongly criticised the English for plundering Muslim ships visiting Mecca and the Red Sea and went so far as to contrast their policy with that of the Portuguese who did not, according to him, attack ships at sea except those which had failed to take out Portuguese passes granting safe-conduct.[13] The English occupation of Bombay was viewed with some resentments, as were the earlier efforts of the Portuguese to convert the locals to the Christian faith. Imperial officers were constantly on their guard against any possible growth of military power on the part of European nations in those trading cities where they were likely to come into strong competition with Indian merchants.[14]

Places where Europeans were allowed to establish fortified settlements were either outside the political control of the Mughals or devoid of any commercial importance. Sir Thomas Roe had perceived this very clearly when he pointed out to the Company in 1615, that if a suitable natural harbour was found in an unoccupied territory, it would be discovered at the same time that the surrounding country was barren and untraded. It was no easy task, he commented with prophetic insight, to attract trade and merchants to such a place from existing and flourishing commercial centres.[15] The East India Company did not systematically adopt any ideological viewpoint which sought to provide any kind of moral justification for armed trading. But there was always an underlying assumption that if it did not do so, the Company and its servants would expose their commercial capital and even personal safety, to the exaction and violence of arbitrary rulers. In the political world of contemporaneous Asia, as perceived by the Court of Directors, European traders appeared as victims rather than as aggressors. There are innumerable examples illustrating this deeply-held belief. In 1675, the Company's factors in Rajapur reported that all favours from local rulers have to be bought, and the people in those parts of the coast being Hindus were even more grasping than Muslims.[16] A later governor of Bombay thought that without a naval force, the Company's Malabar settlements would be quickly overrun by the coastal kings. As he put it rhetorically, 'if no Naval Force no Trade, if no Fear no Friendship' – the Company must judge whether the trade of the whole coast, Persia and Mocha, was worth the expense of keeping a naval patrol.[17]

Although there was a close similarity between the methods followed by the Dutch and the English in realising the political aims in Asia, there were also important dissimilarities in their history and areas of operations. The VOC laid the foundation of its imperial system within three decades of the Company's inception. For the English Company, a comparative development did not take place until the second half of the 17th century. Again, the possession of Batavia in 1619, and a strong territorial base in Java and the Spice Islands, enabled the Dutch to avoid the necessity of seeking similar bases in the Mughal Empire. The East India Company, on the other hand, felt vulnerable without fortified settlements in the Indian subcontinent, partly because it wished to avoid payments to the local redistributive enterprises, and partly because the Directors wanted the Company to become a redistributive enterprise in its own right. The most explicit formulation of such ideas and the strength of Dutch influence on the latter were to be found during the period of Sir Josiah Child's governorship, which in many ways represented a break from the previous tradition of peaceful trading. The Company's aversion to the policy of provoking conflicts in India was stressed with special emphasis when the third Anglo-Dutch War broke out in 1672. There was a distinct danger that the extension of hostilities to the Indian subcontinent might easily lead to military intervention by the south Indian rulers on behalf of one European nation or other. If the English remained on friendly terms with the coastal powers, it was highly probable that the Dutch would be deterred from attacking Madras for fear of a diplomatic breach with them. So far as the Indian rulers were concerned, Fort St George was asked by the Court not to forget that "*we are not only in their country upon termes by which we possesse what we there have, but also under their protection*".[18] This was an important statement, indicative of the mood of the anti-war sentiment within the Court of Committees. But as the Company's political relations with the Mughal rulers deteriorated in the 1670s, there was an increasing call for a more war-like policy. With Josiah Child's accession to power in the 1680s, the non-belligerent attitude was to be sharply reversed.

The political ideology of the Company underwent a complete change and soon a concerted attempt was to be made to create a privileged position for itself in the Mughal Empire by the force of arms. The acquisition of Madras and Bombay provided a tempting opportunity for making the Company relatively independent of the Mughal powers. The burgeoning volume of the Company's trade in the 1670s had greatly raised its stakes in the Indian affairs, which were being threatened by the interlopers at home and by the Dutch in Asia. It was becoming apparent that some vigorous counter-measures would have to be adopted to meet the growing challenge.[19] Also, for the first time in its history, the direction of the Company was in the hands of a man who was a political thinker and had a fixed plan of action. The changing emphasis was visible with the first election of Josiah Child to the governorship in 1681. For the rest of the decade, he and his faction remained in uncontested control of the Company's decisions on trade and war. Child's ardent advocacy of a policy of dominions in Asia was founded on his belief that the commercial success of the Dutch Company was due to its political strategy.[20] His own war policy was aimed at winning a formal recognition from the Mughal Empire, of the Company's right to trade as a sovereign power. That right was to be upheld by the establishment of a fortified settlement in Bengal, a province that was increasingly assuming a crucial place in the Company's trade. By becoming a local territorial power, the Company would be in a position to raise revenues, which in its turn would make the English "a nation in India". To trade in India as mere merchants by courtesy of the local rulers was to make a very silly figure, unbecoming of a national organisation, and the Court predicted confidently that the new policy would enable the Company to survive beyond the lives of men's youngest grandchildren.[21]

After the Company-Mughal war, a discouraged Court wrote to Madras in the summer of 1690, hoping that the Mughal Emperor was as weary of the war as they were. For though he was a very great and rich prince who attached little weight to trade, yet they had reason to believe that *"he draws more annuall profitt from trade especially from his manufacturers within the land than all the princes upon the face of the earth and it is no great pleasure to a great prince to see such multitudes of subjects starve for want of employment"*.[22] A year later, after the peace terms were finalised, the members of the Court of Committees admitted that the attempt to wage war on *"that Great Monarch the Mogull was a very dangerous thing to do"*. But they thought that it was a just war which had prevented the Company's affairs from being totally ruined by the English interlopers and the extorting Mughal governors.[23] The old attitude which saw the Company as a victim of political oppression rather than an imperial force in search of territorial possessions was back again, and the desire for local revenues and the freedom from having to pay tribute to the Asian redistributive enterprises also remained. These aims were to be realized through prudent management and by negotiation. The use of force was to be held in reserve as a strategic deterrent in a finely calculated game of power before being actually used, and the servants were seldom allowed to forget that its financial implications on the commercial balance sheet had a decisive weight on the Company's final policy.

The Structure of the English Market

In England, three methods were used to dispose the Asian merchandise brought by the English Company: (1) candle auction to sell in the domestic market of England, (2) re-exportation to other European markets, and (3) distribution among the shareholders as dividends in kind.[24]

For the candle auction, the merchants of the Company usually gave a notice in writing to the Royal Exchange in London, stating that on a particular day, such and such commodities would be sold at such a place. The selling of commodities by the candle auction was an ancient custom in England. The following is the account of the candle auction given in the Court Minutes. A piece of candle was set up lighted in some place easy to be seen, and the bystanders who came to purchase commodities were required to make an offer for such goods. One by one, they offered and they did it in outcries, one offering more than others, still having a regard to the burning candle. Declaration was made regarding the payment so that he who made the last offer upon the going out of the candle, had the bargain. If it did fall out when there was a confusion of voices made, the candle was set up again by the authority and in like manner it was determined accordingly.[25] Usually, the time for the payment was in four instalments with a six months' gap. Sometimes, if the buyer was interested to clear in one instalment, ten per cent discount was allowed on the total payment. In the General Court of sales held on 29 May 1635, 200 bags of pepper were disposed of through candle auction. First, an offer of sixteen pence per pound at 24 months as period of payment was made for pepper. But the Court turned down the offer and resolved to reduce the time without raising the price. Finally, one Daniel Harvey purchased the whole stock of pepper at 16 pence per pound, the period of payment being twenty-one months from the date of auction, and the pepper was ordered to be delivered to him.[26] In the initial phase, the commodities were invariably sold through the candle auction. But from 1630s onwards, public sales were gradually discontinued and imports began to be given as dividends among the shareholders. As an example, finding calicoes in some quantities unsold in its warehouses, the Company in 1637, in the General Court of Sales, decided to distribute them in kind as dividends among the shareholders.[27]

From the 1650s, the East India Company adopted the practice of auctioning its goods in four quarterly sales held in London, and the economic response of the buyers at these sales provided the necessary information about the state of the market and possible future trend in demand. Similar auctions were held at Amsterdam. The regulation of the volume of trade at the Asian end was largely a function of this simple mechanism located in Amsterdam and London, which acted as a central clearing-house for the East India trade in Europe. The Company's quarterly sales were attended by dealers from Holland, Germany and Eastern Europe. They knew intimately the actual conditions in these distant regional markets, the volume of stocks left in the hands of retailers, the prices of substitute goods, the precise time for shipment through inland waterways before they froze up in winter, and changes in consumer tastes.[28]

In the early part of the 17th century, the Company built all its ships in either of its two shipyards on the Thames – Deptford and Blackwall Yard. The Company's first ships were purchased privately as and when required. Each had a limited life-expectancy, normally four voyages to Asia over 8 to 10 years. Losses from wear, tear and wreck took their toll, and suitable ships were soon at a premium, some costing as much as £45 per ton. In 1607, the Company therefore decided to build its own ships and leased a yard in Deptford for this purpose. Initially, this new policy seemed to work, as the first ships cost only about £10 per ton. However, the ship-building and repair yards at Deptford soon proved expensive to run. The Company, ever eager to save money, had second thoughts. Later, in the second half of the 17th century, it went back to the practice of hiring vessels. The practice of direct construction was discontinued and the Company began to hire from ship owners who bore all the risks. In most cases, the owners who chartered their vessel to the East India Company had them built at Deptford and Blackwall itself.

In the provision of the Company's export goods, as for instance broadcloth and silver, the Company never even considered going either to the producers or to the primary sources of supplies. There already existed in England and in the Continent, a well-known dealer-network that was perfectly capable of supplying the Company with the necessary quantities of the export goods according to its own time-schedule and at the cheapest possible costs. By offering its import commodities in public auctions at specified time-intervals and in one definite location, the Company was able to set up a simple institutional arrangement whereby the buyers and sellers could make contacts. It is, of course, a truism, that no trade or complicated economic exchanges can occur unless both sides to the buying and selling operations know when and where they can meet.

If the market is characterised by slow means of transport and communication, it becomes difficult to stabilise prices without the stock-holding, which would tend to smooth out excess supply or excess demand. The distance which separated the supply and consuming markets in East India trade, and the long time-span elapsing between commercial decisions and their implementation, made it notoriously speculative. The instability of the pepper trade in 16th century Europe arose precisely because the quantity and the timing of pepper supplies arriving from the Indies were not always predictable. The resultant fluctuations in prices made it a profitable commodity to speculate in, provided one was lucky in guessing the future course of the market. The VOC and the English East India Company had their full measure of experience of the extent to which the pepper trade needed careful regulation, in order to avoid heavy financial losses. From the middle of the 17th century, their managerial committees continually strove to strike an equilibrium between the supply and demand of all their import commodities.

The quarterly sales were admirably designed to remove the irregularity and the seasonal nature of the supplies. The Company's main homeward fleet generally arrived back from the Indies during August and September, though a few ships could arrive earlier or later than these two months. It was clearly inadvisable to try to sell the entire stock of goods brought home by the summer and autumn ships in one single auction. By spreading out the stocks over the whole year, the Company not only hoped to prevent a sudden slide in prices, but also provided the buyers with a means of predicting the market. In some cases, the Committee of Warehouses was prepared to go as far as to give a definite guarantee that once a certain quantity of a particular commodity was sold in an auction, no further stocks would be released in the market before a specified date. Such an assurance at once reduced the risk of market fluctuations arising from the Company's own action, and it encouraged the buyers to offer higher prices at the public sales. It is interesting to note that the underlying assumption in the economic behaviour of the Company and its associates in Europe, were typically monopolistic. The crucial decision variable was the control over supplies, and the demand was treated more or less as a given factor which varied according to a known random function.[29] Supplies were controlled over time, according to calculations that took into account the strategy of the rival Dutch or French Companies, the cost of holding inventories, the elasticity of demand and the level of current prices.

A second and equally powerful argument in favour of the public auction system in selling Asian imports, came from the nature of the information it provided to the buyers and the sellers. Before the sales actually took place, a printed list of the total quantity of each type of goods offered, and the prices at which bids were to be invited, were circulated. A potential buyer thus possessed complete information on two very important points, the quantities available and the seller's price offer. During the auctions, prices were determined by competition among the buyers present, again in the full knowledge of rival bid prices. It was possible, of course, for the dealers to form a ring and depress prices. But it is significant that in relation to their London sales, the Court of Directors never referred to the formation of rings, although such complaints were frequent about market transactions in Asia. Since the members of the Directorate themselves could have organized rings as interested purchasers of the Company's goods, it is possible that they were not anxious to publicise their existence if rings did occur. By taking the realized bid prices as market indicators, the Company was spared one of the most difficult tasks facing an oligopolist, the determination of the price of his products. The Company always adjusted its orders about future supplies of particular Asian commodities, on the basis of prices received in sales. With the increased demand of the eastern luxuries in the European markets, the English Company enhanced the volume of export from the East and re-exported to other European countries and the Middle East. This was the first step towards the creation of a multilateral trade system centred in London. The commodities of India exchanged for bullion, in turn, formed the basis of the Company's investments in the Asian trade. Therefore, a large portion of the goods reaching London was re-exported to other European markets.[30] The English Company made huge profits on the sale of Indian commodities in England and Europe, especially on cotton textiles. For example, in the 1630s, a piece of cloth bought in India for seven shillings was sold in London for a pound, i.e. a profit of about 300 per cent. A pound of clove or nutmeg bought in India for eight to nine pence was disposed of in England for six shillings, at a profit of about 800-900 per cent. There was a saying that, "a sheep could be bought in England during the Middle Ages for a pound of ginger... pepper corns were so valuable, they were used to pay rent and buy land". This shows clearly the enormous gain made by the English Company through the trade with India.

Organising the Supply

In organising the supply of Asian imports, trading companies had two choices. They could either buy at the local wholesale market in the port towns, or in the secondary interior markets where they had branch factories, or they could approach the producers directly. Both alternatives were tried out at various times. There were differing viewpoints as to which of the two methods was most efficient and economical. In the early years of the English trade in India, one group of factors led by Sir Thomas Roe favoured the idea of concentrating all commercial activities in Surat. They did not oppose outright the possibility of establishing factories in the interior. But such a policy, as Roe outlined in a letter to the Company in 1616, should carefully take into account the nature of the goods and the problem of transport costs. Bulky commodities that eat much in carriage should be procured from sources nearest to the port. Fine goods, on the other hand, were much better able to bear the cost of lengthy transport.[31] Roe saw no reason to maintain a separate factory in Agra, even though the region around the town produced the best variety of indigo. In his view, it was more economical to give a higher price for it in Surat than to undertake the entire risk and cost of carriage from Agra, because *"the people of this country can transport it much cheaper"*. There were dealers in Surat who regularly supplied indigo to the Red Sea traders. Once the English demand was known, Roe believed, they would be perfectly capable of providing the necessary quantities at Surat at competitive prices. The significant point in Roe's argument was the free operation of the market mechanism, that the supply would adjust to demand and prices would respond to the scale of the operation. This is what one would expect in any well-organised wholesale market.

There were two interconnecting markets in indigo – one situated in the area of production, and the other at the port of shipment. The most important determinants of prices in either of them, apart from the size of the crop, were the number of buyers and the prices prevailing in the Middle Eastern markets. In 1670, for instance, the Surat factory asked the Agra agent to make contracts for 400 bales of indigo, as they were *"informed by the lately arrived ships from Basrah that the esteem and price of said commodity is much risen there, which news will certainly encourage the merchants here to buy up great quantities and then the price will also rise"*.[32] This is not the only evidence of the practice of speculative stock-holding. Two years later, the Company's broker, Bhimji Parekh, informed the Surat factory that the orders for Agra indigo must be completed by November, otherwise the Armenians and other merchants would 'engross' the stocks and the Company would be forced to buy from speculative dealers at inflated prices.[33]

It was not always that the selling side of a particular commodity was so concentrated that the suppliers could influence prices at will. But whatever chance there was for such an occurrence, could be minimised through advance contracting. Much has been written about the Indian advance-payment system, under which merchants received a down-payment on the signing of a formal contract, and they in turn undertook the prior financing of the products and the producers. A whole nexus of credit relationships permeated Indian economic life, and it was an important instrument of social control. For the European traders, it had the added attraction of ensuring a certain measure of standardisation. This was a problem that was particularly acute in the textile trade. It is significant that even in the 1670s, when for a brief period, the English Company attempted to by-pass the Surat cloth merchants and approach the producers directly in the cloth districts of Broach, the advance system was kept intact. In Coromandel and Bengal, where the Company's servants had much less experience of the commercial conditions in the upcountry areas, forward contracts with large wholesale merchants were the general rule. The exact nature of the financial objectives which each party to the bargain attempted to realise, can be studied from the numerous contracts to be found in the Company's records. The main feature of the actual negotiations preceding the formal signing of the contract, was the bidding process through which agreement was reached over prices. The merchants were initially invited by the Council to submit tenders, sometimes individually, but mostly as a group. After examining their prices and the samples, the factory made its own counter-offer, which was either accepted or rejected by the merchants according to their assessment of the current and future state of the market. The price formation in the forward market was evidently a fairly sophisticated operation, and involved very careful calculation of risks.

The Global Trade and Monetary System

The trading world of Europe and Asia in the 15th and 16th centuries were precariously dependent on a monetary system based on metallic currencies. The dependence on gold and silver for international financial transactions was cast into new dimension by the discovery of silver mines by Spain, in South America, in the 16th century. Many scholars believe this to be the beginning of the present-day global economy.[34] Potosi, called 'Villa Imperial de Potosí' during its Spanish Colonial days, a small town in present-day Bolivia having an area of less than 46 square miles, became the epicentre of global trade in the 16th century. In 1545, silver mines were discovered here. Soon, it produced an estimated 60 per cent of all silver mined in the world during the second half of the 16th century. Potosi's deposits were rich, and Spain minted it into the peso de ocho, the Spanish dollar, also known as the piece of eight. This peso de ocho was so widespread that even the United States accepted it as valid until the Coinage Act of 1857.

The ultimate destination for the majority of silver produced in these South American mines, was China. Silver from the American mines flowed mostly across the Atlantic to Europe and made its way to the Far East. A popular route was around the Cape of Good Hope into the east, but sometimes it came over land. Major outposts for the silver trade were located in the East Indies.[ii] Silver found its way across to other parts of the world as well.

---

ii The present-day Philippines

India and Europe both received a fair amount of silver. This silver was often locally traded for other commodities such as gold or crops. In India, silver flowed from the south to the north, and gold flowed the opposite way. Often silver and gold were manufactured into jewellery or hoarded as treasure.[35]

China was the ultimate destination for this silver. In exchange, the Chinese traded their popular goods such as silk, porcelain, and of course, tea. China had a high demand for silver due to its shift from paper money to coins in the early period of the Ming Dynasty.[36] Also, the bimetallic ratio of silver to gold was about two to one, which meant that European merchants made a large profit just by bringing silver.[37] Only by the 1640s, did the bimetallic ratios in China converge with the rest of the world.

For the English East India Company, if there was one aspect of its trade that attracted more attention and polemics at home than anything else – before the competition of Indian textiles with domestic English products became an acute political issue – it was the Company's export of gold and silver. The use of precious metals for internal currencies as well as for international trade and payments, meant that the stability of the European monetary system depended to a large extent on a number of related factors, such as the bimetallic ratios in one country, the relative movements in the rates of exchange and the level of internal prices. The monetary effect of the East India Company's trade with Asia was observed by Sir Isaac Newton, then Master of the Mint. *"When ships are lading for the East Indies,"* he wrote in a memorandum to the Treasury in 1717, *"the demand of silver for exportation raises the price to 5s 6d or 5s 8d per ounce or above. But I consider not those extraordinary cases"*.[38] Newton's reference to the seasonal rise in the price of silver, above the price fixed by the English royal mint, was just one aspect of the currency problems created by the Company's exports.

Similar cases were to be found elsewhere. In Portugal, when the East India ships were preparing to sail, a mark of silver rose to 7,200 reis, whereas at the royal mint in Lisbon, it was rated at only 6,400 reis. In Spain, silver commanded a premium of 5 per cent for domestic payments, which temporarily ceased with the arrival of silver shipments from American mines. This favour shown by Sir Isaac Newton to the East India Company was not a one-off affair. Apparently, he owned shares of both the East India Company and the South Sea Company. These two, along with the Bank of England, formed the holy trinity of the English economy at that time. In 1720, during the South Sea bubble, he lost more than £20,000.[iii] He famously remarked that he could calculate the motions of the heavenly bodies, but not the madness of people.

The East India Company financed its imports from the East Indies in three ways – by exporting goods, by borrowing in Asia (sometimes against bills of exchange issued in the Indies and payable in Europe), and lastly, by shipping gold and silver from Europe. These operations were not always bilateral. Gold was imported into India by the Company's ships. In Europe, the Company's purchases of precious metals are divided into two well-defined periods. From 1660 to about 1695, the Company bought both gold and silver almost exclusively in London, mainly from the goldsmith-bankers, although foreign centres were not entirely neglected. From the mid-1690s, however, the transactions of the Committee of Treasure became much more diversified and the big commercial houses of Cadiz and Amsterdam came to the forefront. A list of the Company's suppliers from 1665 to 1760, shows that the bulk of the Company's bullion and foreign coins was purchased through the agency of a few well-known goldsmiths of the period, the rest being supplied by innumerable small

---

iii Over $3 million in today's money

traders. The Letters Patent granted by Charles II in 1660, allowed the Company to buy and export foreign money and treasure to the value of £60,000.[39] But in December, the Council of Trade had put forward a proposition to the king that he should withdraw the penalties on the export of gold and silver, because the restrictions were injuring trade by preventing English merchants from bringing their money into the kingdom, where it ran the risk of being detained, and inducing them to leave it instead at Amsterdam or Leghorn. The document was endorsed that "this freedom is important to the East India and Turkey Companies more especially".[40] By an Act of 1663, foreign gold and silver were allowed to be exported without fee or duty.

In the early 1660s, the Committee of Treasure was buying Spanish reales and bar silver in both London and Amsterdam. The Company's connection with the Royal Africa Company provided a useful means of procuring gold which the India-bound ships often collected directly from the West Coast of Africa.[41] The Royal African Company was an English mercantile (trading) company set up by the royal Stuart family and City of London merchants, to trade along the west coast of Africa. It mainly traded in gold and African slaves. The most common practice adopted by the Committee for the purchase of bullion in London during this period was to invite tenders for reales at a certain rate, and to seek out individual bargains with the traders and bullion dealers. Edward Backwell, the leading merchant banker of London, was the Company's most important supplier until 1676, when his name suddenly disappears from the account books. Of the foreign Jewish bankers, four had substantial dealings with the Company during this period, supplying mostly gold. They were Jeronimo Miranda, Alphonso and Gomez Rodriguez and Solomon del Medina.[42]

Monetary System in India

Jean-Baptiste Tavernier, whom Gibbon described as the wandering jeweller who had read nothing but had seen so much so well, aptly devoted a whole chapter in his book to the description of the gold and silver trade of India and its currency practices.[43] His accounts, supported by more detailed evidence in the records of the trading companies, indicate the existence of a fairly sophisticated monetary system which the Mughals had established in large parts of India. Not only did most of the important trading towns possess a mint for the coining of silver or copper money, but the Indian bullion dealers had carried to a high level, the intricate art of testing and establishing the intrinsic worth of various foreign coins imported into the country.[44] Thomas Rolt, the English President of the Surat factory from 1677-82, testified to their expertise when he observed in 1682 that the Surat sarrafs "are certainly the greatest masters of their art of any people in these parts of the world".[45] The Company's servants had learnt from practical experience that the Indian sarrafs and bankers, apart from being skilled traders in precious metals, also wielded considerable financial powers. On monetary matters, they could exercise almost a monopolistic influence. In the words of a Masulipatnam factor, it was a strange abuse that the sarrafs of India had the power to raise or lower the price of bullion as they pleased.

The basis of the Mughal currency system was the silver rupee, which was both a money of account and a current coin. Gold was also coined in a fixed ratio to silver, but its currency for transaction purposes was limited, as the value of gold coins, known as muhar or ashrafi, was determined by the market price of gold in terms of silver. Thus, the currency standard in areas of Mughal rule was based unambiguously on silver. But on the coast of Malabar and in much of southern India, the gold standard of former Hindu kingdoms still prevailed. It was silver which bore a fluctuating value in relation to the money of account, the gold pagoda. In Malabar, the Venetian sequins[iv] also passed as current coin, and difficulties were experienced by the English in attempting to make their payments in Spanish pistoles and imperial ducats.[46] The acceptability of certain types of coins for commercial transactions in Asia was closely related to the confidence which merchants were prepared to place on their intrinsic metallic content, as it eliminated the bullion dealer and the need for laborious and time-consuming examination and the assaying of every individual coin types.

The precious metals came into Surat in two forms – ingots and coinage. Abyssinian gold was sold in Surat in 1618 at 22 to 23 mahmudis a tola[v] but the occasional influx of gold from Arabia tended to depress gold prices from time to time. In 1628, the English succeeded in landing gold clandestinely and saved £10,000 in customs-duties. In February of that year, the English reported a fall in the price of gold, and in November, they had gold amounting to £44,000 on their hands as 'unvendible'. The low price continued in 1629, and between 1635 and 1646, the English 20 shillings-piece advanced from 20 mahmudis to 21 1/4 mahmudis only. The gold coins brought in were sold by weight. In 1652, the English standard gold was selling in Surat at £3. 12s. 0d. per oz. Gold was also brought in from the Guinea Coast as a part of the new investment in 1658. By 1676, however there was an unprecedented fall in gold prices, partly as a result of Aurangzeb releasing Akbar's hoarded gold. The gold rupee called 'sunny' formerly worth Rs 15, was selling in 1676 at Rs 11 to Rs 12. In 1677, the English lost about 3 per cent on the sale of their gold.

---

iv A sequin was a gold coin weighing 3. 5 grams[0. 12 oz] of . 986 gold, minted by the Republic of Venice from the 13th century onwards.

v About 185. 5 grains

The English also brought in gold and silver for turning them into coins at the mint. The English imported chests of silver for its conversion into local silver currency at the Surat mint, or for sale to magnates such as Virji Vora, and other sarrafs or moneychangers. They also brought in reales. Sir William Foster explains the rial as the Spanish dollar or reales,[vi] which was at that time the only European coin in general esteem throughout the East Indies, owing chiefly to its uniformity of weight and the purity of its silver.

A few characteristics of the Indian markets in bullion and currencies was noted by leading English economists of the period, such as Lipton. The peculiarity of the East India trade was that it absorbed the precious metals in excessive quantities. Secondly, the hoarding and concealment of precious metals was an obsession not only with the people, but also with the Mughal government. This deprived the markets of a large quantity of the precious metals, which otherwise could have been in circulation through investments and profits of trade and industry. Surat absorbed a significant share of precious metals, as was revealed during Shivaji's raids on this city in 1664 and 1670.

The European East India companies were the symbols and manifestation of the new developments that were taking place in the history of Western nations from the beginning of the 17th century. These were expressed in the art of ship-building and navigation, in settlement of colonies in the New World, the ability to organise and manage distant commercial ventures, and in new forms of financial institutions. The trading companies contributed to all these activities. In Asia, the impact was no less significant. In areas such as the Indonesian archipelago, both the Dutch and the English followed a mixture of commercial and coercive methods to procure their return cargo of pepper and spices. But in India and China, normal market

vi More correctly, the piece of eight reales

transactions were the main form of trade. The huge influx of bullion which resulted from the new demand, was only one indication of the growth in income and employment. The export of textiles turned the coastal provinces of India into major industrial regions, and the bullion imported by the companies passed directly into circulation as payments for the export goods. The contribution made by the merchants and the producers to government revenue and taxation was the main reason, as the Court of Directors and the Mughal historian Khafi Khan agreed alike, why the ruling powers in India encouraged European trade.

References

[1] Thomas Babington Macaulay, *The History of England in the 18th Century* (1849), London: Folio Society, 1980, p. 183.

[2] Fernand Braudel, *Civilization and Capitalism,* vol. 2: The Wheels of Commerce, London: Collins, 1982, p. 436.

[3] John Keay, *The Honourable Company,* London: HarperCollins, 1993, p. 219.

[4] Philip Lawson, *The East India Company,* London: Longman, 1993, p. 21.

[5] Els M. Jacobs, *In Pursuit of Pepper and Tea: The Story of the Dutch East India Company,* Amsterdam: Netherlands Maritime Museum, 1991, p. 16.

[6] Keay, The Honourable Company, p. 113.

[7] David Landes, *The Wealth and Poverty of Nations*, London: Little, Brown and Company, 1998, p. 143.

[8] See Furber, 'Rival Empires of Trade', p. 91.

[9] Daniel Defoe, Anatomy of Exchange Alley, quoted in Maureen Waller, 1700: *Scenes from London Life,* London: Hodder & Stoughton, 2000, p. 243.

[10] East India Company to Fort St George, 9 June 1686, quoted in Pincus, Whigs, p. 12.

[11] East India Company to Fort St George, quote in Chaudhury, *The Prelude to Empire,* p. 68.

[12] The embassy of Sir Thomas Roe to India 1615 – 1619, ed. W. Foster (London, 1926), p. 250, 303.

[13] Muhammad Hashim, Khafi Khan, Muntakhab-ul-Lubab, printed in Sir H. M. Elliot and J. Dowson, *The history of India as told by its own historians* (8 vols., London, 1867-77), pp. 344-5, 354.

[14] Bengal Public Consultations, 17 June 1718, vol. 3, p. 534; Abstract of Letters Received from Bombay, 30 October 1718, vol. 449, para. 56, p. 303.

[15] The embassy of Sir Thomas Roe, p. 303.

[16] Factory Records Surat, 20 April 1675, vol. 88, p. 43.

[17] Abstract of Letters Received from Bombay, 20 December 1718, vol. 449, para. 30, p. 322.

[18] Despatch Book, 29 September 1673, vol. 88, p. 69.

[19] In 1686 Child wrote to Madras that the interlopers and the Dutch were responsible for disturbing the Company's ancient 'peaceable way' and that as to these two parties "we look upon the Mogoll's Governours but as instruments which we hope to compel by fair means or foul to use us better hereafter", ibid., 9 June 1686, vol. 91, p. 145.

[20] For Child's views on this point, see ibid., 14 January 1686, vol. 91, para. 25, p. 37, 47; ibid., 9 June 1686, vol. 91, p. 142, p. 145; ibid., 28 September 1687, vol. 91, par. 36, p. 419.

[21] Ibid., 11 September 1689, vol. 92, p. 64.

[22] Despatch Book, 30 May 1690, vol. 92, p. 103.

[23] Ibid., 13 May 1691, vol. 92, para. 2, p. 161.

[24] Court Minutes, Vol. III (1644-1649), p. 103.

[25] Court Minutes, Vol. I (1635-1639), p. 48.

[26] Court Minutes, Vol. 1 (1635-1639), p. 58.

[27] EFI, Vol. VI (1637-1641). p. 312.

[28] Despatches from England 1721-1724 (Fort St. George), 2 February 1725, para. 21, p. 123; Despatch Book, 15 February 1716, vol. 97, para. 13, p. 780; ibid., 27 January 1742, vol. 108, para. 76, p. 515.

[29] Despatch Book, 6 January 1738, vol. 107, paras. 41-2, p. 371.

[30] Chaudhuri, The English East India Company, p. 173.

[31] Original Correspondence, 1 December 1616, vol. 4, No. 411; Letters received, iv, 249.

[32] Factory Records Surat, 10 May 1670, vol. 3, p. 65.

[33] Factory Records Surat, 20 November 1672,vol. 3,p. 31.

[34] Flynn, Dennis; Giráldez, Arturo (1995). "Born with a 'Silver Spoon': The Origin of World Trade in 1571". *Journal of World*

History. University of Hawaii Press.

[35] Frank, Andre (July 1998). *Reorient*. Berkeley: University of California Press.

[36] von Glahn, Richard (1996). "Myth and Reality of China's Seventeenth-Century Monetary Crisis". *The Journal of Economic History*. 56 (2): pp. 429–454.

[37] Atwell, William S. (2005). "Another Look at Silver Imports into China, ca. 1635–1644". *Journal of World History*. 16 (4): pp. 467–489.

[38] State of the gold and silver coin, 25 September 1717, in Shaw, Select tracts and documents, p. 190.

[39] *Court Minutes of the East India Company* 1660-1663, p. 62.

[40] P. R. O. State Papers Domestic, 12 December 1660, vol. 23, No. 85.

[41] Despatch Book, 12 September 1660, vol. 85, p. 321; 'Articles of agreement between the Royall Company and the East India Company made the 16th day of October 1662', ibid., vol. 86, p. 171. K. G. Davies, *The Royal African Company* (London, 1957), pp. 41-46.

[42] For the background of these London merchant bankers, see R. D. Richards, *The early history of banking in England* (London, 1929). On the Jewish merchants in England, see articles in Encyclopaedia Judaica (Jerusalem, 1971).

[43] W. Crooke, 'Introduction', in Tavernier, Travels in India, p. xxxiii.

[44] Ibid, p. 1, 13.

[45] Original Correspondence, 23 January 1682, vol. 41, para. 13, p. 5.

[46] Factory Records Surat, 29 August 1672, vol. 3, p. 15.

Epilogue
The Decline of Surat

By the end of the 17th century, the English factory at Surat was well past its prime. Many factors contributed to it losing its glory as the headquarters of the English trade in the East. The high-handedness of the Mughal officials and their illegal squeezing of Indian traders and merchants was obviously the most important factor, causing many to either migrate away from Mughal dominion or limit their trading activities. The Maratha war of independence made travel in the countryside unsafe, and the procurement of local textiles and other trading items difficult. Sea piracy was at its peak, making ships, both English and Indian, equally vulnerable. Added to this was the rise of the three towns of Bombay, Madras and Calcutta, which gradually eclipsed Surat.

In 1661, the centre of the East India Company's trade was still Surat. The Chief of the Surat factory carried the title of President and the area of his authority extended to the subordinate factories at Broach, Ahmedabad and Tatta in Sind in the north, Karwar, Kayal and Rajapur further south down the coast, Gombroon and Isfahan in Persia, Basra in the Persian Gulf and Mocha in the Yemen.[1]

The closing-down of a few outlying factories in early 1661 was undertaken in the belief that a reduction of overhead costs would enable the main settlements to function more efficiently and provide commodities required by the Company for its direct trade with Europe and for its trade with Bantam in the Indonesian archipelago. As a port on the western seaboard of India, Surat had no serious rival. It was the hub from which sea-lanes radiated to all the famous ports of the Indian Ocean and beyond. On the landward side, caravan routes from the north, east, and south converged on the city. During his visit to Surat in 1689, John Ovington, who acted as a chaplain to the English factory, saw goods from Agra, Delhi, Broach and Ahmedabad for sale in town, which attracted merchants of all nations, Europeans, Turks, Arabs, Persians and Armenians. *"Surat is reckoned the most famed Emporium of the Indian Empire,"* he wrote, *"where all commodities are vendible, though they never were there seen before... And not only from Europe, but from China, Persia, Arabia, and other remote parts of India. Ships unload abundance of all kinds of goods, for the ornament of the city, as well as enriching of the port"*.[2] It was not without reason that John Fryer commented in 1664, that the Surat Presidency was superior to all others in the East Indies, even the newly independent Agency of Bantam *"being not long since subordinate to it"*.[3]

With the acquisition of Bombay from the Portuguese in 1661 and its actual occupation four years later, strenuous efforts were made to attract trade to that island. But the Company's dream of making Bombay an effective rival to Surat remained unfulfilled for more than a century. It is not easy to suggest any single cause for Bombay's commercial failure during this period. Unhealthy climate was certainly one factor, but perhaps a more fundamental explanation can be found in the geographical location of that city. In an age when land carriage was an indispensable complement of sea transport, the bond between towns and roads was as vital to trade as the sea routes. The space and convenience afforded by Bombay's deep-water harbour was off-set by the steep and rugged hills, the western ghats, which enclosed the island only a short distance from the sea. Surat, on the other hand, was much nearer to the caravan routes, passing through the rich and fertile plains of Gujarat, towards the cities of upper India, and easily acted as the catchment point for goods coming down to the coast for shipment overseas. It was difficult for a new port to displace a city of such strength as was Surat, particularly if it is inhabited by some of the most skilled and enterprising business communities in the world.[4]

The settlements in Gujarat and northern India had developed in response to the needs of the Company's textile trade. When the basis of this trade changed and moved away to southern India and Bengal, their decline followed swiftly. It would be a mistake, however, to look upon these withdrawals as an indication of a general relaxation of the Company's long-standing insistence on buying goods in the cheapest market. It was just that the factory system had outlived its usefulness in that area, and it was found cheaper to exercise supervision over the broker or his sub-agents through the periodical inspection of the investment areas carried out by factors sent from Surat or Broach.[5] The two Gujarat factories were supplemented by a number of settlements created on the Malabar coast. Agriculturally one of the most productive regions of India, the narrow coastal belt stretching southwards from Goa to Cape Comorin attracted the European merchant companies for a number of reasons. Kanara and Malabar were the home of that rare spice, cardamom, and produced a coarse sort of cinnamon known as cassia lignum. But more than anything else, there was the fact that the coast was the world's second greatest supplier of black pepper. Both the Dutch and English East India companies looked to Malabar as an alternative to the Indonesian archipelago for the purchase of pepper. In the later part of 17th century, the two English settlements in Malabar, at Tellicherry and Anjengo, both of which were fortified, supplied the bulk of the English pepper supplies from the Indian subcontinent.[6]

However, a sea-power cannot establish positions of strength far from the sea. The withdrawal of the Company's inland factories in Gujarat, the emergence of Bombay as its administrative headquarters in the 1690s and the foundation of Calcutta and its subsequent fortification, were all part of a single objective. One of the remarkable features of the typology of the East India Company's settlements was that in spite of a divergent history and chronology, there was a close similarity of development which could not have been the result of chance or accidental factors. On the coast of Coromandel and in Bengal, the Presidency towns founded by the Company enjoyed a much greater measure of commercial success as local trading ports than did Bombay in western India. The meteoric rise of Madras from an inconsiderable town which was acquired from a local chief in 1639, to the position of a leading port in Coromandel three decades later, was an object of justifiable pride to the Court of Committees.[7] Even Alexander Hamilton, a sea captain and a country trader, who had nothing good to say about any of the Company's settlements in India, admitted that Madras was enriched by the migration of Indian merchants and that the trade and industry of the town supported an estimated population of 80,000.[8]

In the 1680s, with the expansion in the Company's textile trade, the Court of Committees began to refer to Bengal as the rising investment area in India. Although factories had been established at Balasore, Hugli, Kasimbazar and Dacca over the previous three decades, the productive capacity of the province, as seen in the lower prices of export goods, convinced the Company that here was an area, the full potential of which was not yet properly utilised.[9] Of course, no one engaged in the maritime trade of Gujarat and Coromandel could have been long unaware of Bengal's contribution to Asia's international trade. It was the granary from which the deficient areas of India were fed.[10] The demand for luxury garments in the princely households in the subcontinent and beyond, was met from the handlooms of Bengal. The silk weavers of Gujarat depended for their supply of raw material on the importation of silk yarn from the northern district of Bengal. The commercial importance of the area for the European trading companies, stemmed from its three staple products – the high-quality cotton textiles known as muslins, raw silk, and saltpetre. However, the early attempts of the Company to open trading relations with Bengal in the 1620s had failed, because the factors approached it through the overland route used by merchants from Agra and other upcountry cities, when the economics of transport called for the cheaper and easier passage by sea. But here again, the Company experienced initial difficulties. Even though the province had a magnificent system of rivers and inland waterways, Bengal was virtually a landlocked region for the overseas trader who came equipped with deep-water sailing ships. All deltas with large silt-carrying rivers tend to be dangerous to shipping: Bengal was no exception. Apart from the river Hugli, the coastline, indented as it was, by thousands of creeks and channels, did not offer a single passage of safe navigation to large ships.[11] Even the mouth of the Hugli, with its constantly changing shoals and sandbanks, was considered so dangerous, that it was not until 1672 that the Company was able to induce any of its sea captains to sail up to the busy commercial town 150 miles from the estuary of the river, to which it had given its own name. The navigational problems of Bengal were eventually solved for the Company, as were the complicated logistics of trade, which involved close co-ordination with Madras over the time-table and distribution of shipping and cargo. Soon, Bengal emerged as the premier trading region of the East India Company in the eighteenth century.

Between 1660 and 1680, the centre of gravity in the Company's commercial policy moved to the south, from Surat to Madras. By the turn of the century, the economic ascendancy of Madras was being challenged by Bengal. During the same period, a similar movement also occurred in the other area of English trade with Asia, the East Indies, where the fierce age-old contest over the mastery of the pepper trade slowly gave way before the rising, promise of trade with the Chinese mainland. The immediate task before the Company in the 1660s, was to secure a sound base for its pepper trade, and to strengthen the mechanism on which this trade rested. If the Company's servants made persistent attempts in these years, both in Bantam and Surat, to trade at Achin, Kedah, the ports of Indo-China and Siam, and even at Formosa, it was because of their awareness that the pepper trade of Java and Sumatra had wider ramifications in South East Asia. But the support of the Court of Committees at home for local trading between India and the East Indies was conditional on the ability of the factors to buy pepper more profitably, by selling imported Indian cotton textiles in the local markets. Part of the difficulties faced by the Surat factory on financial allocations, was because of the fact that in the 1670s, the Company was diverting a greater proportion of its export funds to Bengal through the Madras Council. Bengal was a province which was free of the local wars which were beginning to devastate the Deccan and parts of southern India.[12]

The period from 1683 and 1705 was a disturbing one for the Company. The first notable check came in the form of a severe financial crisis in England towards the end of 1682. In April 1683, the Court described the effects in a letter to Bengal, *"The enclosed is a copy of our last[letter] by the Herbert, since which many Accidents have happened to the affairs of this Company not only in the loss of Bantam to the Dutch and the Johanna outward bound... but more especially by an extraordinary and unparalleled Fail of Credit in all the publique Funds of this Citty (London) which hath caused the failure of diverse Goldsmiths in Lumburd Street".*[13] As it turned out, the monetary stringency and its effects did not last long, but the impact of the large orders placed two years earlier had yet to be felt. By the end of 1683, the market for East India goods was severely depressed, and even the Company was surprised by its extent.[14] With the receding threat from interlopers, the old emphasis on maximising prices by adjusting supplies to demand conditions returned. The volume of imports for the next few years continued to be cut-back until the war with Mughal India suddenly brought all trading activities to a practical standstill.

Oppression by Mughal Authorities

The political chaos towards the end of the 17th century affected the Gujarat merchants adversely. The local Mughal administration fleeced the Gujarat merchants to augment their dwindling resources. There is a reference of a similar nature from an earlier period as well. In 1535, an imperial firman was issued to Mir Sabir and Mir Kalan, to the effect that the peasants, merchants, bankers and Bohras of town Besangarh have complained against the agents of Sipahdar Khan for unlawful realization.[15] Due to the frequent Maratha raids and plunder, the towns and countryside of Gujarat became quite insecure. To maintain the security and peace within the four walls of the cities, huge amounts of money were demanded from the merchants by the officials. Whenever there was threat of a raid against the city, the officials forced the merchants to pay money. According to Ashin Das Gupta, *"the forced contribution was no innovation but the sustained pressure which began to develop was certainly new"*.[16] Upon Jahangir's death in 1627, Prince Shah Jahan, who was in the Deccan, marched to Agra by way of Gujarat. The factory records mention that when Shah Jahan reached Surat, his men demanded and secured a forced loan from the townsmen. The English paid 6,000 rials while several of the merchants borrowed money from the Company to lend the amount to the prince. After reaching Ahmedabad, the prince ordered the city gates to be locked for two days to prevent the rich Hindu merchants from fleeing and collected twenty lakhs of rupees from them. Mirat-ul Haqaiq, the diary of a Mughal official Itimad Ali Khan, provides vivid accounts of forced realization of money from the merchant community by the local administration in the subah of Gujarat.[17]

In 1645, Aurangzeb was appointed the Subahdar of Gujarat. The account of Mirat-i-Ahmadi, a Persian history of Gujarat by Ali Muhammad Khan, gives the impression that Aurangzeb was sent to Gujarat to deal with a near-revolt like condition, because immediately after reaching Gujarat, he assembled a large number of soldiers for the establishment of order and the chastisement of the refractory elements. It was the Kolis who were creating troubles in the province. To deal with them, Aurangzeb had to raise troops at his own expense, for he wrote to the emperor that he had spent much more than he had received as income. Shah Jahan rewarded him by increasing his mansab by a thousand horse.

In 1646, Prince Aurangzeb was called back to the capital, as he was to be given charge of the Balkh and Badakhshan campaign. On the recall of Prince Aurangzeb, Shah Jahan appointed his brother-in-law, Shaista Khan, to be the subahdar of Gujarat. The Kolis renewed their insurrection within a short time, and Shaista Khan took ruthless measures to suppress their movements. In 1648, Shaista Khan was transferred to the Subah of Malwa and Prince Dara Shikoh was given the charge of Gujarat. Dara however, ruled through a deputy, Baqir Beg, titled Ghairat Khan. Prince Murad Bakhsh was the last of Shah Jahan's sons to serve as the subahdar of Gujarat. Shah Jahan's last years were marked by an acute war of succession. In 1654, when Shah Jahan fell seriously ill, Prince Murad Bakhsh marched with an army to capture the flourishing port town of Surat. The Surat fort was captured, and before his final departure from Ahmedabad, Prince Murad extracted five and a half lakh of rupees from Manikchand and his brothers, the sons of the jeweller Shantidas.

On 7 August 1725, the governor of Surat, Hamid Ali Khan, forced the merchants to pay money for security reasons. The merchants showed reluctance. The governor ordered for the demolition of the houses of Moolchand, a silk-cloth seller, as well as the homes of Jeevandas and Kishoredas, who were money-lenders. And when they all agreed to pay the amount through Khushhal Chand Jauhri, the nagarseth, the order of punitive action was withdrawn.[18] In another incident on 8 August 1725, seven Mughal and Kashmiri merchants were imprisoned by the governor without any reason and were only released when they paid fifty thousand rupees to the administration.[19] The Bohra community had also suffered from such kind of forced contributions. Nawab Hamid Ali Khan forcibly collected forty thousand rupees from Ismaili Bohras and eighty thousand rupees from Sunni Bohras on 11 August 1725 at Ahmedabad, and humiliated them as well.[20]

Three Maratha attacks on Surat took place during the reign of Aurangzeb – in 1664, 1670 and 1706. The first two attacks were led by Shivaji, in which the city of Surat was thoroughly ransacked. These attacks were also an open assertion of Shivaji's authority vis-a-vis the Mughals, and it clearly showed up the decaying state of the Mughal administration in Gujarat. Factory records and the accounts of travellers provide sufficient details of the sack of 1664. The city of Surat, which was not fortified till then, was subjected to systematic plundering raids by Shivaji. The President of the English factory, an eye-witness to the events, describes the situation in these words, *"From that time, none of his (Shivaji's) party dared to come near us, but continued a great deal of tyranny and cruelty to townsmen, cutting off the hands of some and the heads of others, day and night robbing and burning down the city, until the 11th, which day he made a general fire round about the town..."*[21]

While the plundering raid on Surat was on, a member of the English factory named Anthony Smith, was made captive by the Marathas. However, once his low official status came to be known, he was released. "*When he (Anthony Smith) came away, he could not but guess, by the money heaped up on two great heaps before Sevagee's tent, that he gathered 20 or 25 lakh of rupees that the day. When he came away in the morning, there were brought in near upon 300 porters laden each with two bags of rupees, and some he guessed to be gold: that they brought in 28 sers of large pearl, with many other jewels, great diamonds, rubies and emeralds... and there, with an incredible quantity of money, they found out the house of the reputed richest merchant in the world (his name is Virji Vora – his estate having been esteemed to be 80 lakh of rupees), that they were still, every hour while he was there bringing in loads of money from his house.*"[22] The spoils, secured by the Marathas through this, have been estimated to be around ten million of rupees.[i]

Though Surat was deserted by its Mughal officers, the President of the English factory, George Oxenden offered stiff resistance and defended the lives and goods of his people. The English factory at that time, had one lakh of rupees in cash and valuable stock of goods. J. C. Bruce, the historiographer of the East India Company, has given a detailed description of the sack of Surat. He writes that, "*The commercial arrangements were unexpectedly interrupted in January 1664 by a sudden attack on Surat by Sevagee's army commanded by the chief in person. On his approach, the governor shut himself up in the castle, while the inhabitants fled to the adjoining country. In this emergency, Sir George Oxenden and the Company's servants shut themselves up in the factory with their property, which they estimated at 80,000, and after testifying it called in the ships' crew for defence. When attacked, they made a brave and obstinate resistance, and this opposition not only*

i One crore rupees

preserved the factory but also the town from destruction. Sevagee however, carried off immense booty".[23]

The way the Mughal officers surrendered the city without offering any resistance to the Marathas, strengthened the impression that besides the laxity of administration for which this problem could not be tackled, some of the Mughal officers were in league with the Marathas, which made the latter's task easier. The Mirat-i-Ahmadi reinforces this suggestion when it states that the nazim of the Subah, Mahabat Khan, arrived in Surat after Shivaji had left the town. Mahabat Khan came with an army consisting of contingents supplied by the local zamindars. The subsequent conduct of Mahabat Khan would bring little laurels to the Mughals. He stationed himself at Surat for three months and started collecting peshkash from the region. The tax-paying subjects thus, instead of being provided with protection and relief, were subjected to further exactions. Mahabat Khan after collecting rupees three lakhs as peshkash, left the port town of Surat.[24]

This event provided opportunity to George Oxenden and his council to seek for further trade concessions for themselves. They sent a petition to the emperor for remission of the custom-dues. In view of the losses to the merchants, Surat received an imperial firman to the effect that all the Surat merchants, Indian as well as foreigners, in view of the losses they had suffered, were granted exemption for one year from custom duties on all imports and exports. At the same time, as a further mark of royal pleasure, the English and the Dutch merchants were given, after the expiry of the year, a remission of 1/2 per cent in the 2 1/2 per cent duty payable by them on all imports.[25]

Six years later, in October of 1670, Shivaji raided Surat for the second time. In March 1670, six months before Shivaji's raid, Gerald Aungier, who had succeeded Sir George Oxenden as President of Surat factory, described the situation at Surat in these words: *"The town of Surat is at present in a most distracted condition, occasioned by the fear of Sevagee whose late success and conquest, as also his near approaches, being sometimes within 20 leagues of this place,... hath made all, in general, provide for themselves, some by flight betraying their pusillanimity. Others demonstrated a resolution to defend themselves and their estates by fortifying their houses and keeping soldier to guard them."*[26]

The English council at Surat wrote to the deputy-governor of Bombay to provide them 35 to 40 'white Portuguese' soldiers who were in the services of the Company. Accordingly, white Portuguese soldiers, with an English sergeant were sent from Bombay to Surat by the end of March. Meanwhile, the alarm at Surat had considerably diminished, owing to the arrival of Bahadur Khan, the subahdar of Gujarat, with 3,000 horses, to protect the town from Maratha attack. Aungier, therefore, as an economic measure, sent back the soldiers to Bombay. The presence of the subahdar, however, was not without its embarrassments. As Aungier expressed in his letter to the company, *"It eased us of the present fears, but cost us. The French and Dutch and all the merchants deare for our protection, gave presents to him, which is a civil kind of plunder demanded by these great Umbrawes (Umara) as a tribute due to them"*. The Dutch presents were worth Rs 3,000 to 4,000 and those of the French, Rs 15,000. The English Council, accordingly, thought it prudent to add presents to the value of Rs 1,500 to the few European toys and rarities with which they had hoped to content him. A considerable part of the letter to the company had to be devoted to explaining the necessity for this means of obtaining favours. Besides this, the English company emptied its warehouses at Surat of all goods that were ready for despatch to Europe and there was little of value left in the factory. The company was, however, facing considerable risk in obtaining goods from outside the country, owing to the frequent robberies. The factory record mentions that "*the thieves and inland Rajahs taking the opportunity of plundering cafilas (caravans) are robbing merchants under the name of Sevagee*". The brokers at Ahmedabad and Agra also hesitated to send goods to Surat. To meet this situation, the council had to make forward contracts for the sale of all the company's broadcloth, tin and copper that was expected to arrive on the ships. Khwaja Minaz, on behalf of Virji Vora, took the cloth, and Nanchand,[ii] the tin and copper, obviously causing loss to the Company.

The Mughal administration could not prevent the second attack on Surat by Shivaji which took place on 3 October 1670. The situation, by then, had become so grim that Gerald Aungier, the President of the Surat factory, wrote, "*The distraction in the town was so great that there was neither governor nor government*". At the time of the raid, the President and the Council of the English Factory were at Swally. The goods brought by the ships had largely been unloaded, while the council had almost emptied their warehouses at Surat of all goods that were ready for despatch to Europe. Though the English factors made adequate preparations to secure the interests of the Company, they were not willing to desert the factory. Hence, it was decided to send one of the Council-members, Streynsham Master, with forty seamen taken from the ships. On the third day of raid, 5 October, though the English reached Surat. Streynsham Master was wise enough to decide to send a present to Shivaji consisting of scarlet, cloth, sword blades, knives, etc. besides an undisclosed amount of rupees. The present was sent by two of the servants of the company. The factory records mention that "*Sevagee sent for them and received them with the peshkash in a very kind manner, telling them that the English and he were goods friends, and putting his hand into theirs, he told them he*

---

ii Virji Vora's grandson

would do the English no wrong and that this giving his hand was better than any promise or agreement to oblige him there unto".[27]

In a matter of days, Shivaji's army took possession of the entire town except that of the English, the Dutch and the French houses, as well as the two serais of the city where foreign merchants and travellers kept their goods. While the Marathas were raiding the city of Surat, many of its residents took refuge at Swally. Even the Shahbander and the qazi of the city had taken refuge there. Most of the eminent merchants of Surat, including Muslims and Armenians, had fled to the port under the protection of the English.[28]

During the period 1670 to 1680, Surat could not recover from the Maratha raid. The Marathas also sent a letter to the officers and chief merchants of the city demanding an annual tribute of twelve lakhs of rupees. The Marathas had hardly departed from the city, when the poor classes of Surat fell to plundering what was left, so much so that there was not a house except for those that had armed guard, which was not ransacked. Even Streynsham Master, with his seamen, had some trouble and they could barely prevent these hungry people from plundering the English factory.[29]

The lawlessness that followed resulted in a disruption of trade and the merchants of Surat, along with the English and Dutch companies, suffered immensely. Many of the goods that the English company had brought from England remained undisposed. There was also considerable difficulty in dealing with the gold and silver received, owing to the insecurity. It was initially proposed to coin the bullion at Surat, but the council were forced to keep it at Swally, not daring to risk the danger of sending up such a tempting commodity. The Surat mint was also constantly closed owing to the frequent alarms. In these circumstances, an attempt to get the Company's creditors to accept payment in bullion naturally failed. Trade between Surat and Persia also suffered due to these disturbances at Surat. Persians did not dare to send ships at their own risk. Aungier, in his letter of 21 November, summed up the situation as follows:

"The care of all men, at present, is met not with what they shall get by trading, buying and selling, but what they can save from fire and plunder by hiding and running away. Eminent merchants have suffered not only here but elsewhere, so that the cittys of Agra, Dilly, Brampore, Orungabad and Ahmedavad, the only marts of trade in India, are in the same condition with us here, caused by the fatal jealousies between the present Great Mogul Orengzeb and his Sonne Sultan Mazem, now prince of Orangabad, who in defense of his life, often attempted by his father, stands up on his guard with a vast army and privately setts on Sevagee with other Rashboots and Jentues to rebel against him, at whose outrages he winkes but hitherto hath not offered any open act of hostility against his father. How long things will stand thus between them, wee are not able to foresee, but certaine it is that till a firme peace be settled trade cannot recover the lively vigour it had before".[30]

Fear of another incursion by the Marathas continued throughout the decade. Besides frequent scares of such kinds, the disturbances caused by the hostilities between Shivaji and the Mughal forces caused considerable obstruction to trade. Aurangzeb sent Mahabat Khan to the Deccan with an army of 40,000 against Shivaji, and though hostilities took place mainly in Deccan, the general insecurity affected trade in and around Surat. Even trade to foreign ports was affected, and freights for Persia and Basra was very low. In the middle of 1672, information reached that the Maratha forces under Moro Pandit had taken Jawahar, near Thana, from the Kolis. This was followed by the news of the capture of Ramnagar. Messengers arrived with letters from Shivaji, demanding for the third time, the chauth or fourth part of the revenue, amounting to four lakhs of rupees. The message ended with a threatening note that if this was not sent speedily, he would march up with his army.[31]

Realizing the danger, the governor convened a meeting of all the eminent Hindu and Muslim merchants and proposed collecting a sum of Rs 45,000 to raise 500 horses and 3,000 soldiers for the defence of the town for two months. This was agreed to, but not apparently carried out. The English council wrote that they heard of *"no soldiers being employed but there are officers employed in taking an account of every Baniya house in town, of which the Governor no doubt will make good employment to his particular benefit"*. When news of Shivaji's letter spread, a panic rose among all merchants of Surat and most decided to send their families out of Surat. The governor summoned another meeting to consider how to meet Shivaji's demand. He proposed that the merchants in the city should collect one lakh of rupees, which they declared to be impossible. After a long deliberation, it was decided to raise Rs 60,000 to be sent to the Marathas with a promise for the remainder. But the merchants, apprehending that the governor might keep all the money and not send anything to the Marathas, sent him word that it could not be done. The people had lost confidence in the credibility of Mughal officials.

It was this uncertainty about the safety of Surat and the lack of confidence in the administrative capability of the Mughals, which was responsible for the shifting of the English Company's headquarters from Surat to Bombay during this period. Haji Zahid Beg's son, one of the richest merchants in Surat, declared his resolution with an oath in the presence of Governor Aungier and Matthew Gray, that he would go with his family to Bombay.[32]

Even the death of Shivaji in 1680 could not bring any respite to the subah from the Maratha attacks as they had gained strength by this time. In 1706, the Marathas made incursions into Gujarat under their leader Dhana Jadhav. The Marathas overpowered the Mughal forces, and the naib of the subah, Abdul Hamid Khan, along with the mansabdars, were made captive. The ransom was fixed for each captive. The imperial authority did not intervene at this juncture. Three lakhs of rupees were fixed as ransom for the naib. He wrote to his peshkars and servants for the arrangement of the sum. The sum was collected not only from his relatives, but also from his treasury. When Aurangzeb came to know of these arrangements, he issued a royal order stating "You should not allow any man of the Diwan as far as possible to spend [even] a rupee from the treasury". Abdul Hamid Khan remained in the captivity of the Marathas for some time and was freed only after the payment of the ransom by his own family members.

The failure of the Mughal officers to defend Surat against the Marathas was rooted in the weakening of the imperial administration in the subah at large. It appears that the gravity of these attacks could not be truly gauged by the Mughal Court, and thus, adequate provisions could not be made for the defence of Surat. It clearly demonstrated the slackening of imperial control over the administration of the subah. Towards the end of March 1674, the English Council decided to open up a factory at Dharangaon in the East Khandesh district. This factory was looted and burnt by the Marathas in January 1675, and goods worth Rs 3,554 perished in the conflagration, while weavers fled with Rs 5,681 advanced to them.

The last decade of the 17th century and the opening years of the 18thcentury also saw European piracy in the Indian seas. The English pirates were considered to be most notorious and it was believed that the servants of the English factory had secret dealings with them. In 1695, a large vessel called the Ganj-i-Sawai which belonged to the emperor and was mainly engaged in pilgrim traffic, was captured by the sea pirates and this enraged the emperor. An imperial order was issued to put a ban on all trade by the European Companies at Surat. Not only this, the Sidis of

Janjira were instructed to invade Bombay, and the English company's servants were to be put in prison until the value of the goods plundered from the ships was compensated. Relations between the Mughals and the English became cordial only when the latter agreed to supply escorts to the Mughal merchants and pilgrim vessels to the Red Sea. The agreement was followed by an imperial order for the reopening of the port to all the three companies. For nearly three years, the English company suffered financial loss due to the enforced cessation of trade caused by the frequent confinement of the factors. The retaliatory measures taken by the Mughal authorities, however, could no larger prove effective in taming piracy. As a result of European piracy, the customs-revenue of the Surat port as well as the pilgrim traffic, suffered. In the absence of a strong naval force, Aurangzeb could not formulate any well-defined policy. Instead, he decided to compel the European companies at Surat to bear the responsibility of suppressing piracy at sea. All these together, ultimately led to the decline of Surat towards the end of 17th century. But this did not lower its contribution in standing against all odds for nearly a century, as the sole, brightest, flag bearer of the English East India Company in India.

Conclusion

For the English East India Company, the transition from a relatively weak body of merchants, continually short of capital and threatened by the greater political power of the rival Dutch organisation, to the status of a great trading corporation was a process that stretched over many years. What is indisputable is the fact that very few business organisations have survived for so long and were able to maintain their position as successfully as did the East India Company. During the greater part of its history as an active commercial enterprise, the East India Company was a

State within a State. Its total trading capital, after 1709, was permanently lent to the Crown, and the interest on the loan was secured by assigning to the Company the duties on salt and paper. The possession of a legal monopoly by the Company, firmly and unambiguously debarred the entry of competitors in the home market. The Company could rely on the diplomatic support of the Crown and its ministers, to bring pressure on foreign European governments to subdue small rival companies on the Continent. In India and elsewhere in Asia, it had established a number of trading settlements which possessed semi-sovereign status, distinguished by an elaborate procedure of government, courts of law, a municipal system, as well as a military force. In these circumstances, it is not surprising to discover that the Company's organisational structure and bureaucratic apparatus shared many of the attributes of a great department of state. All this happened long before the Battle of Plassey.

As the renowned historian and compiler of state papers preserved at the Bombay Secretariat, G. W. Forrest, pointed out, the English enterprise, after roaming over the Indian seas, first furled its wandering sail at the port of Surat, and there, founded a small factory which afterwards grew into that stately fabric of an Empire in the East. The story of that small factory growing into a nucleus of an Empire is fascinating. It was Surat that provided a threshold for the British to enter into the western parts of India.

References

[1] Original Correspondence, 7 December 1661, vol. 27, No. 2905; ibid., 7 August 1661, vol. 27, No. 2893.

[2] John Ovington, *A voyage to Surat in the year 1689*, ed. H. G. Rawlinson (London, 1929), pp. 131-33.

[3] Fryer, A new account of East India, I, p. 219.

[4] Original Correspondence, 11 March 1695, vol. 50, No. 5984. On Bombay's slow commercial progress, see also Original Correspondence, 15 March 1679, vol. 39, No. 4563, para. 105, p. 26.

[5] Despatch Book, 15 March 1678, vol. 88, p. 529.

[6] Factory Records Surat, 28 August 1682,vol. 108, p 146-53; Original Correspondence, 28 July 1684, vol. 44, No. 5206, para. 29; for the treaty between the Company and the Queen of Attinga, see ibid., 29 June 1694, vol. 50, Nos. 5921-2.

[7] For the foundation grant of Madras, see 22 July (August) 1639, Original Correspondence, vol. 17, No. 1690. For the Company's reference to the rise of the town, see Despatch Book, 20 December 1699, vol. 93, pp. 258-60.

[8] Alexander Hamilton, *A new account of the East Indies*, ed. W. Foster (2 vols., London, 1930), 1, p. 199, 203. (First published in 1727.)

[9] Despatch Book, 28 August 1682, vol. 90, p. 21; ibid., 5 September 1683, vol. 90, p. 218.

[10] Factory Records Surat, 23-6 July 1616, vol. 84, printed in Letters received by the East India Company from its servants in the east, vol. iv, p. 327.

[11] Thomas Bowrey, *A geographical account of countries round the Bay of Bengal 1669 to 1679*, ed. Sir Richard Temple (Cambridge, 1905), p. 172.

[12] For the effects of these local wars on Surat investment, see Original Correspondence, 3 April 1678, vol. 39, No. 4541. These years was the direct consequence of the Company's decision to fight competition with a trade war.[Ibid., 28 August 1682, vol. 90, p. 27.]

[13] Ibid., 2 April 1683, vol. 90, p. 128.

[14] Ibid., 16 November 1683, vol. 90, p. 4L.

[15] Blochet, Suppi. Pars. 482, ff. 452b, 453a.

[16] Ashin Das Gupta, Indian Merchants, the chaotic and confusing political situation around 1720s has been graphically depicted by Das Gupta. The account is primarily based on Dutch sources.

[17] Itimad Ali Khan, *Mirat-ul Haqaiq*, Bodleian Library Oxford, Fraser Collection, 124. A microfilm copy is available at the centre of Advanced Study in History, AMU.

[18] Mirat-ul Haqaiq,p. 348b.

[19] Mirat-ul Haqaiq,p. 348b.

[20] Mirat-ul Haqaiq, p. 349.

[21] *English Factories in India,* 1661-64, ed. William Foster, Oxford, 1906-1927, p. 301.

[22] *English Factories in India,* 1661-64, ed. William Foster, Oxford, 1906-1927, p. 308.

[23] J. C Bruce, *Annals of the East India Company,* II, p. 144.

[24] Ali Mohd Khan, Mirat-i-Ahmadi, ed. S, Nawab Ali, Vol. I, Calcutta, 1928, p. 256.

[25] EFI 1670-77,p. 190.

[26] Sir Charles, Fawcett, (ed.)The English Factories in India, 1670-77, (The Western Presidency), Vol. I, Oxford, 1936, p. 189.

[27] English Factories in India, 1670-77, pp. 196-97.

[28] Charles Fawcett, Op. cit, p. 197.

[29] English Factories in India, 1670-77, p. 197.

[30] Charles Fawcett, Op cit, pp. 203-204.

[31] Charles Fawcett, Op cit, p. 220.

[32] M S, Commassorit, Op. cit, p. 287.